THE
ERN MALLEY
AFFAIR

MICHAEL HEYWARD

Introduction by
ROBERT HUGHES

ff
faber and faber

First published in 1993
by Faber and Faber Limited
3 Queen Square London WC1N 3AU

Photoset by Wilmaset Ltd, Birkenhead, Wirral
Printed in England by Clays Ltd, St Ives Plc

Michael Heyward is hereby identified as author of this work in
accordance with Section 77 of the Copyright, Designs and
Patents Act 1988

A CIP record for this book
is available from the British Library

ISBN 0-571-16781-0

T

1001 177127

2 4 6 8 10 9 7 5 3 1

THE ERN MALLEY AFFAIR

To Penny, William, Anna and Alice

Their words are clews that clutched you on the post
And you were hung up, dry, a fidgety ghost
                    Ern Malley, 'Young Prince of Tyre', 1943

For lucid Ern, ye penguins, weep no more!
Henceforth he is the genius of the shore
                              James McAuley,
          'The True Discovery of Australia', 1944

'All Australians are anarchists at heart'
                    Harold Stewart, 1989

Contents

List of Illustrations

Acknowledgements

I could not have written this book without the kindness and goodwill of those people who shared with me their intimate knowledge of the events I wanted to investigate. Harold Stewart not only answered hundreds of questions about Ern Malley, but taught me how to appreciate Kyoto, the city he loves. I thank him for his patience, wisdom and generosity. Max Harris offered me his enthusiasm and support from the outset, and made his personal papers in Adelaide and Melbourne available to me. I regret that when the book was finished he was not well enough to read it. Norma McAuley kindly allowed me to read James McAuley's papers and went out of her way to make my research pleasant. Barrett Reid offered me unfettered access to the papers of John and Sunday Reed, and gave the manuscript the benefit of his skilful reading.

I am grateful to the many people who assisted me with their advice, criticism, insights and recollections, in particular to C. L. Abbott, John Ashbery, Colin Badger, Libby Baulch, Amanda Beresford, John Bray, Peter Carey, Manning Clark, Peter Coleman, Michael Cook, Peter Craven, Alan Crawford, Tim Curnow, Laurie Duggan, Joan Dunbar, Ronald Dunlop, Geoffrey Dutton, Ninette Dutton, Brian Elliott, John Forbes, Gwen Friend, Dorothy Green, Diana Gribble, Richard Haese, Gwen Harwood, Bill Henson, Graeme Hetherington, A. D. Hope, Donald Horne, Robert Hughes, Hugh Kenner, Sir John Kerr, Kenneth Koch, Dame Leonie Kramer, Elisabeth Lambert, James Laughlin, Mavis McAuley, Douglas McCallum, Laurie Muller, Jinx Nolan, Sir Sidney Nolan, Vic O'Connor, Peter Porter, Jeff Prentice, Bill Pritchett, Peter Ryan, Peter Schjeldahl, Julie Simpson, John Sinclair, Bernard Smith, Jim Somerville, J. I. M.

Stewart, Beverley Tivey, John Tranter, Albert Tucker, Tess van Sommers, Catherine Veitch, Russel Ward, Larry Wieder and Amy Witting. I am particularly grateful to my editors, Robert McCrum, Clare Forster and Craig Munro. My greatest debt is to Penny Hueston: this is also her book.

I am grateful to the Commonwealth Fund in New York where I held a Harkness Fellowship in 1990 and 1991, and especially to Robert Kostrezwa. I also wish to thank the Literature Board of the Australia Council for their provision of a Writer's Project Grant which enabled me to visit Harold Stewart in Japan, the staff of the Baillieu Library at the University of Melbourne, of the La Trobe Library at the State Library of Victoria, of the National Library of Australia, of the Barr Smith Library and the Mortlock Library in Adelaide, and of the Mitchell Library in Sydney.

I am grateful to John Ashbery for permission to quote his words about Ern Malley; to John Auld for permission to quote the words of Frederick T. Macartney; to the ABC for permission to quote from John Thompson's radio features, 'The Ern Malley Story' and 'Alfred Conlon'; to Colin Badger for permission to quote from his work; to Niall Brennan for permission to quote from his work; to Joan Crawford for permission to quote the words of Alan Crawford; to Brian Elliott for permission to quote from his unpublished letters; to the Estate of Donald Friend for permission to quote from the Diaries of Donald Friend; to Max Harris and Angus & Robertson Publishers for permission to quote from his work; to A. D. Hope for permission to quote from his unpublished correspondence; to Donald Horne and Penguin Books Australia Ltd for permission to quote from *The Education of Young Donald*; to Mrs E. E. Ingamells for permission to quote from the work of Rex Ingamells; to Alister Kershaw and Angus & Robertson Publishers for permission to quote from his poetry; to Peter Nixon for permission to quote from the unpublished papers of Adrian Lawlor; to Norma McAuley, c/o Curtis Brown (Aust) Pty Ltd and Angus & Robertson Publishers for permission to quote from the work of James McAuley; to Lady Nolan for permission to quote from the unpublished letters of Sir Sidney Nolan; to Vic O'Connor for permission to quote from his unpublished letters; to the National Library of Australia for permission to quote from Catherine Santamaria's interview with James McAuley; to Peter Porter for permission to quote from his letters to me; to the Estate of Sir Herbert Read for permission to quote from his work; to Curtis Brown Ltd, London, for permission to quote from Henry Reed's 'Chard Whitlow'; to Karl Shapiro for permission to quote from his unpublished letters; to Jim Somerville for permission to quote from the work of Oliver Somerville; to Harold Stewart for permission to quote from his book of poetry *Phoenix Wings*, from his unpublished papers, from his letters to me, and to reproduce the Ern Malley collages. The poems of Ern Malley and other associated material are reproduced by kind permission of Harold Stewart and Norma McAuley c/o Curtis Brown (Aust) Pty Ltd.

INTRODUCTION: The Well-wrought Ern
ROBERT HUGHES

Every literary editor dreams that one day an authentic genius will drop through his or her letter-box, an unsolicited angel descending in a buff manila chariot. One day late in 1943, as an Australian literary editor named Max Harris was going through the morning's mail, he opened such an envelope. It contained a sheaf of poems, typed on coffee-stained paper, and a covering letter from someone he had never heard of: a woman named Ethel Malley. *Dear Sir*, it began, *When I was going through my brother's things after his death, I found some poetry he had written. I am no judge of it myself* . . .

Harris, the twenty-two-year-old, very precocious John the Baptist of poetic modernism in Australia, editor of a small-circulation literary magazine which he had christened with the truculently surrealist name of *Angry Penguins*, began to page through the poems; idly at first, one imagines, and then with mounting excitement. He went through them again.

Years later Harris would tell me that, the second time around, he *knew* that the history of Australian poetry had changed; its map was redrawn. Harris's generation in Australia had found its 'marvellous boy', its classless genius coming from nowhere and cut off in his prime, a sort of Rimbaud-cum-Keats. Just what the place needed, given its indurated conservatism amid the cultural doldrums of World War II: a dead hero.

Ethel's brother's name was Ernest Lalor Malley, Ern Malley for short. A highly Australian-sounding handle: *Lalor* recalling the leader of the Eureka Stockade, a revolt of the Ballarat gold-miners in 1854 at which the abortive Republic of Victoria was proclaimed; *Malley* a homophone for the tough mallee-scrub of the Victorian semi-desert. Ern was born in England in 1918,

Ethel presently explained; the Malleys had emigrated to Australia after the war; now both parents were dead. After high school, young Ern had worked as a garage mechanic, drifted to Melbourne, sold insurance, and lived all alone in a rented room in South Melbourne. 'I remember I was worried at the time whether he was looking after himself properly because he was never very strong,' wrote Ethel, preparing the ground for her brother as the Antipodean Chatterton, the fiery soul in the enfeebled frame. At night, he would read in the Public Library. 'He was always a little strange and moody and I don't think he had a very happy life, though he didn't show it.' And then he died aged twenty-five on 23 July 1943; and only the poems, which Ethel was going to throw away but then decided to keep and pass on to Max Harris, survived him. Did Harris think they were any good?

Was Ned Kelly Irish? The Pope Catholic? Ern Malley, Harris would presently write to Ethel,

was one of the most remarkable and important poetic figures of this country. It may be rather hard for you to realize that Ern was, in my opinion, a great man, and in the opinion of many people a major poet . . . I have written a big survey of his work which I hope to publish . . . in my journal before it is put out in book form.

Harris was not the only one to respond to young Malley. Almost everyone in the *Angry Penguins* circle (about twenty writers and painters, and especially the artist Sidney Nolan) did so, with varying degrees of conviction. Some of the poems were wilfully obscure; others limpid; some ribald in a clever-clever way – exactly the unevenness of tone you might expect from a young writer working towards his own voice; but the Gift, all agreed, was there. In any case, no plebiscite was needed. Harris was the editor, and what he felt went. He did not just publish Ern's poems, as he had promised Ethel; he devoted a whole section of the autumn 1944 issue of *Angry Penguins* to them. It bore a beautiful cover by Nolan, in full colour (a *Verve*-like gesture for an Australian little magazine, against wartime scarcity), illustrating lines from Malley's *Petit Testament*: 'I said to my love (who is living) / Dear we shall never be that verb / Perched on the sole Arabian Tree.'

No young Australian poet ever had a more auspicious launch for his work. His early death, clearly, was a tragedy. But then it became apparent that, behind this tragedy, a comedy lurked. Ern Malley was not dead, for he had never lived. He and his entire *oeuvre* had been made up, in the course of a single afternoon in a military barracks in Melbourne, by two young poets, Corporal Harold Stewart and Lieutenant James McAuley. When this was revealed to an overjoyed Australian press, the kangaroo-droppings truly hit the fan. For the first and possibly the last time in Australian history, poetry became front-page news, and Ern was translated into an immortality he might never have achieved if he had lived.

The Ern Malley affair was, without question, *the* literary hoax of the twentieth century. Its unfolding, replete with bizarre twists of accusation, argument, counter-argument, involving literary figures overseas (Herbert Read, for instance) as well as Australian ones, and culminating in legal grotesqueries – the prosecution of Max Harris as editor of *Angry Penguins* on the grounds that some of the works of his Poet Who Never Was were obscene – is the subject of Michael Heyward's fascinating account.

In the visual arts deliberate forgery is almost never 'pure', dissociated from profit. The forger fakes a picture or a sculpture to make money, only sometimes claiming – and usually as an excuse, after he has been found out – that he did it as a private homage to the original artist, or to prove the ignorance of experts. There have been a few exceptions, such as Hans van Meegeren, the Dutch forger of Vermeers, who really does seem to have done his work in order to show up what he resentfully believed to be the purblindness of an art world that would not recognize his own talents. But there is no profit in poetry, and so the memorable literary hoaxes have always been (at least in a monetary sense) disinterested, except for two: the Hitler diaries, exposed in 1983, and Clifford Irving's 1971 forgery of the autobiography of Howard Hughes. Both of these belong to the era of big-bucks celebrity publishing, as art forgeries do to the much longer era of big-bucks art collecting. Both were aimed at personal profit and corporate greed. Neither of them made a *literary* point.

Not so with the 'classic' literary forgeries, such as Ossian, Thomas Rowley – and Ern Malley. Even if Thomas Chatterton (1752–70) had meant to make some money from his imaginary fifteenth-century monk-poet of Bristol, Thomas Rowley, he did not do so: only one poem by 'Rowley' actually saw print during Chatterton's short lifetime, before he gulped arsenic and died at the age of seventeen in his London garret. Nor was Chatterton trying to discredit the antiquarians of his day, some of whom were anxious to accept his forged drafts and letters as genuine. Far from having a satirical purpose, Chatterton's hoax was the product of romantic desires: one for fame, the other for union with the primal stem of English literature.

In 'Thomas Rowley', Chatterton hoped to construct a purely English poet whose language contained none of the Frenchification of Chaucer. He would reconstruct what he adored, shelter under its benign fiction. Parody had no part in Chatterton's impulses, and his forgeries are lies told in the service of a naïve and passionate sincerity. Hence his appeal to the far greater imaginations of a later English Romanticism, particularly Wordsworth and Keats. It was no small thing for a hoaxer to have 'Endymion' dedicated to his memory, or to be eulogized by Wordsworth as 'the marvellous Boy'.

Like Chatterton, the Scots poet James Macpherson (1736–96) would have been content to disappear behind his hoax: *Fingal, an ancient epic poem in six books* (1762), which purported to be his translation from Gaelic of the work of a blind third-century warrior-bard named Ossian. *Fingal* very soon became a rallying point for Scots cultural nationalism. Though the piercing eye of Samuel Johnson marked this work for a fake almost at once, it developed a longevity and influence that no critic could kill – particularly when Ossian crossed the Channel and made his posthumous way to Europe. There, some of the greatest figures of the time (Goethe, Schiller, Klopstock, Chateaubriand, even Napoleon) took him up, finding in Ossian the true rugged voice of primitive Europe, a Nordic Homer. 'I am not ashamed to own,' wrote Thomas Jefferson from Virginia in 1773, 'that I think this rude bard of the North the greatest poet that has ever existed.' Painters responded to him, because their patrons did. The so-called *primitifs* who followed Jacques-Louis David were particularly fond of Ossianic themes, and one of them, Anne-Louis Girodet-Trioson, produced for Napoleon's own house at Malmaison a vision of Ossian receiving slain Napoleonic officers into Valhalla.

Macpherson, his creator, was buried (admittedly at his own expense) in Westminster Abbey. Doubts about Ossian did not keep him out, although after his death in 1796 a committee sat on the vexed question of Ossian's historicity and concluded that the ancient bard was, indeed, somewhere between a fake and a pastiche. This did absolutely nothing to stem Ossian's popularity; editions of *Fingal* continued to appear, and as late as 1866 Matthew Arnold was still singing his praises.

No such magnificent fate befell Ern Malley. But then, he lived (or at least, was invented) a long way from Europe, in a small society that had no Goethe, Girodet or Napoleon – or Westminster Abbey, or Matthew Arnold, for that matter. Moreover, his relation to the past was quite different from Ossian's or Rowley's. They had been brought into existence in order to enlarge and glorify the achievements of the past, and to substantiate ideals of national identity. The well-wrought Ern was created to debunk the present, or at least a part of it; his sole aim was to make his admirers look idiotic, and he wasn't meant to reinforce some earlier idea of 'Australian culture' as such, since his creators despised most earlier and all popular Australian poetry, from the bush ballads to the nationalist Jindyworobaks, nearly as much as they detested the 'obscurities' of international modernism.

And yet, 'Sometimes the myth is greater than its creators,' Max Harris said (or always said he said) when a reporter woke him the night the hoax broke. He was right. The basic case made by Ern's defenders was that his creation proved the validity of surrealist procedures: that in letting down their guard, opening themselves to free association and chance, McAuley and Stewart had reached inspiration by the side door of parody; and though this can't be argued on behalf of all the poems, some of which are partly or wholly gibberish, it contains a ponderable truth. You can argue about the merits of 'Durer, Innsbruck 1495', the first poem Max Harris read in that sheaf half a century ago, but it would hardly be possible for a fair-minded person to say that it doesn't make poetic sense.

Nevertheless, as Sigmund Freud allegedly said to Salvador Dali the one time they met, 'It is not your unconscious that interests me, but your conscious.' Ern's elaborate self-consciousness is only a reflection of that of his inventors. Michael Heyward is surely right when he points out, in his summing-up, that the energy of invention that McAuley and Stewart brought to their concoction of Ern Malley created an icon of literary value, and that this is why he continues to haunt our culture. 'Were Ern Malley real he would not be half as alluring as we now find him. As poet and cipher he represents, with whatever perversity or futility, the definitive moment in Australian literary modernism . . . he is the only genuinely avant-garde writer in a country which has never sponsored a literary revolution.' And, one should add, he is a sublimely funny and touching act of literary criticism.

It seems strange that no Australian writer has done full justice to Ern Malley before – but the reason is obvious: he is so deeply wound into Australian culture that, up to now, those who wanted to write about him were all, in some way or another, *parti pris*. The controversy occasioned by Ern's long shadow was still mildly radioactive when I was in my twenties; one was expected to take sides, even in the early 1960s, on the basis that any sort of cultural conservatism was repressive and a bad thing. This polarization was increased by the fact that James McAuley, a poet of remarkable gifts in his own right, had turned into an ultramontanist Catholic conservative as he matured, so that it was almost obligatory for the young to defend Ern's libidinal poetry against its real authors. It has taken Michael Heyward, a younger critic still, to have the first complete and detached word on Ern Malley; and his book is definitive.

PART I The Story

1 The Death of Ern Malley

It is easy to imagine the death of Ern Malley – the small, bare room at the back of the house in Dalmar Street, the chenille cover smoothed across the slender figure in the bed, the walnut veneer wardrobe with its oval mirror reflecting the lino floor his sister Ethel had swept and polished that morning. Now she sat on the single bedside chair in what was left of the winter light. Her mouth was shut tight and she dabbed at her eyes with a damp white handkerchief. Ern was all that remained of her family and she had nursed him to the last – but there were secrets in his short life she would never prise out of him now. There was a time when Ern longed to escape from his sister, and her prim, church-going, lower-middle-class world in Sydney's western suburbs – but he had come home to die and Ethel had done her best.

She was wrong about the secrets. She had no idea, as she ferried the young man cups of tea and bowls of vegetable soup during the long, difficult weeks of his dying, that in the very room where she now sat, Ern had hidden something quite extraordinary. In her grief she did not foresee the moment a few days hence when she would drag Ern's battered suitcase out from under his bed, open it and prod at the lining in a place where it seemed unusually thick until – Gracious! What have we here? Banknotes? Love letters? War documents? – it came apart and she could pull out a handful of sheets, some of them dog-eared and others folded double, on which her brother had typed his poems.

Poems! A few miles away, on the shelves at the State Library, were books Ethel had never heard of, T. S. Eliot's *The Waste Land* and Ezra Pound's *Cantos*, but the battles the champions of *vers libre* had won in Europe had hardly begun in Sidney in 1943, and in all of Dalmar Street it is safe to assume that only in the mind of the wasted youth with the hollow cheeks and staring eyes did 'The Hanged Man' ever have special significance.

Forty Dalmar Street, Croydon, Ethel Malley's home, was an unremarkable, liver-coloured brick-veneer. It had a low fence, a rose bush in the front yard surrounded by a lawn of buffalo grass and at the side two thin concrete strips to accommodate an absent motor car in its journey from gate to garage. With its pubs and shops and factories, Croydon was sleepy and predictable, so far from the European front and even from the war in the Pacific, where some of its sons were serving. Mind you, Ethel had approved when, a few months after Ern's twenty-first birthday, Britain declared war on Germany and Australia's prime minister, Robert Menzies, instantly followed suit. The great land mass that contained Ethel Malley's rose bush and concrete drive was coloured red on the map – it was as if Australia was not just a member of the British Empire, but Britain extrapolated. Ninety-eight per cent of its population of seven million was, like Ethel and Ern, of British descent.

The war in Europe came at the end of a miserable decade in Australia. Thanks to the depression, the old dream of a working-man's paradise had gone sour. The country was in hock to English banks and living standards withered. For several years in the early thirties, while Ern Malley was wearing out the knees of his pants around Sydney's inner west, the population of the country actually declined. Yet this was the decade when Australia turned modern, when the great steel parabola of the Sydney Harbour Bridge took shape, when people with the cash to buy them equipped their homes with telephones and gramo-phones and wirelesses. They caught the flying boat to London if they could afford the ticket or caught up with Hollywood's latest offering at the cinema – Australians were reputedly the world's most avid movie-goers – but more of them were down-and-out than in any other decade this century. In Sydney, homeless men lived in sandstone caves in the Domain or walked to Melbourne looking for work, shooting rabbits on the way to stay alive. At the worst of the depression somewhere between a quarter and a third of able-bodied Australians could not find work.

This was a pinched, puritan world, washed over by sunlight and surf. Back in 1922, when D. H. Lawrence paid the country a visit, he was intoxicated by the primitive, unassimilated beauty of the bush, and wrote hymns to it in *Kangaroo* – but Australians themselves he found 'raw . . . so crude in their feelings – and they only want to be up-to-date in the "conveniences" – electric light and tramways and things like that. The aristocracy are the people who own big shops.' Ten or fifteen years later the place had not changed much, except that it had grown poorer. Nothing had modified that abrasive complacency or the relentless pressure to conform. With the approval of the various temperance movements, pubs shut at six o'clock. Drinkers rushed the bar and guzzled in the precious minutes before closing time. It was illegal for restaurants to serve wine after eight p.m. No one who was not Australian could believe this regulation, which was rigidly enforced.

Lawrence thought 'Australia would be a lovely country to lose the world in altogether' and that if he ever got back he'd settle in the bush with its 'hoary, weird attraction'. But losing the world was precisely what terrified some Australians. Henry Lawson declared in 1899 that any talented Australian writer would be well-advised 'to study elementary anatomy, especially as applies to the cranium, and then shoot himself carefully with the aid of a looking-glass'. Christina Stead left for London in 1928. Patrick White fled in 1932, determined never to return, though he did after the war. Strict censorship was in place, and thousands of books were banned – by writers ranging from Defoe to Joyce, from Huxley to Hemingway. And once the war started, of course, all books, newspapers and magazines were subject to military censorship.

The trouble with the rest of the world was that it wasn't Australian. It couldn't see the manifold attractions of God's own country down under. But Australia could take on anyone in the green fields of sport, where the genius of Bradman or Phar Lap was self-evident. And, when the Empire summoned, Australia would confront its enemies on the red field of battle. The day after Menzies committed his country to the second European war in a generation, several thousand men turned up at the Victoria Barracks, Army Headquarters in Melbourne, to volunteer. Loyalty dissolved distances. Air raid precautions were taken, should Hitler turn south from Poland. Railway bridges and aerodromes were guarded. People tried to think of ways to give the Hun some hurry-up. By mid 1940, the Inventions Board of the army was receiving an average of 500 letters a week with proposals for the best way to defend Britain. Most of these were *Boys' Own* fantasies, like 'the electrification of the English Channel' or igniting oil spread on its waters.

Eighteen months later, there was no need for fantasy. In 1922, Lawrence had noted that Australians were 'terribly afraid of the Japanese' and believed if 'there was a fall in England, so that the Powers could not interfere, Japan would at once walk in and occupy the place'. Now the worst was happening, and the country was beside itself. Like most of her neighbours, Ethel Malley – who had not heard from Ern for months and had no idea in which city, in what squalor, he was holed up – was waiting in a cold sweat for the Japanese to kick the country's front door down. In a trail of blood and smoke and flashing bayonets, they scooted down the Malay peninsula and on 15 February 1942 took Singapore, the fortress Churchill said would never fall. Ethel trembled to think how Tojo's army would swarm down Parramatta Road to Croydon. In shop windows she saw silhouettes of Japanese bombers and posters of leering soldiers, all teeth and slit eyes.

Four days after Singapore, the nightmare arrived in the form of Japanese Zeros, flying in tight formation, which strafed and bombed Darwin until the harbour was a boiling lake of fire and oil and blood and bloated bodies. Thousands fled south, convinced not only that the British lacked the wherewithal to protect them but that the top Australian brass had no intention of defending the thinly inhabited north. Villas on Sydney's affluent

North Shore were abandoned by their petrified owners, who headed south and inland. Some of the braver ones who stayed hurled socks filled with sand out of trenches in Hyde Park, and paraded with sawn-off sticks held rigid on their shoulders.

It seemed just a matter of time before the Rising Sun was hoisted where the Union Jack had first flown over 150 years earlier. Then, on 21 March 1942, US General Douglas MacArthur, who had abandoned his doomed forces in Corregidor and scrambled his way to Melbourne, was cheered by the locals as though he were a liberating commander entering the city in triumph. Weeks and months passed. The Japanese never arrived. In the next four years a million GIs came to Australia instead.

The threat of invasion and the arrival of American troops transformed Australia's cities, which ceased to be sedate, suburban havens, orderly by day and deserted by night. There were occasional food shortages, black markets, the sensation of living life on the seamy side. Charcoal-burning taxis packed with soldiers and girls slid around the eerie, browned-out streets. Some of these soldiers had dark skin, a fact the *Sydney Morning Herald* nervously acknowledged when it published, on 9 September 1942, a photograph of two of them above the caption: 'Their physique is outstandingly good and they are very cheerful about their tasks.' Hundreds of milkbars opened to serve coffee and orange juice and doughnuts to boys from the Bronx or Texas who wore rings and leather jackets and dark glasses, and bought flowers for the astonished local girls. The girls dyed their hair blonde, held hands with the Americans in public, and wrote agonized letters to their Australian sweethearts in Changi or on the Kokoda trail. They danced with the Americans cheek to cheek under the spell of countless crooners, or jitterbugged insanely; 15,000 of them married GIs. Hollywood came to life on the nether side of the Pacific.

The parks of Melbourne, Sydney and Brisbane were invaded by prostitutes who worked their trade in daylight and darkness. Terrible brawls would break out between Diggers and the Yanks,

7

which the universally despised provos or military police, would try to break up – until the brawlers joined forces and attacked them. The *Sydney Morning Herald* reported that by night 'young girls sat on the curbs in the city's principal streets, with their stockingless legs poised so that their knees would support their drink-sodden heads. Some sang; others argued; all shouted to every passing car. There were couples in doorways, on dust bins, and on grass plots off the pavements, under the full glare of street lights.' In Melbourne Albert Tucker, a painter in his early thirties, scored canvases with images of leering belles pursued by men through aquamarine streets, of victory girls in the savage caress of their soldiers. The public fascination with violence and danger turned into terror in the month of May 1942, when three women were strangled and abandoned semi-naked in the suburbs of Melbourne. An American soldier, Corporal Eddie Leonski, was arrested, and the suspicions of many were confirmed. The Americans might be saviours, but they were strangers too. After a public court martial Leonski was hanged at Pentridge Gaol on 9 November 1942.

The country's moral guardians were naturally outraged that the stringencies imposed by the thirties had vanished, and the old order was collapsing. 'The present decay of morals and the menace of social disease accompanying it are unprecedented,' thundered the Most Reverend James Duhig, the Catholic Archbishop of Brisbane, appalled that 'public parks and even church and school grounds' were 'invaded for immoral purposes'. Even artistic expression, some thought, was riddled with sin. In Melbourne the Catholic weekly the *Advocate* lashed out at the hellish decadence of contemporary painters, poets and musicians in Australia. 'THE FLESH, THE DEVIL, AND MODERN ART,' blared a headline. Work by some Australian poets was nothing but 'excursions into the subconscious mind of decadent perverts'. And jazz was evil: born of 'moll-houses, barrell-houses, gin and drugs', it carried 'eroticism to an extreme' and was 'frankly frightening'. Crooning was 'the most obviously anaemic manifestation of a decadent civilization'. The *Advocate* wanted it stopped, and now. On Friday, 23 July 1943, a chill midwinter's day, the *Sydney Morning Herald* complained of 'regular orgies in back rooms in the suburbs'. But not in Ethel Malley's spare bedroom, where Ern tossed and turned in his narrow bed for the last time, as his sister sat by his side.

She was the only mourner at his funeral. The next day, cleaning his room, she found his poems. There was a side of Ern she had never understood, but this! Gingerly she returned the sheets of paper to the trunk. She was going to donate what few possessions Ern had to the Salvos, and burn the rest, but something told her the poems were different. For a month or two she tried to work out what to do with them. Sometimes she opened the suitcase and read one. The phrases flashed by her like trains along the western line, but Ethel began to have an idea. On 28 October, three months after her brother's death, she put the first few poems in her shopping bag. Later, walking home from the shops with half a pound of sausages and her copy of the *Australian Women's Weekly*, which had an interesting recipe that week for onion roly-poly, she called in at the local library to talk to the elderly librarian who – and you have to appreciate the odds against this but the story could not be told without it – actually knew about a magazine that published poetry by young people. *Angry Penguins* it was called. He had a copy with the periodicals.

That night, sitting at her kitchen table, Ethel Malley wrote the letter that made her famous. *Dear Sir*, she began, *When I was going through my brother's things after his death, I found some poetry he had written.*

2 Enfant Terrible

In 1939 Max Harris set out to spark a revolution in Australian literature. He was eighteen years old, a poet and an anarchist. Harris was small and swarthy but tough too – he'd earned a reputation as a handy schoolboy footballer, a rover difficult to bump off the ball. He had an oval face and high forehead, wiry black hair, 'soft deep eyes and absurdly long eyelashes', a smooth baritone voice – like Dylan Thomas, whom he slightly resembled, he seemed the very image of a poet. 'Slender and handsome as Flecker's Hassan or a Syrian sweetmeats-vendor', as the writer Hal Porter remembered him, he cut a boisterous, exotic, indefatigable figure. Harris came out of nowhere as the self-appointed loud-hailer for a new poetry. His city, Adelaide, the only city in South Australia, was half a continent away from Sydney and Melbourne. There was no apprenticeship, no stepping quietly from the shadows. He got up one morning and talked his way into fame.

Born in 1921, Harris was Jewish, a country boy from Mt Gambier on the south-eastern coast of South Australia, where his father owned a wholesale butcher's business. There is not much to Mt Gambier except its blustery winds and bottomless Blue Lake, where in 1864 the bush-balladist Adam Lindsay Gordon covered himself in glory by soaring on horseback over an old stock fence on to a narrow shelf of rock high above the glittering water. Young Max left at the age of thirteen, when he won a scholarship to one of the most prestigious schools in the country, St Peter's College in Adelaide. Defined by the elegant, rectangular grid of streets that Colonel William Light set down beside the Torrens in 1837, Adelaide was small and snobbish, the most polite, Anglophile city in Australia. The cornerstone of its civic satisfaction was the fact that, unlike other Australian cities, none of its handsome sandstone buildings had been constructed with convict labour. No transportee ever served his sentence in South Australia. Many of Adelaide's most prominent buildings were clustered around Victoria Square, the green heart of Light's plan. In the centre of the square stood a grim statue of the ample monarch herself, scowling over this refined outpost of her empire, the Athens of the South as some fondly called the city.

St Peter's, a public school in the English tradition, was one of the jewels in Adelaide's crown. Here Harris rubbed shoulders with the sons of the Wasp establishment – future graziers, stockbrokers, doctors, lawyers and politicians. The scholarship boy did well at Saints. The English master, J. S. Padman, encouraged his bent for poetry, and introduced him to Geoffrey Grigson's magazine *New Verse* where he first read David Gascoigne, Ruthven Todd and Dylan Thomas. In his final year, as the star English student in the state, Harris took off the prized Tennyson medal, inaugurated by the Laureate's son, a former Governor of South Australia and Governor-General of Australia. After a stint as office boy and then copy boy on the Adelaide *News*, Harris went to Adelaide University in 1939 to study English, German and Economics. A dazzling future lay before him.

In the late thirties, as Harris discovered his vocation, news about the new was trickling through to Australia. Poetry started to emerge, though readers remained hostile and suspicious, from its traditional hinterlands of loyalist sub-Miltonic warbling on the one hand, and bush balladry and foot-thumping yarns on the other, the rough-hewn territory of Adam Lindsay Gordon, Banjo Paterson and Henry Lawson. These were the two main streams of Australian poetry, and the second had been livelier by far; but Harris had no intention of swimming in either, impatient with the idea that the 'bush' was the 'true' Australia, antidote to the cities where most people lived, and the authorized source of Australian verse. Harris ached to be modern, but there were no local models. There was still effectively no audience for poetry hailed as revolutionary on the other side of the world a generation earlier, like Ezra Pound's first *Canto* (1917), Yeats's *The Tower* (1921), T. S. Eliot's *The Waste Land* (1921).

There had been Australian poets with distinctive voices who worked in tremendous isolation, like John Shaw Neilson, who can sometimes sound a bit like the French symbolists he never read. Neilson, who died in 1942, was a shy itinerant labourer with no inclination for literary debate or galvanizing theory. In the opening years of the century, his contemporary Christopher Brennan wrote poetry in Sydney that was highly conscious of Europe – his god and master was Mallarmé – but Brennan remained a bizarre and eccentric figure, whose considerable gifts disintegrated in an alcohol-sodden haze. His symbolist vision was couched in the idioms of Wardour Street; his modernity was lathered in a foam of fustian.

The vitalist poet Kenneth Slessor first read T. S. Eliot in 1928 when he was in his late twenties, and was tantalized by the same idioms that were inspiring young poets everywhere to etch out maudlin scenes of decay and dessication. Yet Slessor's haunting lament *Five Bells* – one of the best poems ever produced in Australia, and which could not have been written without Eliot – did prove that new kinds of poetry were possible. *Five Bells* was the first major Australian poem that sounded as though it were written in the twentieth century. It appeared in 1939, the same year that Patrick White's first novel *Happy Valley* was published, and a year before Christina Stead's masterpiece, *The Man Who Loved Children*, came out in the United States. And in 1939 the famous *Herald* exhibition of international modern art, Australia's Armory show, toured Adelaide – where Harris saw it – and then Melbourne, Sydney and Brisbane. This exhibition was a watershed for many artists and writers who had previously encountered modern European painting only in reproduction. Among the artists represented were Picasso, Matisse, Chagall, Ernst, Dali, de Chirico, Braque, Cézanne, Gauguin, Seurat, Van Gogh, Bonnard, Vuillard, Modigliani, Gris, Léger, Signac, Derain and Vlaminck. By the time the show finished touring in

1940 there was no question of it returning to Europe. But it stirred such hostility in the art establishment that for the duration of the war it remained in its crates in the cellars of the Art Gallery of NSW. J. S. MacDonald, Director of the National Gallery in Victoria, opposed any purchases from the show and remarked, 'As owners of a great van Eyck, if we take a part in refusing to pollute our gallery with this filth we shall render a service to Art.' Only a handful of the paintings remained in Australia after the war.

The problem Harris faced, like every Australian writer who grappled with the question of how to connect with the world across the oceans, was that the cultural life of Australians was haunted by their distance from the centre, from London, Paris, New York, or some other fabled city. The centre was metropolitan, sophisticated, and elsewhere. It was also, of course, indifferent to Australia. This provincial isolation was the breeding ground of the cultural cringe, as the critic A. A. Phillips defined it in the fifties: the assumption that local art of any kind had to receive accolades overseas before Australians would acknowledge it as worthy to be called their own. In this mood of insecurity, in which art often aspired to imaginary standards and trends detected in largely imaginary places, creative work that exposed itself to international influence tended to pastiche. Australian artists in pursuit of the avant-garde stepped into an impasse, because the instant they imitated the 'new' and the 'original' their own work ceased to have the very qualities they valued above all. The cutting-edge kept moving out of reach.

None the less, by the time Harris got to Adelaide University, and Australia prepared to immerse itself in another European war, the debates over modernism – about ideas which had originated elsewhere, between the several dozen people in the country who were qualified to enter into them – had begun to grow vigorous. The arguments about art and culture in Australia in the thirties and during the war are legendary not for their originality or even coherence but for their sheer ferocity. And the contradictions between these two aspects of provincialism, flaccid imitation and savage position-taking, went unexamined in the hurly-burly.

In 1938, while still at school, Harris had poems accepted in the first *Jindyworobak Anthology*, a publication dedicated to fostering a 'national' poetry. Among his contributions was a lurid pastiche of Dylan Thomas which concluded:

And the aching
drub of the separator, the pitched cadence
of the singing milk on pails, and the brooding cows
hollow bellowing filter heavy and leaden to the sense
that drooping sheep stir from the arms of stiff gums.

With clanking buckets, round shouldered, from the cowshed
    Dawn comes

The anthology drew comment in the *Bulletin* where the anonymous reviewer (almost certainly the poet and playwright Douglas Stewart, a staunch and influential defender of the bush tradition) cited Thomas and complained that Harris, 'the most interesting of the *Jindyworobak* contributors, spoils a good cow-cocky dawn with this false modernity'. His mixed praise, heady stuff for the seventeen-year-old, helped Harris fix his image as a rebellious outsider in a parochial world. 'I am afraid that my position in relation to Australian poetry is a strange one, and as the *Bulletin* suggested comparable to that of the young Dylan Thomas in England,' he wrote in April of the following year.

By then he was 'secretary of the Jindys and chief ally with Ingamells in his work'. The 'Jindys' were the Jindyworobak Club, a radical nationalist cultural movement based in Adelaide, sympathetic to the right and led by its founder Rex Ingamells, a poet and 'quiet fanatic' in his mid-twenties. Each year the club advertised its aspirations for a new culture in the anthology that bore its name. 'Jindyworobak', an Aboriginal word meaning 'to join', promoted an Australianism supposedly exclusive of *all* European culture, attuned instead to the Aboriginal heritage which would replace it. Even earlier evangelists for the bush, like the bush whistler Henry Kendall or Lawson or Paterson were off the mark for Ingamells, who saw himself as the harbinger of a new dawn in Australian culture. Repressed, Anglophile Adelaide was the perfect matrix for the revolutionary theology Ingamells devised. Irked, no doubt, by the pseudo-English accents he heard in 'society' and by the automatic prestige of green fields, white swans and any English poetry, he urged the elimination of 'English idiom' in Australian writing in favour of an indigenous terminology. Dell and dale, oak and elm were out: gum, scrub, bush and billabong were in.

The key term in Ingamells' mythology was 'Alcheringa', which he defined as 'the dream-time of long ago'. Devotion to the spirit of the Alcheringa was all-embracing: the poet Ian Mudie, an adherent, uprooted all the roses in his garden because they were 'so aggressively foreign'. Ingamells, deeply impressed by Lawrence's *Kangaroo*, had a mystical vision of Australia in part inspired by that novel – a place of primitive splendour corrupted by pathetic Europeans:

Australia is still the Unknown Land, unknown except to a few renegades from the Gangrened Clan. It is the most ancient block of ground on the surface of Earth; and, as if mankind were struggling from centres of mad sophistication, through desert and range bushland, to primeval simplicity and mystery, it is the furthest from human appreciation. At present it is as though the very heart of a strange peace and beauty were reached but not seen, not known, unrealized because the creatures who have, by dint of overweening egotism, encroached upon it still cling to the cumbersome trappings and impedimenta of evacuated and crumbling citadels of craziness and apathy: the propaganda and lying advertisement that filled the whited halls of Commerce and Humbug are blared forth in the very fastness of Hope and Wonder. We, the Australian People, are the hollowest of shams, the most pitiful pretentiousness that the tragic spark of life has contrived; the most ashen gutter the brief candle of spiritual existence has given to the dreams of civilization.

The idea that Australians lived in a fake culture, the 'hollowest of shams', defenders of the butt-end of Europe in a land they did not understand, was pervasive in the thirties and forties, though it did not always find such apocalyptic expression. Much of what the Jindys produced was simply nature poetry, traditional in form, with an Australian accent. Dry creeks, dusty gumtrees, sleepy goannas and startled galahs, in metre and rhyme. But Ingamells' attempt to create an Australian idiom from scratch also generated self-parodic nonsense. His jog-trotting aboriginoid diction, culled from a range of sources, trod the same turf as the Boojum and the Snark:

> Into moorawathimeering,
> where atninga dare not tread,
> leaving wurly for a wilban,
> tallabilla, you have fled.
>
> Wombalunga curses, waitjurk –
> though we cannot break the ban,
> and follow tchidna any further
> after one-time karaman . . .

In 1943 Harris dismissed Ingamells as a writer of jargon, and compared Jindyworobak with 'Jabberwocky'.* He knew from the outset he was only fellow-travelling with the Jindys. Harris wanted to promote a literature open to international writing: 'Each moment of isolationism is a nail in the coffin of Australian culture,' he proclaimed. As early as 1939 he declared himself a disciple of 'the present *attitude* to poetry as expounded by T. E. Hulme, elaborated by Michael Roberts and carried into effect both in painting and poetry by Herbert Read. I also am in agreement with Read when he says that the poet can subscribe to one, and one creed alone – that of the shifting process of reality.'

*The movement was scoffed at even by other cultural nationalists: 'there must surely be something wrong with a theory which is not accepted by any of the writers who are most effectively tackling the problem it sets out to solve,' remarked A. A. Phillips in *Meanjin* in 1949 (Vol. 8, No. 1, 65). Jindyworobak is now dead, but there is none the less a corner of Australian culture that will be forever Jindy: it is one of many attempts that have been made to reconcile European and Aboriginal culture in Australia. The poet Les A. Murray once described himself as 'the last of the Jindyworobaks'.

Hulme, the English philosopher and poet who argued for a dry, hard, 'classical' art, and steered Ezra Pound into imagism, died in the trenches in 1917 when he was thirty-four, but his influence endured. *Speculations*, Read's posthumous edition of his writings, appeared in the twenties, and Roberts also published a critical study of Hulme. In 1936, Roberts' highly influential *The Faber Book of Modern Poetry* appeared and Read, now a romantic anarchist whose prolific writings on art and literature were at the peak of their prestige, published his famous introduction to the International Surrealist Exhibition in London. Announcing his familiarity with 'advanced' English literary thought, Harris anticipated the tenor of the renaissance he was about to superintend. The romantic figure of the poet as free-wheeling outsider filled his vision. The same passage where Read conjured 'the shifting process of reality' also painted a seductive portrait of the artist, 'disenfranchised by his lack of residence in any fixed constituency, wandering faithlessly in the no-man's land of his imagination'. Since this more or less described the sense of isolation any Australian poet might feel, it is hardly surprising it caught the young Harris's eye. Ern Malley, who spoke a 'No-Man's-language appropriate / Only to No-Man's-Land', knew this passage too.

Harris took note of Ingamells' crusading style. In 1939 he contributed to the Melbourne monthly newspaper *Bohemia* a credo which began: 'Artistically I am an anarchist. I am 18.' He announced his programme for literary reform – whoever wanted to 'write true *Australian* poetry must put himself into relation with the general stream of *European* poetry and feeling, must learn his craftsmanship from sources external to his hopeless Australian heritage'. In the next issue, he defended the 'grotesque' in art, dilated on the unconscious, and characterized his own poetry as '*Australian* surrealism'.

Ingamells published Harris's first book of poems, *The Gift of Blood*, in 1940. Some of the work was over-rich but it showed promise all the same. The title came from the short verse drama that opened the book in which Isaac, a German-speaking Jew, declares his brotherhood with a German named Ludovik, who turns out to be a Nazi. At the close of the play Isaac shoots his adversary, and chants the phrase 'the gift of blood'. Here, and in the poems which followed, Harris's accelerated confidence, billowing rhythms, and rhetorical ambition came out of Thomas, Hopkins and Eliot, as well as the German poets Rilke and Moerike:

In the soft stillness, as a Christ, I leave you to the quiet
beloved, to become as the faded trees on the chintz curtain,
with no sunlight to betray the dust and the aged stain –
from the curling hill I watch you in the slow night
moving as the apparition of my desire, and not as you are;
now traced in the light of fear that still glows in the lone
horror of stilled engine thunder and untrodden stone.

In the saddened heart that has loved and been refused,
there is at this time refusal to defy and belief that dark
joy is bedded in the shadows of the hills and the cold remark
is but dying leaf-crackle against the sky where the greys have
    fused.

Two years later he had another collection, *Dramas from the Sky*. In his rage for the contemporary, Harris may have misjudged his own gifts which were essentially traditional: an ear for cadence and an eye for the lyric phrase. *Dramas from the Sky* attempted to turn the nascent surrealism of *The Gift of Blood* into a system of composition. Harris couldn't help showing off his credentials. Among the poems was 'The Pelvic Rose', dedicated to Salvador Dali and in debt 'to the thought of Miltonic Arianism, to Aldous Huxley's essay on Pascal, to Sigmund Freud, and to *The Golden Bough*'. Harris's unacknowledged borrowing, though, was from the English surrealist poet George Barker. The poem began:

the pelvic rose unfolding in the flesh
gropes its roots into the germs of life,
esoteric being about the hair roots of the cells,

spreads wide the set limb, unanswering
the petal's voice, and through the silent orgasm
makes a passage to the precise cross-winds
of thought; burnt to ash of grief
blown pelvic rose is the speck in the eye
from many a backyard fire or the willywilly
hurling the heart with the dead leaf.

By now Harris had rejected Ingamells and the Jindyworobaks outright. In September 1942 Ingamells wrote about Harris to Clem Christesen, a former journalist who had started a left-leaning nationalist literary magazine called *Meanjin Papers* in Brisbane. Ingamells described his ex-protégé as:

a handsome and charming young coot, very conceited but I have never found his conceit insufferable. I'm a bit disappointed about the way he's drifted from Jindy and Jindy spread his name all over Australia; but I'm convinced that Max is utterly honest about it. His nature's such that he's outgrown Jindy, I should say; though it's definitely and strongly coloured him, he's bound up a different alley, which looks very like a blind one to me at times. But he's brilliant, there's no doubt about that, and lately seems to be losing a great deal of shallowness and show in his verse. He'll bust through with something smashing some day, and no doubt he's building steadily all the time. At present, though, I think he's not yet out of his fantastic phase; he's still posing, pridefully full of his own greatness. Mind, I'm not condemning this. It'll work out, and Max will quite justify himself. He's following out perfectly Masefield's dictum to me regarding high achievement: 'Remember – bold design, constant practice, frequent mistakes.'

It was a generous assessment, but deference from the tribal elder of poetic nationalism to the Poet Laureate Masefield gives Ingamells away: 'Jindy' was really an outbreak, long after the event, of Georgian poetry in phoney dialect.

Harris, meanwhile revelled in notoriety. He led with his chin and thrived on attack. 'I am iconoclastical, harsh, scraping people's sensibilities,' he wrote. 'There are numerous instances where I've got myself heartily disliked for my outlook and approach. Such offending is inevitable.' When *The Gift of Blood* appeared, Harris felt sure the book would 'cause hostility, criticism, dislike. I am fully aware of people's reactions before I launch it – but I must publish all the same.'

He saw himself as an 'enfant terrible', and made a stir when he gave a talk at Adelaide University on the subject of 'Surrealism, the Philistines and You' in which he 'suitably insulted all bourgeois possibilities by comparing the ballet with the circus and Greek sculpture with window-models . . . After a preliminary talk on the political and intellectual point of Surrealism and some illuminating remarks on women's dreams, Mr Harris recounted some of the more incredible antics of the Dadaists'. The result, Harris boasted, was itself 'near Dadaistic. There was uproar on several occasions.' His politics were firmly, fashionably, left wing. He was a member of the Communist Party for several years. In late July of 1941, Harris suffered the indignity of being tossed in Adelaide's Torrens River by some brawny loyalists – led by Tony 'Tubby' Abbott, a scion of the establishment whose uncle, Charles, was a prominent lawyer and conservative politician – in a brawl over what role students should play in the event of any 'emergency' interfering with the war effort. A product of the final strike-ridden days of Robert Menzies' conservative United Australia Party government which lost office to John Curtin's Labor Party a few months later, the fracas intensified Harris's notoriety but does not seem to have done him too much harm: at the end of 1941 he was appointed to the position of research officer at Adelaide University, which meant he could continue his studies in economics, and would not be called up.

Harris reported to his friend Catherine Caris, a journalist with the *Australian Women's Weekly*, that 'this town hates my guts', but he was fond of Adelaide, and kicked around with other young artists: Dave Dallwitz, the jazz musician, Ivor Francis, the painter, Geoffrey Dutton, Donald Kerr and Paul Pfeiffer, all poets. His loyal offsider was Mary Martin but his girlfriend was Vonnie Hutton, a dancer whom he later married. It was natural for Harris to be the centre of attention. One of his party tricks was to silence the room by chanting a witty or satirical rhyming poem about everybody there. He made it up as he went along. He loved poetry for its sensuous, exotic qualities and had great slabs of 'The Song of Solomon' by heart.

'Max Harris is probably the most discussed young poet in Australia today,' the blurb to Dramas from the Sky modestly asserted. 'His work is of the utmost importance among contemporary writing.' This was not the opinion of another young poet, Harold Stewart, who reviewed Dramas from the Sky in Sydney in mid 1942. 'Most of the verses', he remarked, 'are what a practising poet would call first rough-drafts . . . There is a fatal facility about all such semi-surrealist verse . . . any poet of talent could produce a hundred lines of it a week for the rest of his life. Once you get the knack, it is no harder to do than a free-association test.' Stewart also complained that the poetry lacked wit: 'a good course of epigrams and a sense of satire would be of benefit,' he advised, and suggested that Harris might be 'really quite an intelligible poet . . . still having occasional lapses. For every now and then, a wicked little bit of an idea, with a very naughty gleam in its eye, peeps around the corner of a phrase and pokes its tongue out when the author is not looking.'

By this time Harris was famous for more than his poetry. In 1940 he announced to an acquaintance that he was 'producing a magazine for the university arts association. We intend circulating on rather a larger scale than usual with such undertakings'. The comic-surreal name of the journal, Angry Penguins, derived from Harris's sequence of poems about the traumas of the Spanish Civil War, 'Progress of Defeat'. Its subtitle was 'death is non-existent: death is bourgeois', and Section VII began:

> We know no mithridatum of despair
> as drunks, the angry penguins of the night,
> straddling the cobbles of the square,
> tying a shoelace by fogged lamplight.

The image stuck – drunken youths in dinner suits, prowling

some European city of the mind by night – and the phrase 'angry penguins' seemed a good deal more surreal in isolation. The patron of the first issue was the Adelaide academic, Charles Jury, a wealthy homosexual bachelor who had palatial rooms on North Terrace opposite the Botanical Gardens, where he held literary soirées. The issue led with a fruity piece by Jury in praise of Harris: 'he shows boundless promise, and what he has achieved is achieved. Like Troilus, he is very young.'

Harris's editorship of *Angry Penguins* (with fellow poet D. B. Kerr, later shot down by the Japanese over the Timor Sea) was a sign of his growing confidence and influence: in his editorial in the third issue he wrote that the magazine was the Australian equivalent of '*New Directions* in America and John Lehmann's *New Writing* in England. Its sole standard is *genuineness now*.' The magazine began to outgrow its coterie beginnings.

Work by young, energetic painters, many of them – like Sidney Nolan, Albert Tucker and Arthur Boyd – from Melbourne, appeared in its pages. In 1942, Harris visited Melbourne, where he met John Reed, a lawyer with a Cambridge degree who lived with his wife Sunday at Heidelberg, in the hills outside the city, on a small farm they dubbed 'Heide'. Born into establishment families, each had a private income, and they found their joint vocation in surrendering their time, their house, their lives and their money to the support of new art and writing.

Heide was a pocket of rural bohemia on the edge of the suburbs, cluttered with books, wet canvases, manuscripts, fresh eggs and milk, fruit and vegetables just culled from the kitchen garden. Fair and strong-jawed, Sunday Reed was imperious, intuitive, seductive, possessive, generous. John Reed was a good-looking man with dark hair and a determined, compact face. He was well known as an activist for the modern movement, an implacable enemy of everything hidebound in Australian culture. His sympathy, in spite of his upbringing, was with the left: 'my life is lived with artists,' he once wrote, 'nearly every one of whom comes from a worker's or lower middle class family'. Harris's friendship with the Reeds flourished. Reed, who was more than ten years older than Harris, became fiercely protective of him. 'He may be egocentric, bombastic,' he told a sceptical acquaintance, 'but it just so happens that if he isn't a genius, he is certainly about as near to being one as Australia has yet produced – and he is only 22.'

Sidney Nolan was the working-class artist with whom the Reeds shared their lives most closely. A lithe, slender, handsome man with piercing blue eyes and a narrow, genial face, Nolan was the son of a tram driver. He left school at fourteen and went to work in a hat factory where he made advertising and display stands. For a time he ran a pie shop. Nolan was an autodidact, a devourer of books, who frequented the great domed Reading Room in the Melbourne Public Library on Swanston Street. He was ambitious, highly gifted, and charming. His transition from factory worker to fully fledged painter was inseparable from his association with the Reeds. He met them in 1938 and went to live with them at Heide in 1941. Their ménage à trois was an open secret among the painters and writers of their circle. John was his patron and champion, Sunday his lover and muse. He and Sunday translated Rimbaud together. She bought him his canvases, paints, brushes. Often while he painted at Heide she would stand beside him talking to him. He painted for her, put her into his paintings, and gave many of them to her.

From 1943, though Harris continued to live in Adelaide, *Angry Penguins* was produced from Melbourne, designed by Sidney Nolan and financed by the Reeds. Harris was paid a modest salary of £100 a year, less than a private in the Australian Army made, and well below the basic wage. Reed and Harris became co-editors of the magazine (though the influence of Sunday Reed and Nolan was equally significant) and founded their own publishing company. *Angry Penguins* spread its wings. It was the plushest literary magazine in the country. Harris was in touch with the American publisher James Laughlin, founder of *New Directions*, and through him obtained work by Dylan Thomas, Robert Penn Warren, and Kenneth Rexroth. The magazine was sympathetic to the ideas of Herbert Read and published his anarchist disciple George Woodcock. *Angry Penguins* also gave attention to the English neo-romantic movement, the New Apocalypse, and printed poetry by Henry Treece, one of its guiding lights and a devotee of Read.

The New Apocalypse was only a year or two older than *Angry Penguins*. Its first anthology appeared in 1939, including work by Dylan Thomas, Norman MacCaig and Nicholas Moore – though Thomas refused to sign the manifesto. Apocalyptic poets rejected the detached, 'cerebral' verse of Auden and Spender, insisting that a poet's images 'should arouse . . . a massive . . . response'. They went in for an elemental rhetoric of blood, bone, seed, womb, water and earth, derived largely from Thomas and George Barker. Treece's work varied the romantic theme by setting its apocalypse in a fairy-tale world of princes and courtiers, wizards and beggars, harps and runes. The movement drew spiritual nourishment from Lawrence, Kafka and Read's critical writings. Its politics were a version of anarchism – hostile to the State, in favour of 'freedom for man, as a complete living organism', as the devotee George Fraser wrote in 1941. Initiates saw their work as the next, life-affirming step after surrealism. Fraser asserted the poet's right 'to exercise conscious control' while agreeing with 'Freud's discovery . . . that it is impossible really to talk nonsense'. The difference between surrealism and the Apocalypse was, Fraser wrote, 'the difference between the madman, who sits back and contemplates all sorts of strange and trivial relationships, freed from the necessity of action; and a sane man who accepts dream and fantasy and obscure and terrible desires and energies, as part of his completeness'.

There was much in Harris's poetry that the New Apocalyptics might approve of, but *Angry Penguins* looked further afield than this British coterie. It ran essays on Baudelaire, Henri Rousseau, Henry Miller; translations of Rimbaud and Seferis; poems by visiting American servicemen, Karl Shapiro and Harry Roskolenko, whom Harris seized on as emissaries from the great, wide world he wanted to conquer. The magazine was hostile to doctrinaire Marxism though it gave debating space to local apparatchiks, and to communist artists like Noel Counihan. There were articles on dance, music, even sociology, with a contribution by the Englishman Tom Harrisson, one of the founders of Mass Observation.

Angry Penguins' romantic ambitions seem quixotic from this distance, though there was nothing else like it in Australia. Harris and Reed wanted to do everything at once. The quality of the magazine was uneven, its editing unreliable, and the blend of pieces not always coherent. It lumped together new work of whatever ilk, local 'modernist' writing, and international contributions of varied quality and persuasion. The magazine published some good Australian fiction writers, Hal Porter, Alan Marshall, Peter Cowan, but its best achievement was to sponsor a new school of Australian painting.

Extending its reach – but not always its grasp – at every opportunity, *Angry Penguins* had found its character by 1943, and Harris defined himself against its activities. He continued to publish in other magazines and took pot shots at other writers. In 1941 Harris attacked Adrian Lawlor, an Englishman in his fifties who had come to Australia in 1910 and soon emerged as a painter, writer and pot-stirrer on the side of modern art. Albert Tucker's portrait of Lawlor, painted in 1939, shows a bald man with a bell-shaped head, high cheekbones and a crescent mouth. When the *Herald* exhibition came to Melbourne in October of that year, Lawlor was its advocate and harangued the crowds from a chariot which he propelled around the Melbourne Town Hall where the show was hung. Lawlor had prodigious energy but his role as apologist for the new was marred by soapbox froth. His polemical defence of modern art, *Arquebus* (1938) has great élan – but is written by a writer in love with the sound of his own voice. Harris, no minimalist in the way he used language himself, attacked Lawlor's 'Tartarean drench of verbosity' in *A Comment*, another war-time literary magazine edited from Melbourne (but with rather less money than *Angry Penguins*: it was printed on brown wrapping paper). Lawlor replied in the next issue by printing a sound-parody of one of Harris's poems under the title 'The dada Dilly'. He delighted in turning Harris's fragrant abstraction – 'may I know you, the faraway sister of time, / dressed in green' – into gut-churning comedy: 'may I show you the faraway blister of slime, / dressed in gangrene'.

But the Angry Penguins could take it on the chin. Among the writers they published was Alister Kershaw, a poet with a sharp tongue who was the same age as Harris. Kershaw fell under the spell of Adrian Lawlor's conversation and identified with his view of the artist as a maverick, accountable only to his own intelligence. He was hostile to the left – 'swinish disciples of equality and fraternity', he called them – and to surrealism. He once gave a public performance at Melbourne University where he primly donned a pair of white gloves before removing a copy of *Worker's Voice* from his bag and attacking it. He then read some surrealist poetry – backwards. In 1943, in the introduction to his first book of poems, *The Lonely Verge*, Kershaw attacked the 'unending self-abnegatory moan' of Auden, Spender and Day Lewis, lamenting that poetry had to 'celebrate collective farming or vilify the aristocracy' to get printed. Only three modern writers were worth reading: Richard Aldington, Roy Campbell and D. H. Lawrence. 'Poetry is a pointing to the essential quick of things,' Kershaw wrote, 'it is the raging hymn of life', and poets the aristocracy who avoided 'cocktail-swilling cretins' and 'the imbecile proletariat'.

In spite of his loathing of surrealism, Kershaw also wrote apocalyptic poetry of grand effect, indebted to George Barker and abstracted to the point of obscurity. His magnum opus, 'Lands in Force', had appeared in the second issue of *Angry Penguins*. His poems, he said, emerged 'from disgust', and his liveliest work was in satire. In September 1943, *Angry Penguins* published 'The Denunciad', in which Kershaw lampooned prominent figures on the local scene. He attacked the bush nationalists as phoneys – 'For no rose ever quite so sweetly smelt / Unless at Broome or Alice Springs it dwelt, / And even then it sweeter smells by far / If it's disguised to look like waratah' – and dished it out to the Angry Penguins themselves:

Around about the 'Angry Penguins' play,
Cheerfully woeful or morosely gay
. . .
Where Sidney Nolan, like a looney don,
Shows them the canvasses he's painted on
Or – if his art must rightly be defined –
His blobs of paint with canvasses behind
. . .
A point about these pleasant little birds
Is that their *only* being lies in *words*

Harris thrived on this sort of thing. The same issue of *Angry Penguins* announced the imminent publication, by Reed & Harris, of his first novel, *The Vegetative Eye*. 'Its original and vital form alone is bound to cause the keenest interest and discussion,' the blurb asserted. *The Vegetative Eye* was 'a work of sensitive and personal prose, with the haunting images and qualities of Kafka and Rilke', while its author was 'already well known in Australia and America as a poet of outstanding powers'. The novel would 'produce a profound effect on the literary world of both countries'.

As chief Angry Penguin, clad in black shirt and white tie, Harris would sweep into the refectory at Adelaide University, an acolyte carrying a pile of books two reverential paces behind him. Educated by the establishment, he was everything a self-regarding provincial city loathed and feared and sneered at: a red, an artist, a bohemian. Harris was young enough to want to push things to the brink without being aware how high the stakes were. John Reed, a true child of power and privilege who had thrown his lot in with the likes of Harris and Nolan, understood the risks of brinkmanship. 'We are in a position . . . where we can either influence the course of events quite considerably,' he warned Harris early in 1944, 'or where, by a single tactical error, we can lose all control whatsoever.' He had no idea that two young poets from Sydney were about to make that sentence come true.

3   Jim and Harold

James McAuley grew up not far from where Ethel Malley lived, in Sydney's depressed, semi-industrial western suburbs. He was a few years older than Max Harris. McAuley's father, Patrick, a lapsed Catholic of Irish stock from Goondiwindi in Queensland, left school at thirteen to work in the bush as a stockman, but gave it up to buy and sell real estate in Sydney, where James was born in 1917. Family legend declared that 'the first McAuley was an Irish soldier who bashed the convicts at Toongabbie'. Patrick McAuley also claimed descent from the Irishman Peter Lalor, the working-class hero who in 1854 led the miners in the Ballarat goldfields massacre known as the Eureka Stockade: James's elder brother John was given Lalor for his middle name. His mother Mary Maude was a church-going Anglican, a baker's daughter from Inverell in northern New South Wales. Patrick McAuley was a severe, remote man in owl-eyed glasses who had 'dammed up his Irish blood / Against all drinking praying fecklessness'. He was cold and silent and formal: young Jim once put his face up to be kissed, but his father turned away in 'curt embarrassment'. The boy learned to hide his 'tenderness'. Patrick was an astute businessman, and did so well in property speculation that after about 1920 he never went to work. He helped around the house, dressed for lunch and dinner, and for their birthdays bought his children shares in BHP, the country's biggest company. Though the family had joined the middle class, they lived frugally. Life was listening to the soapie *Blue Hills* on the radio at lunch, tuning in to the stock report, and songs around the piano in the evening. Mary Maude played the banjo and sang 'Annie Laurie'. James's parents' love was 'daily as the *Sydney Morning Herald*, / Rather than like the eagle or the dove'. The McAuleys had few friends, avoided the relatives, and minded their own business.

James, with his mother's encouragement, showed promise in music and literature – at primary school he wrote a parody of Henry Kendall, and he sang in the choir at a local Anglican church. Like generations of Australian children, he pored over the Ginger Meggs cartoon strip in the *Sunday Sun*: Ginger Meggs taught him to read before he started school. In 1929 he was admitted to Fort Street High School, a fabled institution founded in the mid-nineteenth century. Fort Street took in clever children from all over Sydney and boasted an academic record often better than the plush denominational schools where the wealthy sent their offspring to be educated. Graduates of Fort Street were a special caste: they were outstanding – Bert Evatt and John Kerr attended the school before James McAuley – but they had to fight establishment insiders to reach the loftier echelons of power and influence.

McAuley was precocious, top of his class, prefect and school captain. He had an actor's face, skull-defined, with hooded blue-grey eyes, fair hair, and a wide, confident mouth. He was a brilliant student of the piano but at fifteen decided against becoming a professional musician in order to follow his literary bent. He read widely – the adolescent McAuley lost his religious faith after digesting Sir James Frazer's *The Golden Bough* – and he published poems, stories and articles about contemporary writers in the school magazine, the *Fortian*. In one essay, the sixteen-year-old characterized the 'profound horror' of the modernist poet at having 'his originality tainted and enfeebled by outworn modes of expression', who would risk everything 'for the sake of experiment'. Most modernists, McAuley observed, were Americans, with a 'boisterous "hustling" manner . . . alien to the average English mind', although T. S. Eliot was the exception to this rule. Eliot's poetry was difficult but his 'sins in this regard are more pardonable than those of some lesser poets who substitute ingenuity for genius and obscurity for real subject-matter'. McAuley attacked the poetry of Herbert Read as 'colourless' and 'abstract', presenting, he thought, 'formidable difficulties'.

Fort Street was a haven for McAuley and for another budding poet he met there, Harold Stewart, who came from the same world of the western suburbs that glorified jocks and larrikins, and scorned artistic ambition. Stewart, a quiet, determined boy with a sparkling sense of humour, was small, with a lean, even-featured face, blue eyes, and oiled dark-brown hair he parted down the middle. Born in 1916, he grew up in Drummoyne where his father, who had lived in India until his early thirties and spoke fluent Hindustani, was the local health inspector. Stewart also had musical ability and won a scholarship to the Conservatorium where he studied trumpet for three years before entering Fort Street. While McAuley had all-round abilities as a student, Stewart preferred to go his own way. In a third-year English exam he ignored every question except when asked to define 'irony' in a few lines: then he wrote 'a thirty-page answer'. Since he could hardly be failed, he was given a 50 per cent pass. Stewart himself remembers that he and Jim McAuley were 'rivals' at Fort Street. 'We were both editors of *The Fortian*, and printed each other's poems; though I was somewhat in awe of Jim's highbrow reading and superior intellect, and he somewhat contemptuous of my lack of both. Only after, in our late 'teens and early twenties, did we bury the hatchet.'

In 1935 McAuley won an exhibition to Sydney University and Stewart followed him the next year. To save money the boys would catch the train to Central and walk to the university. The campus was lively but most of the action was extracurricular. Stewart could not connect the tedium of lectures with his determination to become a poet – 'I have never been so bored in all my life, no, not even in the Army' – and he dropped out after a few months, though he kept up with his university friends. In the next few years, until his call-up on 28 September 1942, he scratched out a living doing occasional reviews and broadcasts for the ABC. 'I had no money at all,' Stewart recalls. 'I had to find sixpence in the street to buy a meat-pie to eat.'

He became unpaid art critic for the student newspaper *Honi Soit*, and was friendly with the painters William Dobell, Russell Drysdale and Donald Friend. He wrote a strenuous series of articles for *Honi Soit* on leading figures from the Ecole de Paris, defending and explaining among others, Degas, Cézanne, Van Gogh, Monet, Matisse, Picasso and Braque, whose works had been hung in reproduction in the Sydney University Union. Stewart also reviewed, sardonically but without rancour, the Contemporary Art Society Exhibition for 1941, which featured some artists associated with *Angry Penguins*: 'Among the extreme Expressionists, Tucker employs distortions and cacophonous colour to explore strange mental states,' he observed. 'Nolan has developed . . . the most radically naive vision of any local artist.' Half a century later, Stewart explains: 'That was a period I worked through and by the time I was about twenty-four my interests in art had moved to medieval art in Europe and to Asian art which is of course medieval in its whole outlook.'

McAuley despised lectures too, and rarely went, but kept up his enrolment in English, Philosophy and Latin. 'He did all his own reading,' Norma, whom he would marry in Newcastle in 1942, recalls, 'and a fortnight before exams would prepare by taking black coffee and Benzedrine and not going to sleep.' He cut a glittering figure in his undergraduate days. Friends were in awe of him. 'I thought McAuley was just about the cleverest person I ever met,' the journalist Tess van Sommers told me, with 'his funny little tucked-up monkey face and his blond hair and his irresistible sense of irony and humour.' 'He was so impressive,' the novelist and poet Amy Witting remembers. 'How he called words out of the air was something.' Donald Horne was mesmerized by McAuley, who

had some of the mannerisms of a hypnotist – a careful but slight gesture, sometimes nothing more than a significant stiffening of his long pianist's fingers, would emphasize a point, or he would lower his eyelids, then suddenly raise them, confronting me from beneath blond eyelashes with a piercing stare, his face muscles well controlled to register significant emotion. There were times when his whole body would seem to stiffen and expand, erectile, as if to strike . . . when he spoke the words would bunch up, quick and monotonous, then there would be the briefest of pauses before the key words struck out, slowly stressed. This was 'J. Mc', who wrote verse. Jimmy the jazz pianist was golden-haired, laughing, sometimes frenzied, but behind even the frenzy there was a resilient toughness, a kind of rhythmic control. Metre seemed to be built into his body.

McAuley sometimes used to walk through the city the entire night; at dawn he would join shift-workers and derelicts for a breakfast of rank coffee and Craven A cigarettes at the cafeteria in Central Station. At parties, often held in 'meagre rooms in the western suburbs' where 'everybody drank beer', he would play jazz and blues on the piano – Bessie Smith, Louis Armstrong, Duke Ellington – though he could also improvise versions of Bach for fun. He sang in an alto voice something like Fats Waller but could do a gravelly Satchmo too. McAuley loved pranks: after a party one night he repaired to the university 'and played "Rhapsody in Blue" on the carillon'. At a formal Arts Faculty function, when asked to play 'God Save The King', he riled loyalists by jazzing it. He knew by heart blasphemous songs like 'The Ballad of Joking Jesus' and 'The Bastard King of England', and made up his own nonsense drinking songs. He was a natural parodist. Language danced at his fingertips. To entertain friends he knocked out a letter pastiching James Joyce, unleashing a volley of sexual puns:

Readjoice and begad! A litter half eye scent to Ju-Ju de Sandy Coq. Thangyou and yo sweatheard fo inseducing me. The encounter was most simulating espiciously fo me. I whope she scents me a latter. I arset her fo ein phooeygraph, tooky by dèlight, becoarse eye have scene her butt by moodlight by the riever's side when darkness was diminyrendo. She has a corps delectable, witch would be nice to clammer abit on. I would demoonstrate to her my own pertickler big thick – trick! I shall contrahole her, and if she naughty I will begetting a stick to her. A big joycy bifsteck upper a sole (o mio). You *can* take it with her. At leest *you* cunt, I can. Eye ope she's not an offal sod that I cant get on with, like most of skurts I meat these daze. I would like to have the a-queynt-ance of a nice femurle to sooth my sorrowful s'ole, when I feel sheet on the lever. Becods I am tired of leeving alone (as the prisoner's ballock says). But she will be a newsance too like all these freudulent women. A tun of cares is on my shudders what with one thing and an udder. I am weary of the whoreld and sickert art – titian off to make a whistler turner constable – or drinkwater. Would I had these puns in shillings and pence! Take care of the pens and the shittings will take care of themselves, not to mention the poons. I will mumble-jumble no more. Argott, Kristnamurphy, and the Holy Spillit, Ah blessed Vermin Marey, and all the higher-archies of Heaven: bawls bawls bawls.

Heil Hipbath!
Shame-us

McAuley shared Joyce's mocking fascination with religion – another letter included a droll epistle to the Virgin Mary:

> But then you were faithful to Joseph, except
> For just that one slip with the Almighty, and Joseph
> He didn't mind, though he thought it odd,
> And wasn't altogether proud of it. In heaven,
> I suppose, he's kept in his place, and not *allowed*
> To be jealous. After all,
> It was purely a business affair, you can tell him,
> And he hasn't done too badly out of it.

Van Sommers remembers 'the McAuley group' as 'cliquey. There weren't many women. It was very jokey. I don't remember any impassioned literary arguments at all.' 'It was very chauvinist,' Amy Witting told me. 'If you wanted to be equal with men you walked on knives. They did humiliate you sexually if you challenged them mentally. Girls were conquests or they were ornaments.' Witting was known to everyone by her surname Fraser. 'They called me by a boy's name. They'd let me compete, but they wouldn't let me be a girl.'

McAuley and Stewart spent hours together in cafés over cups of coffee – they were never drinking partners – discussing poetry. They enjoyed each other's wit, and each respected the other's intelligence, but they were not at all alike. Moody and charismatic, McAuley became the centre of attention the instant he entered a room. He dominated any social situation. Stewart was genial but a loner, shy and rather secretive – 'almost without mannerism', Donald Horne remembered. With his 'cheery reliable face . . . he looked like an honest man of the suburbs come to make some repair to the house . . . He could slash out in conversation, although still smiling.' Stewart was renowned for the purity of his dedication to his work. 'He's a very strong character,' Amy Witting told me, 'much stronger than we ever knew then.'

Poetry was the one thing Stewart wanted to do. McAuley gave the impression he could do anything. But the golden boy was also deadly serious about poetry. It was not always easy for friends to connect the dazzling, sardonic heart and soul of the party with the young man who wrote poems of black despair. 'The two halves of his life were quarrelling halves,' Amy Witting, who was close to him in the middle and late thirties, recalls. 'What he loved he hated. He was born under the star Aldebaran. When we read Gérard de Nerval's "Sylvie" I could see he was utterly taken by this reference to the star Aldebaran that flashes alternate pink and blue and he recognized his own sign, I'm sure he did. He was an utterly divided personality.'

The symbolist poets – Apollinaire, Baudelaire, Mallarmé, Stefan George, and de Nerval – mesmerized McAuley. He idolized Blake, whom he saw as the prophet of modern thought, of Freud and Bertrand Russell, A. S. Neill, Aldous Huxley and the surrealists. Blake 'took as his subject the human soul', McAuley declared in 1937, 'and entered into regions which no man before him had explored'. He wrote one of the earliest intelligent articles about Ezra Pound's 'Homage to Sextus Propertius' and described it as 'Pound's outstanding achievement, by means of which he takes his place among the elect of English poetry'. He was also a 'convinced disciple' of Eliot, converted after he opened *Poems 1909–1925* in a café and read 'The Love Song of J. Alfred Prufrock'. Eliot fascinated McAuley by the way he superimposed images of 'tradition' and 'modernity' – though his masterpiece *The Waste Land* carried the method of 'discon-nectedness' too far. In his later poetry Eliot had lost his 'blinding eloquence' and 'macabre wit'. 'It is a melancholy reflection,' McAuley wrote, not able to foresee his own conversion, 'but in the main a true one, that the more a poet becomes reconciled with Catholicism the more his art suffers.'

McAuley finished his arts degree in 1937. His results – first in English and University Medal, third in philosophy – were not good enough to win him a scholarship to Oxford or Cambridge. He was still living at home, had no money, and little prospect of finding a job. He applied to join the fledgling Australian foreign service but was knocked back; they thought he should cultivate his literary talents instead. Then, through the university employ-ment agency, he found a job in the bush, tutoring the offspring of the Osborne family on their long-established property 'Curran-dooley' at Bungendore outside Canberra, several hundred miles from Sydney. It was not an arduous appointment. When he was not teaching McAuley would go horseback riding through the paddocks and the scrub, but he spent most of his spare time sitting in his room writing.

In this isolation the young man lived an intense, dreamy life in his own head. He wrote often to his friend Dorothy Auchterlonie (later Green) in Sydney, and sent her drafts of what he was writing, reports from his reading: Proust – 'the only prose work I know of that is *incredible*' – Virgil, Rilke, Gertrude Stein, *Hamlet* – 'fee fi fo fum' – *The Faber Book of Modern Verse*. He tossed her way whatever bright thoughts occurred to him: 'my chief function in life is not to be a poet – it is to follow the paths of virtue', or 'except for the 17th C lyrik give me the moderns for my money'. He was writing all in a rush: 'In the last ten days I have written six poems, translated two of Rilke's ("Herbsttag" and "Der Aubaumgarten"), set an Elizabethan lyric to music and written a comic song and a comic poem as well.'

He sent Auchterlonie drafts of a sequence of twenty-odd poems called 'Prelude, Suite and Chorale'. Steeped in the disil-lusion of Eliot, the fragrant *cauchemar* of the French symbolists, the brooding inwardness of Rilke, this was McAuley's homage to his romantic gloom. Some of the poems used a system of punctuation McAuley borrowed from George, each phrase separated by an elevated full stop. The sequence constructed a ravaged but dandified image of the poet as an outcast who 'shall be alien where his heart is given / And have no kin; and pass his days unknown'; as a lover whose futile love 'knows no more what it intends', whose tortured love 'hates and will not turn from hating'; as a dreamer who hears 'death's voice', submerged in 'the dawn waste stretch of sleep'. 'Departure', the fourteenth poem in the sequence, made Mallarméan gestures at a kind of perfumed religiosity.

> How often have I sat at evening
> Under the painted alcove of the sun
> The secretary of its facile flame!
>
> And like a Presence in the fading arch
> Your gold hair burned – your body flushed
> Hieratic through the rosy shrine.
>
> In kingdoms hidden by the sun
> 'Tis your bright torch shall sow the dark with seeds
> Priestess of visions which there caverned lie.

'Cheerfulness is not my metier,' McAuley wrote. 'I cannot endow it with the inwrought subtlety that I love. For me, as Gide says: "La tristesse est une complication. Jamais je ne cherchais à analyser mon bonheur." And complications are my meat.' He wanted, he said, his 'verses to fold in on one another with the complex pattern of dreams'. Sometimes the dreams were terrifying: McAuley suffered from nightmares from which he would wake screaming. On at least one occasion he smashed the windows of the room he was in – and a friend remembers him describing a dream in which white butterflies were going to eat out his eyes. 'There was a banished part of himself that he feared,' Amy Witting told me, recalling these episodes. Several years later he wrote three 'Nightmare Songs' – he never published them – in which he summoned up 'a big man in a stove-pipe hat':

> He's my shadow on the wall
> some say he isn't there at all
> It isn't true, it isn't true!
> He's just as real as me or you.
>
> At night he keeps me company
> if *he* weren't there *I* wouldn't be
> He's my shadow twice as tall
> as any man amongst them all.

Even as he abandoned himself to the jejune dramatics of 'Prelude, Suite and Chorale', McAuley saw the limits of his project. He wrote to Auchterlonie about the importance of clarity in verse – 'that inward stir and outward simplicity that I love' – and complained about a remark he discovered in Michael Roberts' introduction to *The Faber Book of Modern Verse*, that 'primarily poetry is an exploration of the possibilities of language'.

That is true of a lot of modern work, and I think it's a pity that it should be so. Such a project is (a) dangerous because it encourages a poet to *use* any devices his explorations hit on (b) fundamentally unfruitful because needs must create means; the exploration of language cannot go very far unless it is informed by a more ultimate purpose. Much of what he says seems to admit this, but the statement is there, and it is a clue to the modern attitude. There is too much verse that is purely verbal in its content (e.g. a lot of Hopkins, Laura Riding, Edith Sitwell and W. H. Auden). Here we find exploration of language as a thing in itself, a world unconnected with the realities underlying the words. Sometimes the results are good fun, they are rarely valuable as art. The good work which these poets do goes beyond this theory of a rootless, self-related language.

He also gave her a critique of his work that parodies the kind of thing it is and dismisses the poems he sweated blood over:

'Aspects of the Moon' is less than I would have expected from J. McAuley – isn't it about time he was put on the reserve list? The present production seems to be a case of a bad attack of Heine which, altho a variation on his usual *Eliotism*, does not become him very well. The spurious, faded, 19th century scene of the first poem was, after all, done once and for all by Heine, Baudelaire etc . . . The last two lines are a climax of banality to which the proper reply from the astonished reader is obviously: 'Well, fancy that now!' Coming to 'Hecate', it strikes one with wonder that there should be so much that is otiose in so small a place. '*Softly* the dead arise'. The mansuetude of mortality is admirably presented!

It did not take the twenty-one-year-old James McAuley long to realize that his romantic agony – the troubled lover, sliding into death, transcribing his dream world – was hand-me-down. He entertained ideas of publishing the sequence but then dismantled it. The handful of poems he kept have the simple speech that characterizes the poetry of his final years: 'We came from a crooked town, my dear, / And we walked a crooked mile, / And all we found in the end was a tear / A kiss and a crooked smile.' As his work matured, McAuley turned his back on cloudy romantics and cloak-trailing symbolism.

By early 1939 McAuley was at Mount Victoria in the Blue Mountains 'earning a small living as companion to a young man called Butler, who is a half-invalid on account of sinus trouble. He's a pleasant chap with similar tastes to mine – we spend hours dissecting Joyce, Proust and Pound!' He had also finished a novel, called *The Pane Of Glass*, about campus life at Sydney University.* He decided he would go back to university to write his Master's thesis, and submitted it early the following year with the grand title 'Symbolism: An Essay in Poetics'.

An ambitious, equivocal project, the essay not only reveals a disaffection with symbolist theory but a fascination with mysticism. McAuley gives a Freudian reading of Blake but refuses to reduce mysticism to a pathology, a descent into madness or retreat from reality. No Australian poet before McAuley, with

---

*It has not survived but Amy Witting recalls its opening sentence – 'They revolved the filth of Adam, as upon a wheel' – describing some young men talking in a bar. 'You mean they were telling dirty jokes, Jim?' she asked.

the exception of Brennan, was so saturated in European poetry. He thrills to symbolist verse but is scornful of '*le culte du verbe*', the belief in poetry as an ersatz religion or conjuring of the occult. Baudelaire wrote with 'acrid despair' but he was kidding himself: whatever he thought about the power of the word, he 'fails to produce the infinite and gives us only a picture of the world coloured and permeated by his emotions'. And despite the 'compulsive beauty' of Mallarmé's work, he cannot 'present us with any ideal realm of existence – all we can find is the operation of fantasy in the real world'. Visionary symbolism is fake mysticism, McAuley suggests, and surrealism is 'mysticism decapitated' that reads 'like a perverse juggling with images in consciousness: the surrealist may be fooling himself all the time'.

McAuley had high hopes his thesis would unlock the door to an academic career. He was given a first but not judged to be the top candidate, perhaps because, on the eve of the Second World War the Faculty of Arts at Sydney University was not ready for psychoanalytic discussions of poetry in several European languages. Certainly that is what McAuley believed. In the interim, he had taken a job teaching at Shore, the Sydney Anglican Grammar School. He was there when Hitler invaded Poland on 3 September 1939. Dorothy Green remembered talking to McAuley that day. 'He wanted to be a conscientious objector,' she said. 'On the other hand like most young men he didn't want to be shelved off from the general social experience that was about to take place . . . the last thing he said to me about joining up was that he could bring himself to join an ambulance unit.' McAuley spent that night walking around the city with his friend, the lawyer Alan Crawford, wondering what would happen. At dawn they found themselves on Bennelong Point where the Opera House now stands. The narrow world McAuley knew, hostile to his gifts and suspicious of him, was about to change irrevocably, but he was not ready to join the war. Shore was Anglophile and loyalist: under some pressure from the headmaster, McAuley resigned early in 1940 rather than compromise his principles and enlist as other teachers at the school did.

Later in that year and through the first half of 1941 he was involved in the anti-war revue *I'd Rather Be Left*: McAuley was musical director, played the piano, and co-wrote a few of the songs. An acquaintance remembers him knocking out a song, when it was required at short notice, in twenty minutes. *I'd Rather Be Left* was performed at the New Theatre League's premises upstairs at 36 Pitt Street near Circular Quay. The league was a beacon for people sympathetic to the left, radicals and communists, pacifists and anarchists. McAuley cut an enigmatic figure there: the historian Russel Ward remembers 'a thin, slight, pale, intense young man with sandy hair and a mouth clenched tightly shut and turned down sharply at the corners as though he had just swallowed a lemon', but thought it strange that McAuley 'earned a precarious living by playing the organ at divine service in an Anglican church in the inner western suburbs'.

I'd Rather Be Left was a smash hit, and ran for six months, attracting a much wider audience than usual at the New Theatre League, even 'several heavily disguised secret policemen who took notes diligently'. Its target was not the massing armies of Hitler but capitalists profiting from the war, and local politicians out to sell the country short. The 'anthem' of the show, written by Alan Crawford, went to the tune of 'There'll always be an England'. It entered the vernacular and was reputedly sung 'as a sort of mock wake or dirge at the first meeting of Curtin's Labor cabinet' after Robert Menzies lost office in October 1941:

> There'll always be a Menzies
> While there's a B.H.P.
> For they have drawn their dividends
> Since 1883.
> There'll always be a Menzies
> For nothing ever fails
> So long as nothing happens to
> The Bank of New South Wales . . .

If *I'd Rather Be Left* was an accurate mirror of McAuley's radicalism in 1941, then his recension was swift. Later he would say that his politics lacked a reality principle until the war provided one: they were like a 'film running in your own mind'.

The question of how to earn a living was just as urgent. McAuley's last resort was to train as a school teacher. After he left Shore he went to live with the poet Alec Hope and his wife Penelope at Woolwich, and in 1941 he enrolled at the Sydney Teacher's College, where Hope lectured in English. A graduate of Sydney University, Hope had also been to Oxford. He was ten years older than McAuley, a shrewd, sceptical, witty man with bushy eyebrows and a plain, aristocratic face. McAuley took his diploma on an absolute minimum of work, and in 1942 was sent to teach at Newcastle Junior Boys' High School. He loathed teaching but his conscription was as imminent as his abandonment of anarchism and pacifism. When Malaya fell, he wrote, after Villon, the 'Ballade of Lost Phrases'. His halcyon leftist days were over:

> In what museum now abide
> The pamphlets that we read of yore;
> Where are the orators that cried
> 'We will not fight a bosses' war,'
> 'The system's not worth fighting for,'
> 'To Hell with the Jingo profiteer,'
> 'The Empire's rotten to the core,'
> – Where are the phrases of yesteryear?
>
> No longer can it be denied,
> The Left Book Club's become a bore;
> We're social patriots double-dyed,
> And social fascists too, what's more.
> We tolerate Sir Samuel Hoare!
> Churchill now delights the ear,
> And Beaverbrook is to the fore.
> – Where are the phrases of yesteryear?
>
> The Party Line from side to side
> Zig-zagged till our eyes were sore;
> Can it be the Marxists – lied?

Peace to the shades of *Inprecorr*!
The left wing's moulting on our shore:
It will not fly again, I fear.
Freedom has become a whore.
– Where are the phrases of yesteryear?

Envoi

Comrades, we argued, fought and swore:
We might as well have stuck to beer.
The Japanese are in Johore
– Where are the phrases of yesteryear?

On 7 January 1943 he was summoned to the Sydney Show-grounds and bundled into the army. This was the acid test: 'I had to ask myself, now, have I really got any authentic anti-war sentiments?' McAuley remembered. 'Have I got a reason for going to Long Bay Jail instead of joining the Army?' He was made a sergeant and given a posting in Army Education. A few months later his work defending his nation against Japanese domination took him to Melbourne.

The historian Manning Clark was standing among the crowd at the Carlton Football Ground in Melbourne one Saturday after-noon in the winter of 1943. He was distracted from the game by a stranger dressed in khaki standing near by. Clark remembered he was 'timid with people in uniform', even though he was 'used to handling fast bowlers and so on'. This chap was edging closer and seemed to want to speak with him, or worse, pick a fight. Clark had not gone to the war, and soldiers could get aggressive about it. He was 'obviously drunk, this chap in the sergeant's uniform'. He had 'craggy cheeks' and a 'ravaged' face: he looked 'quite old, though his body was young'. By now he had moved so close his voice could be heard above the hum of the crowd. 'When he spoke he spoke very clearly and he uttered the most astonishing sentence.' 'I am', the drunk man in the uniform said to Manning Clark, 'a disappointed radical.' It was James McAuley.

*

The generation that reached adulthood during the war was the first in Australia to believe in its own modernity, to assume its right to comprehend new ideas in literature, art, politics. They knew what to read. They thought that what they thought mattered. They were arrogant, at odds with the sluggish, philistine world around them. But the enthusiasm of Max Harris in Adelaide and Sidney Nolan in Melbourne for modern art and poetry was not duplicated in the steamy, northern air of Sydney, where McAuley, Stewart and Co. had decided modernism was old hat. Donald Horne reviewed *Angry Penguins* in *Honi Soit* on 2 October 1941 and diagnosed its writers as 'preternaturally aged, with all the enthusiastic inexperience of youth . . . They still have the feeling that in writing poetry they are attempting something NEW . . . At least my friends the Sydney poets . . . have given up any obsessions of novelty they may have had.'

'What you hated in those days you hated good and strong,' Amy Witting remembers. This hyper-critical spirit and loathing of modishness was fostered in Sydney by John Anderson, the Scottish free-thinker and Professor of Philosophy at the university. Anderson arrived in Australia in the twenties as a Stalinist and moved through a Trotskyist period before emerging in the thirties as a trenchant anarchist. No academic on an Australian campus has ever galvanized students as he did, arguing that freedom of thought meant abandoning allegiance to orthodoxy, whether Anglophile or Stalinist. To be unaligned was the correct line. Neither Stewart (he had no interest whatsoever in politics) nor McAuley were fervent 'Andersonians', but McAuley flirted with his aesthetic theories for a while, and Anderson's influence in university circles was so profound it was difficult to escape untouched by him. Much later McAuley admitted that 'Anderson taught so many of us to think' and emphasized his 'stress upon the critical spirit as almost the sole value that he could clearly articulate'.

Anderson made a point of riling hidebound colleagues at the university by donning his hat and striding across the Quadrangle in all its mock-Gothic sandstone splendour at the instant the

43

daily rendition of 'God Save the King' began. Outraged pro-
fessors stood bare-headed to attention. In the early thirties he
championed James Joyce's *Ulysses* which was banned in
Australia in 1929.* Attracted to the Joyce who refused the
consolations of God and Nation, Anderson identified with the
non-conformist Stephen whom he in turn identified with Joyce
himself. He nurtured the Dedalean principles of 'silence, exile,
cunning' among students ready to see themselves as young
Stephen Heros and encouraged in them his own policy of
'obscenity, blasphemy, sedition'.

One young man who fell under Anderson's spell was the poet
Oliver Somerville, a friend and contemporary of McAuley and
Stewart. Somerville had things in common with both men. He
too was hostile to 'replicas of the innovations of 40 years ago'
and hated 'castrated replicas of surrealism without its political
affiliations'. Like McAuley he loved jazz and was an authority on
the subject. And, like McAuley, Somerville wrote poems that
savoured, he said, of 'moping maudlin moonlit nights'. He
understood the complexity of McAuley's romanticism: 'he has
written sentimentally bad poems,' Somerville remarked to a
friend. 'There's always been a squashy, death-directed streak in
him; but it's neither the only nor the predominant streak . . . Like
us, he sees through the traditional academic futilities – quite as
thoroughly.' He wrote a parody of McAuley's 'Selene on Latmos'
he wickedly called 'Jupiter on Ganymede'. 'Late through the
suburbs wandered the blonde moon / With disenchanted gaze a
little wild' became 'Late through the suburbs wandered the blond
loon / with gin-enchanted gait, a little Wilde.'

A maudlin, flamboyant character, with 'all the outward marks
of genius' as Amy Witting recalls, Somerville was a black-haired,
black-hearted romantic, at home in a time when despair was the
fashion, passion passé, and cold wit the means to express both.
He smoked 'violently' ('as if there wasn't enough pressure to get

*The ban was lifted in May 1937 but reimposed in September 1941 to howls of
protest including Anderson's. *Ulysses* remained off limits in Australia until 1953.

the tobacco in fast enough') and drank the same way. Derelict and dandy, he often wore an overcoat, summer or winter, but underneath might be clad only in an old singlet, trousers and sandshoes. A photograph from the period has him in a silk scarf, book tucked under his arm. Once he climbed a tree outside the university and shouted to those below, 'I'm a monkey! I belong here!' He thought himself an outsider ('I've always been on the fringes of university free-thought, of bohemia, of pedagogy'), a nobody ('I am gregarious or a pallid non-entity', 'the most suburban bank clerk is more alive than I am'), a waif ('I am really, as McAuley once said of himself, "a simple, home-loving soul without a home" ').

Somerville thought McAuley's 'Ballade of Lost Phrases' so much better than anything of his own: 'it beats all mine into the most diminutive recesses of the conventional cocked hat'. He collected his own poems and wrote them out in an exercise book under the title *Thin Jests and Other Verses*. Its centrepiece was his ballade that tore strips from the cult of modernism, which he almost certainly wrote after he saw the *Herald* exhibition of modern art. No work of the period better dramatizes the difference between what passed in Sydney, and in the pages of *Angry Penguins*, as a sophisticated point of view. The two groups had in common their youth and their inheritance of a collapsed tradition that in Australian terms was no tradition at all. But they differed in so much else. What aroused in one group sardonic familiarity stirred for the other the hope of new possibilities. The cities were almost as isolated from each other as Australia was from the world. To the north, in Sydney, a developed instinct for satire, a yearning for the key to the mystery of things. To the south, in Melbourne and Adelaide, a naïve, passionate energy which wanted to believe it had the key. Both outlooks were 'modern' and both informed. They were on a collision course and Somerville's 'Ballade' was one point of impact:

45

The educated mob exudes
Its unepatable caprice;
The avant-garde its tongue protrudes
In agonies of mock release;
Orders for cubist works increase;
Red artists fade to paler pinks;
Art's Jasons find their Golden Fleece;
I wonder what Picasso thinks.

Modigliani's daring nudes
That shattered our neurotic peace
Now publicize the patent foods
That mark us off from ancient Greece;
Manet no more suggests police,
Epstein adorns our skating rinks;
Derain is growing more obese;
I wonder what Picasso thinks.

But I, abhorring prigs and prudes
Alike, to pack in mind's valise
A cold perception which excludes
The biases that never cease
Although I've learned to play with ease
The psycho-analytic lynx,
Before each frenzied masterpiece
I wonder what Picasso thinks.

Envoy

Prince, we have understood Matisse:
Your likeness done by Sargent stinks.
High art is quacked by human geese;
I wonder what Picasso thinks.

As if in response to Anderson's demand for 'obscenity, blasphemy, sedition', Oliver Somerville became the moving spirit behind *The First Boke of Fowle Ayres* – the Only Boke of Fowle Ayres, as it turned out. Its contents were written largely at a café called Sherry's on the south side of Pitt Street, opposite the Sydney School of Arts. Here McAuley, Stewart, Somerville, Alec Hope, Witting and others would meet on Saturday afternoons for on-the-spot readings, collaborations and critiques of works in progress. Swathed in cigarette smoke, drinking coffee, and oblivious to the citizenry around them, they would sit around a laminated table strewn with bits of paper, and cap each other's verses. Somerville bought a printing press second-hand and collected many of the squibs, satires, clerihews, lampoons, limericks, dirty songs, parodies, insults and in-jokes composed at Sherry's and chanted at parties over the years. He needed his own press because no publisher in 'Australia, 1944' (these words appear on the cover beneath the title) would have touched *The First Boke*. Nor was it ever prosecuted for obscenity. But who could be prosecuted? No publisher was listed, no poem signed by any author.

The First Boke of Fowle Ayres was libertarianism with the lid off. It took the mickey out of the puritans, evangelists, and wowsers, whose voices could be heard thundering against dissolution and moral decay. Stewart contributed 'The Virgin Mary Blues' which he co-wrote with Somerville. There was a smattering of McAuley's anti-hymns. Friends from his youth still know all the words and on request sing them softly in bars:

> If I weren't J. Christ
> I'd feel enticed
> To make some good woman a baddie,
> I simply adore
> A crack at a whore,
> But my heart belongs to Daddy . . .

The First Boke included political satire too, like McAuley's dry epigram:

> The Revolution, how betrayed?
> By whom misled, by what dismayed?
> What Stalin did and Trotsky said

Beguiles my sabbath ease in bed.

And while the bell from yonder steeple
Doles out opium to the people
'Tis only just that Marx should be
The opium of the bourgeoisie.

The Boke went underground to avoid prosecution. But anonymous and pseudonymous publication, which projected writing as a higher activity accessible only to those in the know, was common practice. Contributors to *Hermes* routinely published under *noms de plume* or sets of initials. When McAuley wasn't 'J. Mc' ('jay muck' his friends pronounced it) he was 'Glaucon' or 'Proteus'. Harold Stewart signed his work 'Kenning Skald'. Oliver Somerville was 'Padruic'. Pseudonyms also gave camouflage for attack. In 1941, an unknown critic named Dulcie Renshaw had written an article for *Honi Soit* pouring scorn on the literary magazine *Southerly*. The following year she carved up the *Melbourne University Magazine* ('*MUM* is the word'), though she spared Max Harris, a contributor to the issue: his work, she opined, might be 'authentic utterance, and I personally feel that it occasionally very definitely is'. Dulcie also had serious things to say about *Angry Penguins* which, 'despite its immaturities and bumptiousness', was 'one of the few significant occurrences in the field of Australian university publication'.*

Dulcie Renshaw disguised Harold Stewart in her first appearance and then James McAuley. She was the refinement of a technique: anyone guessing her identity would be doubly con-

---

*The names of the contributors to *Angry Penguins* caught the attention of Tess van Sommers and her friend Beverley Tivey, who imagined that an exotic name must be the prerequisite for publication in the magazine. Intrigued by the presence of 'Lola Van Gooch', 'Marceine I. Dickfos' and 'Sunday Reed' ('poor woman, I think she'd been christened that,' Tivey remarked in an interview on 4 July 1989), they decided the formula was to have a first name as lurid as the last was drab. They began to toy with versions: 'I said I'd call myself "Scream",' said Tivey, and 'was hesitating for a surname when Tess said "Hobbs".' They fell about with laughter. The joke – they invented another name that afternoon, 'Augustus Tree' – would have been forgotten; but the girls told the story to their friends, Harold and Jim, by now at the Victoria Barracks, in Melbourne.

fused by the shared pseudonym. But she could be generous too. In the voice of James McAuley, she dismissed most of the contributors to *MUM*: 'None of them shows any background of painstaking and conscientious work with their materials such as characterizes the work of Harris, McAuley or Stewart.'

Whether a joke, a disguise or an honorific, a name signals an identity. Having no name, on the other hand, denies readers the right to assume anything. In a Lilliputian literary world ferociously subdivided into the rival groupings of *Meanjin*, *Angry Penguins* and the Jindyworobaks, it was inevitable someone would decide to publish beneath the banner of having no banner. In July 1943, a magazine appeared in Sydney with the subversive anti-title, *Number One*. It had no editor, no front cover, no price, no pagination, no contributor notes, no public sales, no advertising, no distribution, no policy except not to have these things. The contributors, who went to the length of identifying themselves, were A. D. Hope, Garry Lyle and the anarchist poet Harry Hooton. An unsigned statement in the centre of the issue declared that 'we are as utterly fed up with self-conscious national bards as we are with unoriginal importers of meretricious styles already done to death overseas by their own intrinsic mediocrity'. *Number One* was followed in 1944 by *Number Two*. Oliver Somerville, who printed the book on his press, was now a contributor, along with Hope and Hooton. Hope presented a suite of poems called 'Contemporaries' which pasted the Jindyworobaks and Max Harris. Hope wrote corrosive anti-Freudian satires obsessed with cartoon sexual grotesquerie. Modern life was strip-searched in poems like 'Standardization' or 'The Lingam and the Yoni', though Hope had no apparent yearnings – as McAuley and Stewart did – for more civilized periods. His was a 'Brave Nude World, that had such people in it'.

Number Three appeared in 1948, a commemorative issue for Somerville, who had been killed in a car smash the previous year. Hooton wrote that Somerville attained a 'positive position of anarchism', unlike the other members of 'that Sydney group which included A. D. Hope, James McAuley, Harold Stewart'. Together these three constituted a 'triangle' that 'could not get past the negative critical attitude'. Yet they were 'unquestionably the best three poets of our generation. Their work may be summed up roughly as realistic, classical, intellectual, in contra-distinction to the surreal, romantic, religious, and of course utterly worthless poetry which was issuing from Adelaide and Melbourne at the time – during the war years.'

This was in the future. In the early forties James McAuley and Harold Stewart were looking for the middle of the stream. This was a familiar modernist quest, the nostalgia of the Americans Pound and Eliot for an established order, embedded in history, Joyce's scorn for the provincial backwater of Ireland. Their solution was simple: emigration, exile. But post-depression Australia in the late 1930s was too far away from fantasy land, and too poor to permit easy expatriation. For many of the best minds of that generation escape was forbidden, and the war, for those who stayed at home, heightened the sensation of belonging to a world cut adrift from the world. They would have to civilize themselves at home – the very place, they were convinced, where the materials of civilization were lacking. Here they would have to find for themselves the answers to the problems which beset them. The Penguins felt this too: 'I sometimes think the war forces us to localize what we have walked around in for so long without being aware of it, being compelled to know where home is,' Nolan wrote to Sunday Reed.

McAuley and Stewart felt Australia would not allow them to inhabit the culture they sought as their own. This perception became inseparable from the culture they did possess, and turned them into outsiders whose natural resort was to scorn and subterfuge. Most of what they saw around them they didn't like, though they were part of what they saw. Australians are adept at this double-think, and it helps produce shrewd, disaffected people, convinced the society they belong to cannot cater for them. McAuley and Hope wrote poems on the subject of their nation, built on the assumption that the words 'Australia' and 'culture' were oxymoronic – or merely moronic. 'There the blue-green gums are a fringe of remote disorder', wrote McAuley, as if he were somewhere else. 'A Nation of trees, drab green and desolate grey', wrote Hope, as if no one lived there. 'The people are hard-eyed, kindly, with nothing inside them', wrote McAuley, though he was one of them. 'A vast parasite robber-state', wrote Hope, 'where second-hand Europeans pullulate on the edge of alien shores'. That was in 1939, five years before Ern Malley's 'black swan of trespass' paddled on the same patch of water.

Northrop Frye once suggested that in a colonial society the central question of identity is not 'Who am I?' but 'Where is here?' Here could not be European because here was not Europe. But here could not be Australia because the poets were Europeans whose heritage was at odds with the ancient, enigmatic island continent of their birth. They stood at the edge of Europe, at the edge of the Antipodes. Some of the Angry Penguins shared this dilemma, which the painter Albert Tucker recalled as a terminal unreality. At one instant Australia was real, Europe a fantasy land, abstracted into Art and History. Blink and the positions reversed. Europe – where none of them had been – loomed up as the only reality, and Australia became a cruel fiction where an indifferent fate had dropped them.

Stewart's reaction was to immerse himself in the study of his art. He was a fastidious craftsman. 'He is capable of producing stuff that will put us all to shame,' McAuley wrote in 1938. If Stewart wanted to get to know a poet's work he would sit in the public library transcribing the entire *oeuvre* in longhand just as the ancient scribes used to do. Hart Crane and Mallarmé were two writers he absorbed this way. He read widely but was drawn to certain writers, among them Edith Sitwell, and Arthur Waley who had recently translated the Japanese *uta*. 'I liked Emily Dickinson's "poetic shocks",' he recalls, 'and Edna St Vincent Millay's sonnets, so nicely turned; but always detested Wal Twitman.' He adored Keats, and Marlowe too, the decisive influences on his early work. For a time Stewart dabbled with modern poetry and free verse. He introduced Horne to Pound and cummings, and when the famous *Herald* exhibition of modern art moved from Melbourne to Sydney in 1939, Stewart spent an entire Saturday morning explaining the nine Picassos to him. 'It took me years', Stewart wrote to me in 1988, 'to work my way through the long dark tunnel of modernism before I emerged at the far end into sunshine and fresh air.'

If Harold Stewart ever played apprentice to the sorcery of modernism, it did not show up in the poems he published or the reviews he wrote. His poetry was gorgeous, adjectival, multi-faceted like cut jewels, sculpted into tableaux and set pieces. Stewart made a couple of translations of Mallarmé and Valéry (McAuley introduced him to the latter) but he never wrote post-symbolist verse. He was not interested in 'arbitrary personal symbols for whose meaning the writer (and reader) grope around in the dark', preferring – in his own shorthand – 'le symbolisme qui sait' to 'le symbolisme qui cherche'. Keats fascinated him not so much for his romantic self-projection, but by his luminous, proto-mystical apprehension of tradition. He was deep into Jung, and was intrigued by the symbol of the phoenix – it preoccupies Ern Malley too – the firebird which rises from the ashes of its pyre.

By 1940 the scholar–poet began to emerge, transfixed by Eastern art, literature, and religion, intent on studying 'the universal language of symbols, whose variants are to be found in all the extant and extinct cultures & civilizations, and which have precise metaphysical and religious meanings'. Jung and Keats were the bridges to oriental mysticism that Stewart later burned. They led him to an integrated culture where 'Truth is Beauty' remained a viable equation, the Grecian urn meta-morphosed into a landscape scroll, the personality of the artist subsumed by tradition and technique. In 1942 he wrote a long poem called 'The Ascension of Fêng' – the phoenix of the East – which included this opalescent Marlovian description of the celestial city glimpsed in a flash of lightning:

Now in that brazen zenith hung, the sun
Clashes the cymbals of the solar disc,
And lo! its molten gates are thrown apart
With the struck clangour of a going gong.
Out of the furious crucible within,
Down the exalted regions without cloud,
The empyreal strata of the sky,
A violent instant with electric spur
Strikes, streaking through the astonished air.
Now a vivacious shower of four-point stars
Burns on the dazed salver of the pond,
So that it seems sprinkled with cubes of glass
Sparkling in constellated fervency:
A glittering city of prismatic planes
And clustered corners, as of crystals cut
To send their rays out into angled flight.

McAuley's reaction was more troubled. His confidence and rapport with the European tradition grew but so did his sense of crisis. He was alive to the horror of the war, in Europe and in Asia, and his poetry began to hint at some approaching apocalypse. The romantic dream became a nightmare of hallucinatory vividness. His language became richer and tougher – to spectacular effect in 'The Incarnation of Sirius' which reached its climax with a crazed, appalled, elaborated vision of the birth of the dog-star:

Anubis-headed, the heresiarch
Sprang to a height, fire-sinewed in the dark,
And his ten fingers, bracketed on high,
Were a blazing candelabra in the sky.

The desert lion antiphonally roared;
The tiger's sinews quivered like a chord;
Man smelt the blood beneath his brother's skin
And in a loving hate the sword went in.

The two poets' apprehension of 'tradition' was in their antipodean context purely innovative; each one in his own way assumed an inheritance which did not exist except by force of will. Much of the poetry they saw around them in Australia and despised was either debased Victoriana or second-hand 'modernism': they set out to invent a poetry free from fashion, that belonged to a history they were free to choose for themselves.

McAuley had been preparing a book of poems for some time. In Newcastle he assembled a manuscript called *Poems in Three Dimensions* but could get no one to publish it. He applied for a grant from the Commonwealth Literary Fund but was rejected by the conservative littérateur, Frederick Macartney, who reported to the fund on 10 August 1942 that the book deserved to be published in an 'experimental way' (a phrase he did not explain) but was otherwise not impressed. 'Like the French symbolists,' he said, McAuley was 'more concerned with general effect than with definite meaning' and indulged 'the modern habit of enforcing intellectual disgust by occasional terms of crude revulsion'. Not until 1946, when it spanned a decade of writing and his work had changed several times over, did this book appear, entitled *Under Aldebaran*. Harold Stewart's first book, *Phoenix Wings*, appeared two years later, in 1948. The delay was crucial: it gave both poets the opportunity to cast a colder eye on their apprenticeship to the muse, to make the most of their desires to revise exhaustively. It also meant their poetry did not reach a readership outside their own coterie. Max Harris had a public career, a magazine to blaze his trail. The work of James McAuley and Harold Stewart was invisible by comparison, one of the secrets of the war. Ern Malley, of course, once Harris discovered him, put them all in the shade.

4 A Strange and Sinister Figure

'A Man's life of any worth is a continual allegory,
and very few eyes can see the Mystery of his life'
John Keats, letter, 14 February 1819

At the end of October 1943, Max Harris sat down at his desk
with the day's mail. There was a letter with a Sydney postmark
from some woman he'd never heard of.

Dear Sir,
    When I was going through my brother's things after his death, I
found some poetry he had written. I am no judge of it myself, but a
friend who I showed it to thinks it is very good and told me it should
be published. On his advice I am sending you some of the poems for
an opinion.
    It would be a kindness if you could let me know whether you think
there is anything in them. I am not a literary person myself and I do
not feel I understand what he wrote, but I feel that I ought to do
something about them. Ern kept himself very much to himself and
lived on his own of late years and he never said anything about
writing poetry. He was very ill in the months before his death last
July and it may have affected his outlook.
    I enclose a 2½d stamp for reply, and oblige,
    Yours sincerely,
    Ethel Malley

Harris read the letter at speed and then unfolded the
accompanying poems. A bright red stamp depicting the king
fluttered to the desk. If Ern Malley wrote anything like his sister,
there was no hope for this lot. He began to read:

Durer: Innsbruck, 1495

I had often, cowled in the slumberous heavy air,
Closed my inanimate lids to find it real,
As I knew it would be, the colourful spires
And painted roofs, the high snows glimpsed at the back,
All reversed in the quiet reflecting waters –
Not knowing then that Durer perceived it too.
Now I find that once more I have shrunk
To an interloper, robber of dead men's dream,
I had read in books that art is not easy
But no one warned that the mind repeats
In its ignorance the vision of others. I am still
The black swan of trespass on alien waters.

Harris was stunned. He read the poem over and over, and each time he read it he fell in love with it some more. The language was so beautiful, so seductive after Ethel's comatose prose: 'slumberous heavy air', 'shrunk to an interloper', 'dead men's dream', 'black swan of trespass on alien waters'. Ern Malley had a mind, and a vivid way with words. The last line was a clinker. The other poems in the batch, perhaps three in all, though Harris remembers receiving only two altogether, were just as startling. They had titles such as 'Baroque Exterior', 'Palinode', 'Documentary Film'. Their imagery was bold, sensuous, exploratory. 'Baroque Exterior' began:

When the hysterical vision strikes
The facade of an era it manifests
Its insidious relations.
The windowed eyes gleam with terror
The twin balconies are breasts
And at the efflux of a period's error
Is a carved malicious portico.
Everyman arrests
His motives in these anthropoid erections.

Work of real flair, Harris knew, is a rarer than hen's teeth among unsolicited contributions to a literary journal. But an editor lives on his dream of turning up the next prodigy, and Harris's spine was tingling. 'At this stage I knew nothing about the author at all,' he recalled in *Angry Penguins*, telling the story of how the poems landed on his desk, 'but I was immediately impressed that here was a poet of tremendous power, working through a disciplined and restrained kind of statement into the deepest wells of human experience. A poet, moreover, with cool, strong, sinuous feeling for language.'

The other poems offered further proof of Ern Malley's 'dream of recognition', which also seemed an intuition of his own death. But something like 'Documentary Film', its 'sound track like a trail of saliva', lacks the finish of 'Durer: Innsbruck, 1495' and Harris's claim of restraint is harder to defend. It has moments of throwaway grandeur, brilliant evocations of Dürer's famous woodcut in the British Museum:

> Durer:
> 'Samson killing the Lion' 1498
> Thumbs twisting the great snarl of the beast's mouth
> Tail thrashing the air of disturbed swallows
> That fly to the castle on the abraded hill
> London:
> Samson that great city, his anatomy on fire
> Grasping with gnarled hands at the mad wasps
> Yet while his bearded rage survives contriving
> An entelechy of clouds and trumpets.

'Documentary Film' also includes crude mumbo jumbo like 'the blood-dripping hirsute maw of night's other temple'. But for Harris the poetry was seamless. His discovery dazzled him. Editors on the scent don't muck about. Max Harris put Ethel's shiny red twopenny-halfpenny stamp to use, and obliged her with a letter on 2 November 1943:

Thank you for sending me the M.S.S. of your late brother. I read it through carefully and I was very much impressed with it. I should have no hesitation in publishing the poems you sent me in the January issue of Angry Penguins.

Should my partner, Mr. John Reed, share my enthusiasm I think our organisation would agree to publish a posthumous volume of your brother's work, if it maintained the level of the poems you sent me, and if there is sufficient of it. No doubt if my opinion is borne out by Australian critics I could place some of it with U.S.A. and English poetry journals.

I should be very glad if you would send me any more of his poetry that is extant, and also if you could give me as much biographical information as you can – his life, his work, the nature of his illness, his interest in architecture and art, and so forth. This would be extremely helpful to enable me to get a perspective of his work.

I hope we shall hear from you soon, and that we can make arrangements for the publication of your brother's remarkable work.

Without waiting for Ethel to answer, Harris fired off a letter to Reed in Melbourne on 8 November:

Here's a pretty terrific discovery. I was sent the enclosed poems by one Ethel Malley of Croydon NSW, an almost illiterate woman, who said they were found in the papers of her brother who died in June of this year . . . she didn't understand them thought they were the product of her brother's illness and its effect on his mind. Apparently Ernest Malley died of TB or throat cancer of some sort. He went away to live on his own when he was dying, and these poems are the result. I'm certain that there is no gag in it . . . it's too perfectly done to be a Kershaw–Lawlor gag. I've written asking for complete biographical information plus any other MSS whatsoever that they can discover.

Whatever the circumstances I think these poems, architectural, unified in their language treatment, are among the most outstanding poems I have ever come across. I have shown them to a number of people without saying anything of the circumstances and they have borne out my opinion. It has sharp and surprising hints of D. B. Kerr in it, but I think the treatment of his own death transcends Kerr's treatment of the subject. It is unbelievable that a person going away to die could write poetry of this objectivity and power. I hope to have more information within a week or so and will keep you in touch with it. In the meantime I'd be pleased if you and Sun would look over them carefully and tell me if you agree with me, and also show them to anyone else you think might contribute to an evaluation of them.

TB has all sorts of romantic associations, but throat cancer is a horrible, almost allegorical disease for a poet to be struck down by. The work was too good for Lawlor or Kershaw, who had just slagged the Penguins in 'The Denunciad', to have cooked it up. Malley, Harris believed, wrote too well to be some kind of joke. In fact he reminded Harris of Donald Kerr, the co-editor of *Angry Penguins* until his death in 1942 when he was just twenty-two: earlier in 1943 Harris had brought out an edition of Kerr's poetry under the title *Death, Be Not Proud*. Harris thought Malley had come up with the kind of poetry Kerr might have written had he lived longer. Malley seemed to intuit the exultation and despair of countless young men defending their country who saw death all around them and knew their own lives swung in the balance.

Reed replied to Harris's package the next day, 9 November:

Sunday, Nolan and another friend of ours, John Sinclair all read Malley's poems without first seeing your letter and all were impressed with them, Nolan particularly so. After seeing your letter they held pretty well to their opinions and I think the general feeling is that the poems are genuine, though it is just possible that they are not. Sunday says that when she read them, she did not feel that they were essentially 'new' but were in a fairly familiar idiom and individual words struck both her and Nolan as being reminiscent of Kershaw – for instance, 'wrists', 'hirsute', 'everyman', and 'caught on the unlikely angles Of an awkward arrangement. Weren't you?' etc. It also seems somewhat incredible that anyone so sophisticated and obviously in touch with world poetry should be unknown, but of course your enquiries should do a good deal to clear up these points. Anyhow, the main thing is that the poems are good and if this is so, they cannot have been written as a gag, though of course it is possible, that once written the author may have decided to send them to us under another name for some obscure reason of his own. Apparently poets do that sort of thing. We all agree that they should be published, though with what comment or biographical detail cannot be decided until you get further news . . .

Malley's resemblance to Kershaw, which Harris vaguely sensed, and which Nolan and Sunday Reed brilliantly clarified, was based partly on an accident of diction – the word 'wrist' which Malley uses twice occurs ten times in *The Lonely Verge*, a book sixteen pages long – but also on a shared fondness for slick derision. Though its rhythms are subtler, the end of 'Palinode':

> I snap off your wrist
> Like a stalk that entangles
> And make my adieu.
> Remember, in any event,
> I was a haphazard amorist
> Caught on the unlikely angles
> Of an awkward arrangement. Weren't you?

was the same kind of thing as Kershaw's clever-clever lines in 'Du Côté De Chez Everyman':

> He plucked and held the scented rose
> More thaumaturgic than a cock,
> Invoked its beauty with his nose –
> But kept his eyes upon the clock.

When she received it, Ethel was heartened by Harris's letter. She had done the right thing, and it made her proud to think that Ern was a good poet after all. As soon as she could find time she sat down to write to Harris about her brother's strange life. She sent the rest of the poems and 'as much biographical information' as she could supply. Her leaden, garrulous letter, which she neglected to date, was seven pages long:

Dear Mr Harris,
    Thank you for your letter of reply and your kindness in giving your opinion of Ern's poems. I am very glad to know that you think they are so good.
    Please find enclosed all the rest of the poems I can find. They were in a folder with the couple of sheets in his own handwriting which I

am sending you also. The ones I sent you before I got out of the folder too. Just to be sure, I have added another sheet of paper which he must have been writing on when he was in bed. It wasn't in with the rest of the things and I don't know whether it is any use to you but I am sending it in case.

Certainly you may publish any of them you like in your magazine. I had no idea they might be good enough to publish overseas. I suppose as he numbered the pages he intended it to be published as a book. It is a pity he did not leave any instructions about what he wanted done with them. I am very much obliged to your kind offer to publish them in a book. Do you think it would be a paying proposition? I don't want any money from them myself because I don't feel that they belong to me. I would be very grateful if you would let me know if your partner agrees to publishing them.

You asked me for some details about Ern's illness. I didn't mention in my last letter that his death was due to Grave's disease. If he had only taken better care of himself it need not have been fatal. But while he was away from home he neglected his health. When he was called up for his medical exam the doctors evidently told him what was wrong with him, because he was rejected. But I don't believe he saw a doctor again until he came home last March though I found out later he had been dosing himself with iodine and the doctor said that must have kept him going. He was terribly irritable and hard to do anything for. I was anxious for him to go to hospital where he could be properly looked after, but the doctor said it would be better for a person in his condition to stop at home. The doctor spoke of operating at first but when he refused to have it done the doctor said it would be better not to which I thought was strange.

You asked me also to tell you something about Ern's life. Well, my brother's full name was Ernest Lalor Malley and he was born in England at Liverpool on March 14th, 1918. Our father died in 1920 as a result of war wounds and the family came out to Australia where mother had relations. We lived for many years in Petersham where Ern went to the Petersham public school and the Summer Hill Intermediate High. He did not do very well at school although he was good at other things. Mother died in August 1933 and I could not stop Ern from leaving school after that as he was set on going to work. I have always thought he was very foolish not to have got his Intermediate but he was determined to go his own way. He got a job as a mechanic in Palmer's Garage on Taverner's Hill for a couple of years. He was always clever with mechanical things and I thought he was settled and had got over his wildness. But when he turned seventeen he came home one day from work and said he had given up his job at the garage and was going to Melbourne. I did my best to persuade him but he went. After that I did not see much of him or hear from him as he did not write, but some-one I knew met him in Melbourne and told me he was working for National Mutual selling insurance policies. They said he was living in a room by himself in South Melbourne. I remember I was worried at the time whether he was looking after himself properly because he was never very strong. I wrote to him but he did not reply for a long time. Later, in 1940 I think it was, I did get a letter from him saying that his health was better and that he was making a fair amount of money repairing watches and doing other work on the side. I did not hear from him again until the beginning of this year I found he was back in Sydney. I got him to come home and it was only then I realized that he was ill but even then I had no idea of how bad he really was. He was amazingly active for his condition. Finally he told me that he knew what was wrong and I managed to get a doctor to him. The weeks before he died were terrible. Sometimes he would be allright and he would talk to me. From things he said I gathered he had been fond of a girl in Melbourne but had some sort of difference with her. I didn't want to ask him too much because he was nervy and irritable. The crisis came suddenly and he passed away on Friday the 23rd of July. As he wished he was cremated at Rookwood.

As I said in my last letter I never knew that Ern wrote poetry. He was a great reader and he told me he did a lot of study in Melbourne. He said he often used to go to the public library at night. I wouldn't have thought Ern was interested in architecture and art as you say. If he had brought any books back with him you might be able to tell more from them. I still have the only book he brought with him though he was mostly too sick to read much, it is called Theory of the Leisure Class by Thorstein Veblen. He did have a coloured postcard pinned up in his room which I haven't included because the writing on the back seems to be personal, but if you think it would help I will send it to you.

I am sorry I can't tell you much more about Ern, but as I said before he kept very much to himself. He was always a little strange and moody and I don't think he had a very happy life, though he didn't show it.

If there is anything else I can do to help please don't hesitate to let me know.

Thanking you again for your interest and kindness,

I remain,

Yours sincerely,

Ethel Malley

Harris pored over his El Dorado. He raced through the letter, and then turned to the poetry. Ern Malley, it turned out, had written a book which he called *The Darkening Ecliptic*. There were seventeen poems altogether, all typed except for one in a wavering hand that seemed to be unfinished. The title page of *The Darkening Ecliptic* was inscribed with the oracular command 'Do not speak of secret matters in a field full of little hills – Old Proverb', which Harris later interpreted as 'an explanation of his complete silence on the subject of poetry during his lifetime'.

Here was the thing itself, stamped with the mark of its maker, sole clerk of his metamorphosis. Ern Malley – read *in toto* – was a poet of tremendous energy, death-obsessed, sex-obsessed, neurotic, mannered, expressionist, surrealist, modernist, a phrase-maker with no fear of obscurity, and able to manoeuvre a poem in several directions at once, as if he were taking dictation at a conference of muses. He careered out of control and then, with no warning, managed to do things only real poets can. Malley gave the feeling that poetry was rich, rough, rollercoasting speech, that he might talk about anything: war, politics, love, sex, masturbation, menstruation, nose-picking, astrology, history, art and poetry itself: 'the loaves and fishes, / Or no less miracle', as he described it. His reading – whatever Ethel might say – was very wide, and Malley let his reading shape his poetry. Blake, Shakespeare, Freud, Eliot, Pound, Dante, Mallarmé, Lenin, Longfellow, Marlowe, Keats, Dylan Thomas, George Barker, Henry Treece, James McAuley, Harold Stewart, Alister Kershaw and perhaps even Max Harris were among those writers whose work he stumbled on at the public library.

There was another thing about the sequence read entire. From the opening poem, 'Durer: Innsbruck, 1495', the work seemed to grow more elaborate and involved, tougher and darker in expression, as if it were the field of some huge, obscure battle in Ern Malley's psyche. The degree of difficulty was highest in 'Young Prince of Tyre' or 'Colloquy with John Keats', until Malley burst through into a stunning autobiographical clarity in 'Petit Testament', his final poem. Still, even at his cloudiest, Malley could ungarble himself. This kind of grandstanding from 'Colloquy with John Keats':

> Like you I sought at first for Beauty
> And then, in disgust, returned
> As did you to the locus of sensation
> And not till then did my voice build crenellated towers
> Of an enteric substance in the air.
> Then first I learned to speak clear; then through my turrets
> Pealed that Great Bourdon which men have ignored

sat beside lines which did 'speak clear', like this Marlovian passage from another late poem, 'Egyptian Register', brooding on the insignificance of human life amid the cosmos:

> Nature
> Has her own green centuries which move
> Through our thin convex time. Aeons
> Of that purpose slowly riot
> In the decimals of our deceiving age.
> It may be for nothing that we are.

Here, thought Harris as he absorbed the work, was an extraordinary new voice in Australian poetry. That hyperbolic note, speculative, disaffected, chaotic, and intensely urban, had never been struck before with this confidence, or these resources. What's more, Ern Malley himself, his mind concentrated by his impending death, had theories about what he was up to. 'The couple of sheets' that Ethel reported finding in Ern's 'own handwriting' were headed 'Preface and Statement' and were in a wiry, confident script:

These poems are complete. There are no scoriae or unfulfilled intentions. Every note and revision has been destroyed. There is no biographical data.

These poems are complete in themselves. They have a domestic economy of their own and if they face outwards to the reader that is because they have first faced inwards to themselves. Every poem should be an autarchy.

The writing was done over five years. Certain changes of mental allegiance and superficial method took place. That is all that needs to be said on the subject of schools and influences.

To discover the hidden fealty of certain arrangements of sound in a line and certain concatenations of the analytic emotions, is the 'secret' of style.

When thought, at a certain level, and with a certain intention, discovers itself to be poetry it discovers also that duty does after all exist: the duty of a public act. That duty is wholly performed by setting the pen to paper. To read what has thus been done is another thing again, and implies another order of loyalty.

Simplicity in our time is arrived at by an ambages. There is, at this moment, no such thing as a simple poem if what is meant by that is a point-to-point straight line relation of images. If I said that this was so because on the level where the world is mental occurrence a point-to-point relation is no longer genuine I shd be accused of mysticism. Yet it is so.

Those who say: What might not X have done if he had lived? demonstrate their different way of living from the poet's way. It is a kind of truth, which I have tried to express, to say in return: All one can do in one's span of time is to uncover a set of objective allegiances. The rest is not one's concern.

Here, thought Harris, was the reader's guide into the pathless woods of Malley's poetry, though he had to confess in *Angry Penguins* that he was not sure what some of it meant. A mixture of assertion, paradox, insight, truism and brilliant bullshit, Ern's 'Preface and Statement' is like a manifesto in the electric manner of Pound or Eisenstein. Some of its terms were cant ('concatenations', 'analytic', 'objective') and some were pure pretension ('scoriae', autarchy', 'ambages'). But the 'Preface and Statement' was crisply written all the same, and in a clipped style not a bit like his poetry. It drew a magic circle around *The Darkening Ecliptic*, and made the poems seem even greater than the sum of their parts.

Tickled pink by his find, Harris began to show Malley's work to people in Adelaide. Among these was J. I. M. Stewart, the Jury Professor of Language and Literature at Adelaide University, an Oxonian stranded in the Antipodes by the war. Stewart compensated for this bleak fact by refining his accent and renting a house in the Adelaide Hills that stayed cool enough through the summer for him to write Michael Innes detective stories in comfort. *Hamlet, Revenge!*, that hymn to Scamnum Court, almost the 'stateliest of the stately homes of England', was plotted in a bungalow in the bush. Stewart had created a minor controversy in 1940 when, after being asked to lecture on Australian literature, he declared the category did not exist. In its absence, and to justify his fee, he announced he would discuss the nearest thing, Lawrence's *Kangaroo*. You didn't need to be English to have your doubts about this question. Stewart's sidekick, Brian Elliott, who identified himself in public as a lecturer in Australian literature, gave a talk in late 1944 entitled 'Is Australian Literature Real?' Beside the heading he scrawled the cautious answer, 'Yes, with reservations'.

When Harris submitted Ern Malley's poems for a professorial opinion, Stewart didn't make too much of them. This was, he thought, 'the sort of highly derivative and to me, I'm afraid, rather incomprehensible verse that young men and women were writing at that time in England and America and that young poets in Australia were beginning to go after too'. But the poet Geoffrey Dutton, an original Angry Penguin (now elevated to a flying instructor in the air force, stationed at Parkes in New South Wales), had no reservations. He thought the typescript he had been sent 'marvellous' and wrote back to tell Harris so. 'I was

absolutely carried away by it. I was envious. Here was somebody
who had the real voice.'

Harris also tried to generate some publicity for Ern Malley –
his was a remarkable story which ought to interest the mainstream press. The Adelaide office of the *Australian Women's
Weekly* was a few doors up from Harris's office in Grenfell
Street. Harris immediately thought of his friend Catherine Caris
who wrote for the magazine. One morning, she recalls, he
walked in with a parcel, and put it on the front counter, and told
her about the great poet, now dead, who had written and lived in
total obscurity. Would the *Women's Weekly* like to publish a few
of the poems, and tell Ern Malley's story? Catherine took the
parcel into the office of the editor, a middle-aged woman named
Frieda Young. She kept them and 'read them carefully. I'll never
forget her coming out to me and saying, "Catherine, I think this
is a load of rubbish".' It was a long shot on Harris's part, but
perhaps he was thinking of the thrill it would give Ethel Malley to
see her brother in her favourite magazine.

Harris set about writing a critical introduction to Malley's
work for *Angry Penguins*. 'Ern Malley prepared for his death
quietly confident he was a great poet,' he began. He annotated
each of the dicta in Ern's 'Preface and Statement' and announced:

I have been placed in somewhat the same quandary as was Max Brod in
disposing of Kafka's writings. But with this difference. Ern Malley left
no instructions, no indications of what he wanted done with his MSS. It
was obviously prepared for publication. But he did not even mention its
existence to his sister. Yet this statement assumes that posterity will be
interested in his work, that the search for scoriae and biographical detail
will take place. It is more of a challenge than an expression of his desires.
For my part, I find such respect for the amazing relation of his art and
his dying that I feel I have no right to conceal facts which bespeak
greatness.

In the end Max Brod decided not to burn Kafka's work and
Harris had no intention of putting a match to Ern Malley's
paper-thin corpus. Of the style of the poems he wrote:

What he read or when he read is a matter simply for conjecture. But from his poems there is evidence of tremendous assimilation and integration. The use of remote and esoteric language can at times be dangerous affectation and love of verbiage for its own colourful nature. In his few poems Malley's vocabulary spans innumerable worlds, but his use of language is never logomachical. His wide, difficult vocabulary emerges spontaneously and necessarily from his poetic motives. Appropriateness is the final test, and Malley reveals an acid preciseness in all his handlings with language . . . In one of his best poems, then, we find such relatively unfamiliar words as apodictic, valency, crenellated, enteric, and bourdon. Yet the poem logically demands these words because of its strict autarchical domestic economy. Language is not master; it is creator!

Harris admitted that some people – like J. I. M. Stewart – who saw the poetry before its publication said his work was 'derivative and echoed various contemporary techniques' but added 'I am strongly of the opinion that these critics are completely wrong.' He described how Malley had outstripped the influence of Auden, and in his treatment of the 'personal' transcended '*Angry Penguins* writers and contemporary English writers'. 'There is no hint of the Auden generation who tend towards the impersonal and philosophic as a product of the dynamics of their imagery.' He invoked the poetry of Donald Kerr, and wrote, 'These two, with their diverse spiritual outlooks, are the two giants of contemporary Australian poetry.' He took Malley's line, 'The new men are cool as spreading fern', as the key to his 'sane, personal verse'. But in his pastiche of Ern Malley's critical manner Harris found himself all of a tangle.

Art is not Life, nor is it an imitation of life. It is experiencing at a different level from life; it is life but differs in kind from it. Art emerges from experience at the 'analytic' level of the emotions. Art reflects life at second hand, as it were, when experience and detachment integrate in a dialectical union of 'poetic' or 'analytic' experience. The secret of style then is reduced to faithful reflection, for felicity of language is integral to the 'analytic' experience itself.

Harris concluded with a poem, 'Biography', and an 'Elegiac for Ern Malley' in prose that betrayed the incendiary influence of Malley's work: 'As the earth lay undulating like a lackey, its faded braid and livery dulled with the imprecation of centuries, it had a wild organic vision. The astigmatic eye loomed as high as the sun; the long golden dirndl swept with the rhythms of sin about the purple sex of the penultimate mountain ranges.'

Ethel was nothing if not thorough. What was this extra sheet on which Ern doodled, in bed of all places? The wan title 'So Long' had been scored through and a smudgy 'No' etched in above. The pen fumbled its inconsolable way through the lines before sputtering to an inky silence:

> The wind masters the waves
> As the waves the sea
> And all of it entire
> And none of it to me
>
> I had thought it was finished
> And now it is useless
> Like the writing on graves
> Empty of future
>
> Renew
>
>   the sign
> At the moment of

Harris correctly judged the fragment – unpaginated, unfinished, of uncertain provenance – not worthy of its author, and made no attempt to publish it. Its wan rhymes and metrical regularity must have seemed like a failure of nerve. In his writings on Ern Malley he never alludes to its existence. Ethel was confused by it, but that clarifies the picture: the poem was written in the morbid hours – or minutes, seconds even – before the poet's death, when he was confined to bed, compelled to write but in no condition to assess his work. Malley's failure to finish the poem was evidence of a moment of visionary rapture. The lines, described later as 'a heart-rending unfinished last poem in MSS blotted with the dying poet's tears', were a footnote to genius, their stammering and then silence the description of a death.

Towards the end of November Harris sent all the Malley material to Reed, including his introduction. On 26 November his co-editor replied:

It was a big moment opening up all that additional packet of Malley's work and I can imagine how excited you must have been. He looms up as a strange and, perhaps to us, a somewhat sinister figure as his destructive philosophy – his acceptance and even seeking after death – is opposed to our own life impulse. But he is obviously a poet of some standing and in many ways close to your own expression.

As usual, I am moved to admiration at your spontaneous enthusiasm and vigorous activity in handling the whole situation, but I did feel that perhaps in parts your writing lacked complete coherence.

Reed used a contact to discover if Malley had ever worked in Melbourne for the insurance company National Mutual, but they replied that he was 'quite definitely never . . . connected with them'. Undeterred, Harris referred Reed to Malley's poem 'Perspective Lovesong' and suggested they try to trace the 'princess of Princess Street as she apparently is the only person who can give us any solid information about Malley. If necessary we can plaster the Melbourne papers with the story of the garage mechanic and insurance peddlar who turned out to be a great poet.' Reed was 'reluctant' on the grounds that 'it might be the sort of action that Malley himself would have resented and which "the Princess" might also resent'. Nothing was done.

Instead Reed sent all the poems to Sidney Nolan, whom the army had dispatched to the Wimmera, the flat dry wheatlands and semi-desert country several hundred miles north-west of Melbourne. He had been called up in April 1942, and was posted to the town of Dimboola to guard a garage filled with biscuits, jam, tins of pineapple and bully beef, survival rations should the

Japanese invade. By November 1943, after a period of leave
spent with the Reeds at Heide, he was back in the Wimmera, in
Horsham. Here he read *The Darkening Ecliptic*. On 1
December 1943, Reed reported to Harris that Nolan had 'no
doubt about the quality of the poetry which impressed itself on
him so much that I think a painting will come out of it'. Nolan
remembered he was impressed by the 'internationalism' of
Malley's poems; he felt 'they were the product of somebody
who'd been in Europe . . . who'd come back and was writing in
this way. And since that didn't tie up with what the sister said, I
just had to take it for granted that he hadn't been abroad.' He
told Reed that he had

Been reading the Malley at most opportunities & do find his images
are ones I am in harmony with, or visually practicable, put it that
way . . . For the moment, as much as I can synthesize my thoughts
on the import of his poetry, I think of a critic (probably Spender)
saying the fact that Dante was able to use his poetry to enact a more
coherent world than say Rimbaud did not alter the greatness of
Rimbaud's poetry.

'Visually practicable' are the key words: the random suggest-
iveness of the poetry, no diminisher of its worth, is understood as
a raw potential for pictures. Nolan had started out as a poet and
he felt at home with writers, while painters, he said, 'help you to
see things but I don't know any that help you to paint'. The
French symbolist poet Rimbaud – a key figure for him, who had
already inspired several paintings – provided a natural context
for his interest in Ern Malley. Like Malley, and like Rimbaud,
Nolan saw the artist as an outsider, a rebel who bowed to no one.
There were also distinct similarities between Malley's life and
Nolan's. Perhaps they had glimpsed each other across the room
in the Melbourne Public Library, Nolan with his head full of
Kierkegaard and Malley studying his Veblen. No painter was
better qualified to gaze into Ern Malley's poetry than Sidney
Nolan. Everything in his life had prepared him to grapple with
the work of a self-invented modernist of uncertain identity.

Nolan and Sunday Reed read Ern Malley together. He described his painting to her:

Painted this afternoon instead of swimming, the Malley had started last week on the panel of 3 ply. And now it is finished looking different under the electric light. Malley needs a small painting probably and this is bigger than usual . . . but the landscape he lived in was a strange one when you think of it in colour and practically everything is green with two red rocks rising from it and the Arabian Tree with the two figures perched in it. Perched in a word like trembling when read in a poem; as verbs they have, as I wrote to John I think, an explicit painterly instruction about them. All of Rilke's images are the same . . .*

With its marine greens and vivid reds, the painting was a dreamy, lyrical illustration – as if seen underwater – of Ern's lines in 'Petit Testament' (partly stolen from Shakespeare's 'The Phoenix and the Turtle') which Nolan had written out in a slanting hand:

> I said to my love (who is living)
> Dear we shall never be that verb
> Perched on the sole Arabian Tree
>
> . . .
>
> (Here the peacock blinks the eyes
> of his multipennate tail.)

Nolan stripped the landscape back to its primary elements which he recombined into images of disarming clarity: 'painting as hard as a mirror', he called it. *The Sole Arabian Tree*, with its sensuous abbreviated forms, echoing the conventions of primitive and child art, like something out of Chagall, appeared on the cover of the Ern Malley edition of *Angry Penguins*. Its detail was autobiographical: the pinnacles to the right were based on a

---

*The obsessive, breathless letters Nolan wrote to Sunday Reed while stationed with the army in the Wimmera form a natural continuum with his paintings of the period, and are significant literary documents in their own right. Animated by Nolan's vivid thumbnail descriptions of the landscape, the letters – like the paintings – give the sensation that nothing has come between what the artist has seen and its registration on the page.

distinctive Wimmera landmark, the Mitre Rock, and the two naked figures isolated in the tree signified himself and Sunday Reed, like Adam and Eve in their own lush paradise on the looming plains of the Wimmera. Nolan remembered they both 'had a very intimate relationship with the poems', and that Sunday 'thought they were connected with our own private life. That's why the figures in the tree are herself and myself.' Musing on Malley in the isolation of the Wimmera, Nolan wrote to Sunday that 'of all things loneliness is the most destructive to the human organism, notwithstanding great art and its traditions'. In Malley's charged fatalism the two of them saw an image of their own ambiguous destiny. 'Petit Testament' seemed to comprehend their predicament, Nolan told me. He felt that 'his life wasn't going to work out'; he 'would never be that bird perched on the sole Arabian tree. That was the case with Sunday also. We both knew it. That's not much fun.'

Harris wrote back to Ethel, grateful for the riches she had bestowed on him. He remained polite but made allowance for the fact that she could not grasp the magnitude of the material she had stumbled across. Ethel must have blinked at his opening sentence and was probably miffed by the words which followed:

Your brother was one of the most remarkable and important poetic figures of this country. It may be rather hard for you to realize that Ern was, in my opinion a great man, and in the opinion of many people a major poet. Ern himself, we can tell, from his writing and his preface had no doubts of it.

I have written a big survey of his work which I hope to publish as an introduction to his work in my journal before it is put out in book form. We have tried to trace his life and background to some extent . . . but we drew a blank with the National Mutual who knew nothing of him. We are trying to trace 'the princess of Princess Street' who should be able to throw a great deal of light on his life . . . the books he read, the people he knew and the like . . . We should be very grateful if you could let us have any such information . . . his Melbourne address or the girl. The postcard would be of some help I think if you could send it.

There is no doubt Ern intended his MSS should be published as it is all prepared, titled, and prefaced, for that purpose. We are prepared to undertake the full cost of publishing his book. Although there is not a very great likelihood of it realising substantial profits, we could no doubt come to some agreeable arrangement in the event of it making a profit. Usually with poetry we offer a 50% share of profits made on sales after costs of printing and distribution have been met.

Thank you very much for the information which was quite invaluable and we hope you will send anything else that will help us trace his life in Melbourne when he wrote the majority of his remarkable poems.

It was noble of Harris to offer to split any profits with Ethel after her refusal of payment. Though he thought she was an idiot he was always fair to her. Ethel did not reply to this letter, insulted perhaps by Harris's suggestion that she was too dim to see that she was related to a genius. Harris wrote again, this time in search of a photograph of Malley which Reed had urged him to procure.

I have not received an answer to my last letter from you. I hope it reached you safely. Your late brother's work will soon be on the market. Already a great number of people have become intensely interested in him, and I hope you will give us whatever further information you can. Particularly we are looking for a photograph of him to publish with his work; it is not extremely important that it be a recent one, and we hope you can help us in this respect.

We have not managed to learn his Melbourne address, but I think we now feel sufficiently at home in his aims and ideals to present him adequately.

Ethel replied – on 14 January 1944 – and did her best to answer his questions though her silence about a photograph of her brother was uncharacteristic:

I am sorry I couldn't reply to your last before, but what with Xmas and the New Year I just haven't had a moment to myself.

I never imagined when I sent the poems that you would have so high an opinion of Ern. I suppose it is because Ern was just one of

74

the family but I find it hard to think of him as a great man. It is very kind of you to publish his poetry, but as I said earlier I don't want any money from it. As long as it is published I feel I have done all I can.

Enclosed please find the postcard you asked for though I don't think it will help you much. I'm rather surprised the National Mutual did not have some record of him but then he was only a casual salesman. I'm quite certain that was the firm I was told he was with. I hardly like to say this and I know I can rely on you to treat it as *strictly confidential* but I have an idea that Ern might have got into some sort of trouble in Melbourne and gone under another name. I only mention this because if you come across anything he would not want to be known I know I can rely on you not to make it public. I am sure you will agree it would not be fair to his memory.

Would you please send me anything you publish about Ern as I would like to keep it. How long do you think it would take for the book to come out?

I must close now, hoping you will let me know if there is anything else I can do.

PS: I have tried my hardest to remember the address but all I can remember is that it was South Melbourne but I don't think Princess Street was the name of the street.

There were limits to the information Ethel could pass on. She never gave the slightest hint about what Ern looked like. Harris connected the poet's invisibility with his consciousness of death, and wrote to Reed, after receiving this letter: 'There are no photos of Malley – the couple there were he deliberately destroyed on arriving in Sydney.' The postcard that tumbled out of Ethel's envelope on to Harris's desk turned out to be a tatty colour reproduction of Dürer's *View of Trent*, folded in several places and showing rusty traces of the drawing pin that had fastened it to the wall. This 'old' and 'creased' icon naturally associated itself with the first Malley poem that Harris ever read, 'Durer: Innsbruck, 1495'. Ern was some kind of Dürer freak. Scrawled on the back across the top left hand corner, in the same hand that penned the 'Preface and Statement' was a jaunty couplet, some kind of personal message:

75

Ern –

'The plot is sprung the Queen is took,
One night enjoyed the next forsook.'
                    Remember?
                          – Lois

Who was Lois? What did the words have to do with Albrecht
Dürer and images of Trent or Innsbruck? Or with Ern's poetry?
There was nothing to identify the sender of the card or the source
of the quotation. If Lois was Ern's beloved, she certainly took a
sturdy, rather literary attitude to rejection – there is something
ominous about that sly recrimination, 'Remember?'. Harris
guessed the lines were pinched from somewhere in Shakespeare.
'The handwriting is cultured, the lines very lovely. I do not know
their source but suspect Elizabethan drama – possibly early,' he
told Reed.

Harris did not reply to Ethel, and she never wrote to him again.
In the months until the publication of *Angry Penguins* he
continued to think of Malley as a metaphor for his own
obsessions. He talked the work up at every opportunity, and sent
it around. Through the agency of Harry Roskolenko, he
arranged for three of the poems to appear in an 'Australian Issue'
of *Voices*, a poetry magazine edited by Harold Vinal in
Brattleboro, Vermont. Harris described Malley's death for
American readers: 'Grave's disease is . . . one of the worst and
most debilitating diseases known. The effect is that of the human
machine going faster and faster until it explodes and stops . . .
the diabolical tension, the nervous irritability of the sufferer is
all-consuming. The disintegration of the individual is almost
certain.' He told John Reed that 'Malley will possibly be more
important as a symbol integrated in my own poetry, than he will
be as a poet', and in February 1944, after reading Freud, confided
that 'Malley is of such terrible significance to me because I think
he saw the problem as I saw it, and fought out his slow hypnotic
wrestling match with the angel of death over 5 years. In all
biology – in all sex – I see a huge cosmological symbol of death.'

Harris fervently believed in Malley's death wish, 'the epic suffering of his going away like the elephant to die'. In *Angry Penguins* he remarked that Malley 'deliberately invoked death upon himself to provide the deepening and consummating forces of poetic experience. For the sake of the unity of death and poetry, Malley sacrificed his relationships with the woman he loved, left her, and returned to Sydney . . . he treated death greatly, and as poetry . . . dying at the age of 25 with Grave's Disease.' In Adelaide, immediately the poems were published, he 'addressed the Art Association on Aust. poetry and spent a good deal of his time examining this magnificent new discovery of the late lamented. They tell me he told the tale choking back his manly sobs,' a bemused witness reported.

The '1944 Autumn Number' of *Angry Penguins*, 'to Commemorate the Australian Poet Ern Malley', finally appeared in early June. This rubric possibly created the impression that Ern had fallen in action: at any rate, it asked readers to remember a poet nobody had heard of. Malley's poems led the contents: in Sidney Nolan's design, they were laid out, one per page, in large type with ample leading to simulate the look of his double-spaced typescript. Of 108 quarto pages Malley's poetry, with notes and commentary, filled thirty-five. Among the other contributors were the fiction writer Peter Cowan, the painter Albert Tucker, the left-wing art critic Bernard Smith, and the poets Geoffrey Dutton and Alister Kershaw. There was a clutch of American poets too, as well as articles on Aboriginal art, surrealism, and Marxism. John Reed wrote a piece on contemporary Australian art. *Angry Penguins* ran three reviews of Harris's novel, *The Vegetative Eye*, two of them equivocal. Nolan's cover painting *The Sole Arabian Tree* was reproduced in colour. The run of 900 copies retailing at 5/- apiece cost just over £250 to set up and print. John Reed expected Reed & Harris to *lose* about £100 if the issue sold out. No previous issue ever had.

'I have posted you a copy of Penguins express,' Reed wrote from Melbourne to his co-editor Harris in Adelaide on 31 May. Harris was jubilant when he saw the issue which he thought 'the

most outstanding journal in the annals of contemporary literature . . . It is the outstanding weapon and technical instrument
for articulation in our time,' though he added that 'this no doubt
sounds a little excessive – I see you smiling paternally at Max's
enthusiasm.' *Angry Penguins* was distributed to contributors,
subscribers and bookshops nationwide. Mullens bookshop in
Melbourne ordered a hundred copies. Plans were made to send
the issue to the London publisher Faber and Faber, to Herbert
Read, Kathleen Raine, Stephen Spender. Copies were dispatched
to the Gotham Book Mart in New York, on West 47th Street,
and to the Grolier bookstore in Cambridge, Massachusetts,
where the poet John Ashbery, an undergraduate at Harvard,
found his in the fall of 1945. Harris believed their moment of
triumph was almost upon them: 'It seems to me that the next six
months may well prove decisive in the history of the firm and we
should have our plans and ideas clear and effective,' he wrote to
Reed on 2 June 1944. 'To know yourself on the verge of big
things, yet in this state, is very hell.'

PART II The Hoax

'A poem is good until one knows who wrote it.'
Karl Kraus

5 A Wonderful Jape

All of it – Ethel, Ern, the poems, the life, everything – was a hoax, of course, the biggest literary hoax of the century. It began in Melbourne one Saturday afternoon in early October 1943. Lieutenant James McAuley and Corporal Harold Stewart were at their desks in the general office of L Block at the Victoria Barracks. They were the rostered CO and NCO on duty at their outfit, the Directorate of Research and Civil Affairs. The barracks itself is a handsome, Georgian-style bluestone building, fronted by lawn, palms and ornamental cannon on St Kilda Road, the leafy boulevard that sweeps from the south-east across the Yarra River into the city – but L Block, a little to the west of the main building, was a scruffy old weatherboard shed with a tin roof.

The Victoria Barracks were Land Headquarters, the nerve centre of the Australian Army. From here the Commander-in-Chief, General Sir Thomas Blamey, controlled his forces. The army's top brass and key intelligence units were housed here. Macarthur rested and schemed in the barracks amid his tumultuous reception in Melbourne after his flight from Corregidor. Later he installed himself in the city in the Menzies Hotel before taking his entourage to Brisbane. The Directorate of Research and Civil Affairs, where McAuley and Stewart spent much of the war fighting the 'Battle of St Kilda Road', was an outfit without precedent in the army. It has a notorious reputation and little wonder: surely only specialists in dirty tricks could operate under such lofty cover.* No evidence has emerged suggesting that the

*The term 'Civil Affairs' derives from British Army usage, and denotes military government of a civilian population in wartime.

directorate itself was a clandestine operation or a front, but it is hard to describe what it actually was. No War Diary, no account of its daily activities, was kept. It never had a War Establishment, a formal military hierarchy, and made up its rules as it went along. Its impact on hostilities is debatable, but is less profound than its influence on some gifted men who might otherwise have found themselves firing rifles in the anopheline jungles of New Guinea. The directorate was the brainchild of a man named Alf Conlon, a backroom boy and duke of dark corners, who knew 'that sometimes the shortest way across a square was around three sides'. Conlon knew about Ern Malley almost from the outset: he regarded himself as 'the moving force' of the affair and thought it all 'magnificent fun'.

Ten years older than McAuley and Stewart, Conlon met them at Sydney University where he studied Arts – including Philosophy with John Anderson – and Law and then Medicine before the war intervened. He was a bulky man 'with a solemn, rather owlish expression behind hornrimmed spectacles and a pipe'. The hair on his large head was crew-cut. He had the habit of shoving the pipe inside his nostrils or inserting it in one of his ears. In some accounts it is never lit, in others he sits amid clouds of blue smoke. The spectacles made him look an egghead. 'He was given to using, sometimes very effectively, all sorts of metaphors,' Alan Crawford recalled. 'Many of them would be very bawdy.' Conlon loved polysyllabic words and never raised his voice. 'Sometimes he would admit with a rather shy grin that he'd put over some startling piece of nonsense quite successfully as a bluff.'

Conlon was elected to the Sydney University Senate in 1939 on almost no platform but opposition to compulsory attendance at lectures. ('To hold out specific promises on matters of detail would be quite irresponsible,' he declared in his policy statement. 'I am a supporter of freedom of speech.') His politics were left wing but not Marxist, and he owned a large collection of anarchist and socialist pamphlets. Soon after the war began he was appointed University Manpower Officer, which gave him control over which students got drafted. Then and later he believed his job was to ensure that clever young men were not blown to bits on the front, to preserve an intellectual elite who could influence post-war affairs.

Conlon was in touch with the powers in the land. In February 1942, after Pearl Harbor and the fall of Singapore, he convinced Prime Minister Curtin to establish a 'National Morale Committee' made up of senior judges, academics and bureaucrats, with himself in the chair. Two months later, on 7 April, he was commissioned as a major, in charge of a research unit at the Victoria Barracks, attached to the Adjutant-General's section. The National Morale Committee produced a report on Information which got lost in the bureaucracy and the committee disappeared from sight. Conlon's unit became the directorate.

He began to recruit talent, especially among university friends. Early in December 1942 he rescued Stewart from his job as a sapper drawing ordnance maps from aerial photographs for a field-survey unit out at Dandenong, twenty miles east of Melbourne. McAuley was diverted from Army Education and arrived at the directorate on 12 June 1943. John Kerr was summoned, a labour lawyer with prospects, who went through Fort Street and Sydney University a few years earlier than the poets. He became Deputy Director, Conlon's right-hand man. Scientists, doctors, geographers, anthropologists and cartographers were called in. Sometimes Conlon used to work all night in L Block, 'snatching an hour's sleep at dawn on a rather crummy mattress kept behind the door, and drinking a bottle of milk for breakfast'.

Conlon's directorate, McAuley decided, was like a 'Renaissance Court, with Alf as the Medici prince. People like myself and Harold Stewart were the court poets . . . There were times when I ended up doing a good deal of probably useful work, but in Alf's mind this was not really the nature of the contract.' Conlon gave a new and compelling image of themselves to people who fell under his sway: he 'would switch lights on', McAuley remembered. He thrived on his inscrutability but did not hesitate to manipulate people if he thought it was for their own good. John Kerr described him as 'a kind of spell-binder, Svengali-like' and 'found it extremely difficult to escape his psychological grip. He had a capacity to occupy one's mind and make one feel one's destiny was in his hands.' He changed the lives of both McAuley and Stewart who, in Kerr's opinion, 'were bloody lucky they had Alf to look after them'. Conlon awoke in McAuley an interest in New Guinea so consuming by the war's end that he abandoned his old dream of working in academia – he knocked back a teaching job at Melbourne University and then an appointment at the London School of Economics – rather than give up his work in the administration of Australia's only colony. After the war, when the pickings for poets intoxicated by Eastern religion and philosophy were slim, Stewart lived for a time with Conlon and his family in Sydney.

No one like Major Conlon had ever enlisted in the Australian Army and his Falstaffian mob was not everywhere admired. In January 1943, a new Adjutant-General was appointed and summoned Conlon to ask him what his unit did. 'Well, General, we just bugger about,' Conlon is supposed to have replied, though in other versions he gives the blunt answer, 'Fuck all', or declares, 'It's bullshit!', or is actually speaking to General Blamey, the Commander-in-Chief, or the encounter is something Conlon dreamt up and never happened at all. Not satisfied, Lloyd, the Adjutant-General, tried to make the unit, along with everyone else at the barracks, hold regular parades in the Botanical Gardens across the street. These were such farces they were abandoned to prevent the barracks being held up to ridicule. Harold Stewart recalls

another naughty thing that James and I and other people in the directorate did. We produced a scurrilous magazine called *The Call of Nature*. It was full of satirical sketches and witty poems about all the people in the directorate and in the army and political figures of the time. And of course Dr Conlon had to turn into a fascist dictator and destroy all copies, otherwise we would all have been in jail or shot at dawn or something more drastic. It was dynamite. If a copy had leaked to General Sir Thomas Blamey, Australia would have blown up and sunk slowly to the bottom of the Pacific.

For a time it looked as if the army might disband the directorate, but on 6 October 1943, just when Ern Malley was in the works, Conlon pulled off another coup: the directorate became responsible to Blamey himself, with its primary duty being 'to keep the Commander-in-Chief and certain other officers informed on current events affecting their work'. Its survival was assured, and the legend of Conlon the mecurial operator, advisor to the PM, confidant of the C-in-C, could flourish unimpeded.

For the three or four years of its life the directorate formed a buffer between Blamey and the government. In McAuley's view, Conlon convinced Blamey he was the first Australian general who 'wasn't an appendage to the British Government', and was really in charge of his own army. The directorate did valuable work in consolidating the laws of Papua and New Guinea after the Japanese retreat. It involved itself in the administration of Borneo. It produced maps and geographical surveys and, with the assistance of Cpl H. F. Stewart who performed the duties of an assistant librarian, built up a considerable library. Conlon was fond of Corporal Stewart because he was the only member of the directorate with no ambition to improve his rank. As for McAuley, he briefed Blamey on American affairs for a time, but then turned his attention to New Guinea. He studied the British administration of East Africa, and taught himself to read Dutch to familiarize himself with the Dutch legacy in Indonesia. Through his mentor, Conlon, McAuley had access to real power at the highest levels and in this heady atmosphere he acquired a taste for political intrigue. Manning Clark recalled that McAuley turned up on his doorstep in Geelong in 1943

with a toothbrush and nothing else and proceeded to eat and drink everything in the house and to play on the piano of a neighbour of ours news commentaries made up on the spot. He just went to the piano and started to play and sing songs about the situation in the war and in politics. He was fascinated by the low-down and he had all sorts of the most astonishing information about the relations between the Vatican and Japan, and the domestic politics of Burma. He was reeling off names I'd never heard of. He was in love with political gossip, 'intrigue and conspiracy', the 'low-down'. It was brilliant talk.

The directorate helped fulfil a desperate need in the army bureaucracy for technical advice about how to run a war for which it was not properly prepared, even though the battle raged on the country's doorstep. The directorate was also a law unto itself. It raised the ire of politicians who could not fathom how this over-ranked brains trust was on the public payroll. 'The Directorate has inquired into everything in Heaven and on earth,' snarled the Honourable Member for New England in the House, scandalized by the ample vision of Conlon in Canberra, 'a third-year medical student in civilian life . . . wearing the full uniform of a Staff Colonel'.

To cover his flank, Conlon produced a smokescreen in the form of a report which summarized the activities of his unit up to 1945. Among other things the directorate investigated the 'manpower position in universities', prepared a memorandum on the 'situation in North Africa since the Allied invasion' and on 'Wang Ching Wei's declaration of war'. It analysed 'psychological service in the US Army and the Germany Army' and 'problems of political and economic warfare'. There were memoranda on 'Shinto and Bushido', on 'the carriage of explosives by rail', and the introduction of pyrethrum as an insecticide 'to be grown by prisoners-of-war in camps'. Every so often the fog of the prose reduced visibility to zero: 'The Directorate represents the Army on Inter-Departmental Committees set up to handle problems arising out of the administration of New Guinea, and part of its staff carries out work connected with the government of New Guinea by direction of the Cabinet Sub-Committee, which operates in conjunction with the Commander-in-Chief in connection with problems that are of joint civil and military interest.' It was an impressive report, too impressive by half, but the eye which skims this list half a century later lingers on one tiny item: 'Advice to Adjutant-General on necessity of establishing entomological services for malarial control'.

Such advice was urgent when casualties from malaria could outnumber those inflicted by the Japanese. The war in New Guinea was also fought against squadrons of the *Anopheles punctulatus var. moluccensis*, a highly efficient vector of disease. As many as a quarter of Australian troops in New Guinea contracted malaria (among them Lieutenant James McAuley) and the Japanese were ravaged by it. 'Malaria discipline' and anti-mosquito squads were all the rage. Countless secret army reports were produced by the Allies suggesting ways of countering the problem, the most inventive of which was an Australian propaganda plan to concoct 'travelling Malaria exhibitions in 3 ton-trucks, skits and stage shows at Camp entertainments, judicious posters, rhymes and jingles'. The reports often gave detailed descriptions of the conditions under which mosquitoes flourished, and they were sometimes well written: 'Springs and seepages even if the water is very shallow and especially if concealed by grass are common breeding-places. Ponds, lagoons and sink-holes may be important especially if they have no fish and are not covered with water weed. Sunlight seems to be preferred but some breeding will be met even up dark jungle streams. Man made pools are a common breeding place as in slit trenches, borrow pits, road ruts.' Exposition like this might slow the eye of a skilled reader dutifully researching 'entomological services'.

Conlon reminded A. D. Hope of Christopher Brennan: a compulsive talker who started others talking. The comparison of the bureaucrat with the poet is instructive. McAuley was 'immensely grateful' to Conlon for 'a sense of things opening out, a sense that great enterprises were still possible' and claimed to have written a couple of poems 'directly under the stimulus of this sense of daring'. 'The Blue Horses', a more febrile and suggestive piece of work than anything else McAuley put his own name to, was dedicated to Conlon and given pride of place as the first poem in *Under Aldebaran*. A homage to the expressionist paintings of Franz Marc, the poem celebrates the apocalyptic power of the imagination to obliterate the workaday world which is otherwise nothing but the false construction of a fictional self:

> All things escape us, as we too escape.
> We have owned nothing and have no address
> Save in the poor constriction
> Of a legal or poetic fiction.
> He that possesses is possessed
> And falsifies perception lest
> The visionary hooves break through
> The simple seeming world he knew.

Conlon was asked once by an admirer why he never became a poet and he 'suggested in a way that he *had* written poetry because in the room where we were sitting a poem had been written – I think it was by James McAuley – and the complete poem had been written in one sitting with Alf standing by'. Is that how it worked? Did Colonel A. A. Conlon, brilliant desk soldier and natural politician, 'a strong opponent of any sort of humbug except his own', encourage in the co-conspirators a literary derring-do they might have repressed in ordinary circumstances? He would dream in his cups of what he called an 'intellectual underground', a network of self-styled mavericks and mandarins who saw more and further than mere careerists. The directorate, with its makeshift set-up and improvised agenda, a unit on the fringe of the army filled with people at odds with military life, was a scale model of that dream. It was the perfect place to construct a prototype of the invisible man, the self-propelled outsider, the gifted misfit: Ern Malley, court jester of the court poets, was almost an inevitable outcome of Colonel Conlon's weatherboard theatre of war.

Malley was born in an idle moment that afternoon in the spring of 1943. After lunch McAuley and Stewart had the place to themselves: there were no urgent telegrams to deal with, no research jobs to finish on the double. Here was their chance to do something they'd fantasized about, take *Angry Penguins* down a peg or two. Another issue was just out – they thought it reached new heights of pretension. They set to work improvising Ern Malley, their Primitive Penguin, writing his poems out on an army-issue, ruled quarto pad, tearing each page off as they filled it. They worked rapidly, buoyed by the wickedness of what they were up to, and spurring each other on – but they were stone cold sober.

McAuley did most of the writing 'and probably gave thereby the degree of continuity there might be in the work', but Stewart recalls stages when 'we probably had two pens and two different bits of paper and then put them together'. The hoaxers grasped from the start that they were faking a life and a death, and the paper corpse had to look authentic. Ern's manuscript, an artefact, an item of evidence, would have to seem old, tatty, loved: as if the product of sleepless nights in single rooms beneath an unshaded bulb, and lumped from city to city in a battered trunk. As they wrote, they spilled tea and put their cups down to stain the pages, experimenting to get the correct grubby effect. In black ink, in the manner of his long-abandoned Bungendore sequence, 'Prelude, Suite and Chorale', McAuley concocted 'So Long', Ern's last romantic gasp.

His full name was Ernest Lalor Malley. Ernest was obvious, since the hoaxers were anything but. Lalor was plucked from McAuley's family tree, and gave the right revolutionary edge. Malley, a good Celtic name, also identifies a desert region (the Mallee) in South Eastern Australia, not too far from where Nolan was sitting out the war. Malley, to Australian ears familiar with such affectionate abbreviations as 'footy' and 'telly', suggests a jokey diminutive of 'Mallarmé', no small figure in the tradition McAuley and Stewart were out to guy. The 'mal' in Malley also conjures a writer who knows how to write badly and implies, at one remove, a pun on Baudelaire's *Les Fleurs du mal*.

To set the ball rolling McAuley plucked 'Durer: Innsbruck, 1495' out of his own unpublished poems. Stewart remembers he read the poem intact, and adjusted it only lightly, if at all. The poem identifies Ern Malley as a clairvoyant who can 'see' the scene he imagines by taking the paradoxical action of closing his eyes. In the beginning he has no idea *what* he sees but knows his vision is 'real':

> I had often, cowled in the slumberous heavy air,
> Closed my inanimate lids to find it real,
> As I knew it would be, the colourful spires
> And painted roofs, the high snows glimpsed at the back,
> All reversed in the quiet reflecting waters –
> Not knowing then that Durer perceived it too.

This is *déjà vu* with a difference. The 'slumberous heavy air' and 'quiet reflecting waters' seem like qualities of his own world and of the experience he is in the throes of. How can we tell the dreamer from his dream? Yet Ern does not realize that the vista he disappears into is a work of art, 'perceived' and created by someone else, an inflection of the mind like the poem he is writing. The painting insinuates its detail into him just as the town of Innsbruck, at Dürer's behest, imprints itself on the water below. Ern Malley is a visionary who arrives at the dreadful knowledge that his vision is second-hand:

> Now I find that once more I have shrunk
> To an interloper, robber of dead men's dream,
> I had read in books that art is not easy
> But no one warned that the mind repeats
> In its ignorance the vision of others. I am still
> The black swan of trespass on alien waters.

'Once more' suggests this is not the first time he has witnessed an art he has no knowledge of. As they wrote the sequence the hoaxers picked up on this. In 'Baroque Exterior', as Malley curses his own obliteration, he seems to intuit 'The promise of a new architecture' – only to discover that 'What Inigo had built I perceived / In a dream of recognition'. Ern's spectral genius and his tragedy is to realize that someone else has already dreamt his dream for him. In the process of saying that, he even manages to rehash the opening sentence of Harris's editorial in the second issue of *Angry Penguins* in 1941: 'This is not an easy book.' Ern finds his identity in the understanding that his identity is not his own. This knowledge presumably accounts for his certainty of voice. Listen to it: the withering precision of 'shrunk / To an interloper', the drum-beat of 'dead men's dream', and then the Polonius-like, oh so earnest dissolve, 'I had read in books that art is not easy', which leaves the reader unprepared for the conclusion that, in its ignorance, repeats the vision of no one: 'I am still / The black swan of trespass on alien waters.' We intuit a poet of weird echoes and conjunctions, barely able to control their manifestation in his work, but aware of them in formulations like the final line with its intimations of shocking reversals, loss of self, originality dispossessed. This is a portrait of the artist as a medium whose seance is his poetry. Ern Malley stands in relation to other artists as radio does to static. More sensitive a sensibility you cannot get.

But why Dürer? And this painting by Dürer? The 'View of Innsbruck' was painted early in 1495 while Dürer was making his unprecedented journey, on foot or by horseback, from Nuremberg, his home town, to Venice, to study the work of his Italian contemporaries. He was twenty-four years old, perhaps the same age as Ern Malley – who also travelled south from Sydney to Melbourne to broaden his cultural horizons and push back the frontiers of art – when he experienced his vision of Dürer's vision. The painting, one of Dürer's earliest watercolours, was a breakthrough for the artist, a work of great promise, with the trace elements but without the finish of genius. That afternoon at the barracks the hoaxers conceived of the Dürer poem as 'one of two or three on the boundary-line dividing the end of a supposed middle-period from the poet's triumphant breakthrough into his final phase'.

McAuley had been interested in Dürer since the late 1930s. When he was courting Norma Abernethy they used to buy postcards together. 'We ranged from Picasso's Blue Period in rather haphazard leaps back to the early Renaissance and stray specimens of Gothic. Dürer attracted us considerably: water-colours, drawings, not many of the engravings and woodcuts except a few of the most famous and compelling; the oil-paintings I think not at all.' McAuley admired the 'objective' Dürer, master of rendering 'the object observed with an acute attentive eye' rather than the generator of distortion and gro-tesquerie whom Max Harris cited in *Bohemia* in 1939 to prove that the 'abnormal' in art predates modernism. Such is the 'View of Innsbruck' with its architectonic precision (even the scaffold-ing on the tower is sketched in), its portrayal of the green reflecting water, the gradations of colour in the buildings, the sky and snow-capped mountains behind the town.

Dürer's seductive dramatization of the distance between the cosy township and its mirrored reversal in the river becomes an ideogram of the way Stewart and McAuley played their tricks of illusion to make their portrait of a genius seem real. Fifteenth-century Innsbruck is given substance by Dürer's art because its incomplete, insubstantial image in the river is exact. The painter gives us enough detail to fill in the gaps ourselves. That is the technique the hoaxers used to build their portrait of an artist from the reflections cast by a hundred luminaries, one of them Albrecht Dürer. Ern Malley's 'real' evocation of a 'real' painting by the 'realist' Dürer was a brilliant feint, a way of distracting the reader from what the poem was actually saying – that its author was a chimera. McAuley designed it this way. Later he described the poem frankly as a 'come-on' and added:

What the poem claims is that the poet had often had a pre-vision of Innsbruck before seeing Dürer's picture: not a very credible assertion. But we are now so well trained into Coleridge's 'willing suspension of disbelief' that we exercise it not only where we should but also where we shouldn't. We need as a counterweight a revival of the eighteenth century reading habit of noticing what the poem actually says and asking whether this is sensible. The effect of the reasonably pleasant and accurate description of Dürer's picture was to lull the reader into acquiescence.

Whether or not a poem should be judged by how 'sensible' it is, not many people habitually question the authorship of what they are reading. McAuley and Stewart needed to have it both ways as they set to work that Saturday afternoon. They needed a poem that looked conventional enough not to draw excessive attention to itself but which would also suggest an exotic potential, an appetite for sensation. With its rhythmic assurance, descriptive command, and promise of a subtle intellect, 'Durer: Innsbruck, 1495' would lull almost any reader into acquiescence. Nobody could have intuited a bogus poet on the basis of this poem alone, and yet it foreshadowed the pattern of the entire hoax.

The key principles in their improvisation were free association and conscious interruption. 'We'd think of a line or two each,' Stewart recalls, 'or we'd play with this bit and we'd put a bit in here and take a bit out there. They were all joint efforts, in different proportions, of course. One would have a bright idea and we'd say, "Oh yes, let's adopt that." Or sometimes Jim would get a line and I'd say, "Oh, it'd be much better if we could get that word in there, in that line."' McAuley wrote 'the lungs are divine aquaria' and Stewart, who'd been looking into Egyptian mythology, elaborated this into 'Ra's divine aquaria'. McAuley came up with 'Princess, you lived in Princess St., / Where the urchins pick their nose in the sun' and Steward added the fake coda, 'With the left hand.' The joke was teased out in the next poem with 'that snowy globe / Milady Lucy's sinister breast'. McAuley also 'wanted to do what he called a statistical poem', constructed by choosing a poem like Shelley's 'To a Skylark' and taking out every seventh word all the way through. These words would then be strung together into lines. 'We may have actually tried that in one or two lines,' Stewart remembers. They also decided to write the poem 'Night Piece' twice – it is possible that they preselected its imagery, agreed on the number of lines, and then wrote the two versions individually.

Conjuring their hyperbolic surrealist, McAuley and Stewart parodied or manipulated their own work whenever it suited them. When he read Ern Malley in 1944, Alan Crawford recognized fragments from drafts of poems McAuley had shown him in Sydney, though half a century later he could not begin to guess what they were. McAuley admitted that they borrowed 'one another's style or his field of imagery as part of the playfulness of the thing . . . I can remember starting with some of Harold's Chinese imagery and then getting Harold to fill up with something which was probably aping my field of imagery.' 'Palinode' cryptically suggests the hoax bastardized Stewart's interest in the East and Keats:

> There are ribald interventions
> Like spurious seals upon
> A Chinese landscape-roll
> Or tangents to the rainbow.
> We have known these declensions,
> Have winked when Hyperion
> Was transmuted to a troll.
> We dubbed it a sideshow.

They took pot shots at poets they considered beyond the pale: the 'sunken sodden breeding-grounds' in 'Culture as Exhibit' departed from the opening of 'Little Gidding' by 'Tears' Eliot (as Alec Hope was wont to call him): 'Midwinter spring is its own season / Sempiternal though sodden towards sundown'. Harold Stewart recalls how Hope described that last line as Eliot's epitaph on himself. And 'The evening / Settles down like a brooding bird' in 'Sybilline' was lifted directly from the first line of Eliot's 'Preludes'. The sprawling, chaotic 'Documentary Film' made fun of Pound's *Cantos*, dubbed the *Rantos* by Harold Stewart, which he described as 'a macaronic medley of literary detritus'. 'Documentary Film' bunched 'Melbourne' with 'the Ch'en Plain', and transposed images of the inner Melbourne suburb Footscray against an evocation of the carvings on a Javanese temple:

> The elephant motifs contorted on admonitory walls,
> The subtle nagas that raise the cobra hood
> And hiss in the white masterful face.

The poem concludes with a pastiche of Mallarmé, further proof that Ern Malley was half in love with easeful death:

> The solemn symphony of angels lighting
> My steps with music, o consolations!
> Palms!
> O far shore, target and shield that I now
> Desire beyond these terrestrial commitments.

Shades of Mallarmé also gave the pair the opulent opening of 'Egyptian Register':

> The hand burns resinous in the evening sky
> Which is a lake of roses, perfumes, idylls

though the sands of time that Ern chokes on at the end of 'Baroque Exterior' had blown in from Longfellow. The seed-puffing thistle at the end of 'Petit Testament' was written over Keats's 'seeded thistle' which 'sendeth fair / Its light balloons into the summer air'. And the poets glanced at *Angry Penguins* for inspiration: in Alister Kershaw's 'Denunciad' they found this description of the painter and part-time political theorist Albert Tucker, 'who, like a cockroach, lives / Deep in the cleft of split infinitives'. Thus Ern Malley confessed in his 'Petit Testament': 'Where I have lived . . . the cockroach / Inhabits the crack . . . I have split the infinitive.'

Not all their sources were so literary, though: 'Culture forsooth! Albert, get my gun' modified 'Annie, get your gun' from the musical *Oklahoma*, and the name Albert came from Stanley Holloway's music-hall monologue about poor little Albert Ramsbottom, eaten by the lion at Blackpool Zoo. The whole line also brings to mind Hermann Goering's famous remark: 'When I hear anyone talk of culture I reach for my revolver!'

They also made fun of their research jobs in the directorate: 'I have been noted in the reading-rooms / As a borer of calf-bound volumes / Full of scandals at the Court'. A few of Ern Malley's lines came straight out of their work: 'the scrub-typhus of Mubo' which was laying low Australian troops in New Guinea, for instance, or the 'rabbit's foot' Ern kept in his – can you guess? – 'left pocket' which derived from Harold Stewart's observation that black American soldiers often carried a rabbit's foot for luck. The pair used whatever books happened to be on their desks, the *Concise Oxford Dictionary*, a *Collected Shakespeare*, a *Dictionary of Quotations*. These proved to be insufficient since they made up their own pearls of wisdom too. If only Lenin had actually said 'The emotions are not skilled workers.' They found an ominous Biblical tag in the non-existent Odes of Solomon: 24.8. 'And the Lord destroyeth the imagination of all them that had not the truth with them.'

Handy research material also found their way into the poetry. Their entomological investigations for Alf Conlon had led them to read a US Army report on mosquito control – so they copied out its opening sentence – 'Swamps, marshes, borrow-pits and other / Areas of stagnant water serve / As breeding-grounds' – to kick off 'Culture as Exhibit'. Ern Malley's trick, by providing a new context, was to turn descriptive prose into satire. Later the poet Elisabeth Lambert, the Reed & Harris representative in Sydney, wrote to John Reed:

Someone should try and locate the man who wrote the opening lines of that American drainage report. It might easily be accidental, but on the other hand the poor fellow might be a suppressed poet. In the first two lines he has demonstrated my pet prosody theory. It isn't everyone can toss off a 1st paeon as he has. The whole quotation has a fine flavour. And borrow-pits. What a beautiful word. I'm doubtful just what a borrow-pit is, but it makes a lovely noise. In any case what made Stewart-McAuley think a mosquito unpoetic? I find the whole poem delicious satire.

Among the dictionaries and reference books the hoaxers dipped into was Stewart's copy of Walter Ripman's *A Pocket Dictionary of English Rhymes*, first issued in 1932 and 'Re-issued at a Cheaper Price' two years later.* Rhyming dictionaries,

*Stewart remains a devotee of rhyming dictionaries and showed me his own adaptation: a card itemizing in alphabetical order clusters of consonants in their commonly found formations. Its reader supplies the necessary vowels. The

like graphs of metrical patterns, tend to confuse a characteristic of poetic craft with the art itself. Ripman believed that the corpus of English poetry would have been improved if some of its practitioners had been able to consult his book. He listed instances of 'imperfect rhyme' from the likes of Keats, Byron, Tennyson and Kipling, and noted that they sometimes 'let unstressed syllables bear the rhyme, so that we find *eyes* coupled with *mysteries*, *less* with *thankfulness*. I do not myself regard this as an embellishment of the verse, but it is interesting to observe the practice of the poets.'

Try to *read* a rhyming dictionary and it becomes a Dada poem, like something by Kurt Schwitters: consider the obsessive, subliminal sexuality of Ripman's list: 'hued you'd unsubdued nude denude unrenewed feud lewd allude elude delude exude unreviewed'. But Malley does not go in for sound poetry, concrete poetry, broken syntax, neologisms, verbal diarrhoea or the abandonment of grammar. He is a sturdy traditionalist by these standards. Using Ripman, McAuley and Stewart exploited a standard tool of trade. After all, neither poet needed a lexicon to think up silly rhymes.

Like his makers in their own verse, Ern Malley often rhymes, just as he breaks into metre at will. A handful of the poems use strict and sometimes complex rhyming patterns, and many others include internal rhyme. Some pairings are sophisticated and slick, though Ripman would not have approved: Pericles / knees, wrist / amorist, loyalists / lists. Others could never have been found in a dictionary: adieu / weren't you, singers / lingers, for't / distort. When they came to write 'Sonnets for the Novachord', however, the poets opened Ripman, plucked most of the rhymes out in advance, and assembled the poem around them:

---

possible number of words which may be formed is limited only by the user's vocabulary.

(i)

Rise from the wrist, o kestrel
Mind, to a clear expanse.
Perform your high dance
On the clouds of ancestral
Duty. Hawk at the wraith
Of remembered emotions.
Vindicate our high notions
Of a new and pitiless faith.
It is not without risk!
In a lofty attempt
The fool makes a brisk
Tumble. Rightly contempt
Rewards the cloud-foot unwary
Who falls to the prairie.

(ii)

Poetry: the loaves and fishes,
Or no less miracle;
For in this deft pentacle
We imprison our wishes.

Though stilled to alabaster
This Ichthys shall swim
From the mind's disaster
On the volatile hymn.

If this be the norm
Of our serious frolic
There's no remorse:

Our magical force
Cleaves the ignorant storm
On the hyperbolic.

'All these dreadful rhymes,' Stewart chuckled, remembering
how they thumbed through the dictionary. §8.37 cites '*kestrel*
orchestral *ancestral*' and a few lines down (§8.41) the eye

stumbles on 'disk fisk *risk brisk* frisk whisk'. Further flicking produces (§16.62) *'faith(s) wraith(s)* rathe' and (§2.77) 'tempt *attempt contempt* self-contempt kempt'. Likewise: (§9.1) 'dish *fish wish* swish squish'; or (§15.31) 'haulm(s) shawm(s): *storm(s) norm* form forme deform'; or, next page, (§15.42) 'sauce . . . recourse discourse morse *remorse force*'. The words they chose did not always fall side by side. §17.45 listed 'ocean potion nicotian motion *emotion* promotion commotion locomotion *notion*' and §30.3 'airy hairy dairy vagary canary fairy *prairie* glary glairy wary *unwary* vary chary'. Thus 'alabaster / disaster' and 'frolic / hyperbolic' were fished out of the dictionary. 'Miracle' does not occur in Ripman and 'pentacle' is married to 'tentacle'. Here the poets improved on their source.

They were not seduced by any bizarre couplings Ripman offered: the lists above contain oddities and exoticisms they overlooked. Of course, if chance dictated everything, the pairings they came up with might *not* necessarily be awkward or comic. In fact they gave themselves the maximum freedom: random choice, careful selection, closing the book altogether. The effect of 'Sonnets for the Novachord', a poem full of hints that a game is being played, is not one of enforced gaucherie, but of a coup: getting inside the opponent's guard with a hand tied behind the back.

They wrote all afternoon and into the evening, around nine or ten, perhaps taking an hour off to eat. 'It was a hard day's work creating the poems,' McAuley remarked. There are 424 lines in Malley: assuming they produced his *oeuvre* over a period of eight or ten hours, discarding drafts and false starts along the way, that sets their output at a poem every half an hour, a rate slightly less than a line a minute, no mean feat. Many people, including some who approve of the hoax, refuse to believe this possible. Fans of Malley won't have a bar of it: they deny the hoaxers the wherewithal to write such marvellous stuff so quickly. 'It would have taken Shakespeare a weekend,' scoffed Sidney Nolan as late as 1974. But the speed at which Ern Malley was written does not guarantee either inferior work or the outpourings of genius. It simply makes the poets' disclaimers of merit more powerful.

Imagine Ethel told Harris that Ern bashed his poems out in a day.
Would he have believed her?

Stewart has always vowed that it was not only possible but
repeatable:

two army officers working in the same unit, both distinguished
anthropologists, questioned the possibility of doing this in one afternoon and so we set them the task of doing the same thing, and they had
no difficulty whatever in producing an equal number of poems and lines
of a very much higher quality than ours, in rather less time, if I
remember rightly, but certainly no more than one afternoon and
evening.

A day or so after they were written, Stewart typed the poems
up in the directorate library. Any revisions in the process were
not substantial. The hoaxers did not want to muffle the effect
they were so sure of. Here they refined the delicate condition of
the manuscript. 'We carefully mistyped and erased,' Stewart
recalled, 'we rolled the paper in the dust, we stood our wet cups
of tea on it to make ringed stains, we "aged" the ink in the sun.'
They also graded the poems, according to Stewart, 'so they got
sillier and sillier . . . by the time you got to things like: "In the
twenty-fifth year of my age I find myself to be a dromedary" you
have reached the comic'.

In the McAuleys' flat, at the elegant 'Paris' end of Collins Street
in the city, the hoaxers read the poems aloud 'in fits of laughter'
to Norma McAuley, who doubted anybody would be fooled by
them, and was 'horrified' the poets would be exposed to ridicule
for writing such drivel. She also foresaw legal problems. Was it
false pretences if they received money under an assumed name?
The hoaxers sought advice. They did not have to go far: the
directorate was filled with clever legal minds destined for ample
careers. A delighted Alf Conlon came in on the hoax and then
McAuley approached John Kerr, who had the amplest career of
all. He became Governor-General of Australia and in November
1975, at the climax of Australia's greatest political crisis since
Federation, dismissed from office Gough Whitlam, the Labor

Prime Minister who had appointed him. Kerr gave the hoaxers the green light. He 'laughed and said he doubted whether the law had anything to say on the point, and therefore might predictably say anything, though he doubted whether there was any serious risk.' McAuley and Stewart played it safe anyway, and Ethel refused to accept a penny for her brother's work. 'I don't want any money from them myself because I don't feel that they belong to me,' she wrote.

Kerr and McAuley also toyed with the idea of extending the hoax by inviting 'an important public figure . . . to write an introduction to the poems; but we decided it was too risky and idle talk along those lines was abandoned'. A tantalizing fragment – the VIP they had in mind was Herbert Vere Evatt, the Federal Attorney-General, and Minister for External Affairs, one of the more remarkable politicians to influence public policy in Australia's short history of national government. Born in Sydney in 1894, Evatt was a brilliant jurist who left the High Court in 1940 to take a seat in parliament on the Labor side. A short, portly, ebullient man, with prodigious energy and a blustery manner, he did not tolerate fools gladly. Evatt knew John and Sunday Reed – they nicknamed him 'Judgie' – and sometimes stayed with them at Heide. He and his wife Mary Alice also collected modern Australian art. In 1943, when the Curtin government was at its most popular, he was at the height of his powers: he had been in Washington and London in early 1942, when the situation looked grim, and he went again in mid 1943 to negotiate with Roosevelt and Churchill. Later, in 1945, Evatt helped frame the United Nations Charter, and was President of the General Assembly for two years from 1948. He was a bitter, losing figure in the Petrov affair in 1955, when the defection of a minor Soviet diplomat ignited the Cold War in Australia.

Why would the pranksters want to involve such a man in their literary high-jinks? It is a puzzling question and bemused Alan Crawford who saw McAuley at the barracks in September 1944. McAuley mentioned the hoax and said 'with a kind of sardonic grin' that they'd hoped to get a preface to the poems from Dr

Evatt and 'unfortunately they hadn't been able to do it because the Doc had said he was too busy or something'. Kerr recalled that the idea was probably Conlon's – 'he had a no hands approach to life' – but doubted any approach was ever made. They pulled back from 'making a victim of a man who was a big sort of bloke in the prime of his life', though there was 'a lot of giggling' among those concocting the scheme.

It would have taken some ingenuity for the hoaxers to connect Ethel Malley with Bert Evatt, without letting him in on the story. And it is hard to see how a humiliated Evatt would have profited Conlon, who had no love for him but who needed his co-operation to further his own endeavours in New Guinea and Borneo. Whatever its motivation, any approach to Evatt must have had political implications, perhaps connected with McAuley's steady drift to the right. Given the power of the hoax to galvanize the media, it is boggling to contemplate the fall-out had Ern Malley been published with the imprimatur of the Attorney-General, the chief legal officer in the land. Through the Reeds, Evatt was aware of *Angry Penguins*, though this may have been incidental to the hoaxers' intentions – whatever they were. The anecdote is a strange footnote to events, evidence the joke was becoming a juggernaut.*

They were ready. Stewart practised a fake backhand and wrote out Ethel's first letter. Everything in Ethel Malley's hand was scribbled out by Harold Stewart, while James McAuley used his own undoctored script for Ern. The letter was dispatched, with a handful of the poems as bait, to Harold Stewart's family home at 40 Dalmar St, Croydon, where his sister Marion had been instructed to send it on to Harris in Adelaide. The two poets were delighted with their handiwork – but they had no way of

---

*Kerr's wartime work in the directorate, his walk-on role in the Ern Malley hoax and his sacking of the Whitlam government are a potent cocktail for anyone disposed – as Sidney Nolan, for instance, was – to conspiracy theories about connections between the political motivation of the hoax, and the politics of the crisis in 1975. No evidence has come to light to link the two events, and it is hard to see how any could.

knowing if Harris would rise to the bait. They went about their work at the directorate, and waited.

It did not take long. Marion Stewart forwarded Harris's intoxicated reply to the barracks a few days later. The poets were ecstatic. The grenade was in flight. Now they 'had to get to work and invent a life'. The figure of Ethel Malley, elaborated in her long confessional letter to Harris, was a brilliant feint – it is hard to imagine anyone less likely to harbour a poet in the family home or to foist an elaborate joke on an unsuspecting editor. Ethel was a MacGuffin, an element in the plot to provide distraction while the real story got under way. But what a distraction! Her dogged, costive voice was exactly registered, the measure of a limited mind at full stretch. Her letterese was Joycean in its hand-me-down precision, the sparse punctuation and bunched clichés a minefield for the unwary crashing through the clouds.

Ethel lent the hoax credibility by showing that Ern had flesh-and-blood relatives, and grounded the fantasy of the unknown, self-educated genius in the world of lower-middle-class suburbia that McAuley and Stewart had grown up in, and escaped from. This was and is the true home of Australian philistinism: Ern Malley mocked the romantic myth of the proletarian artist but Ethel anticipated by a decade that formidable icon of the Australian suburban sensibility, Edna Everage, invented in the fifties by the comic genius Barry Humphries. 'Edna was conceived as a character to remind Australians of their bigotry and all the things I found offensive. She was a rebuke. She was a silly, bigoted, ignorant, self-satisfied Melbourne housewife,' Humphries confessed. 'I invented Edna because I hated her.' Stewart himself described Ethel as the 'apotheosis of the lower middle-class female, who always writes in letterese; snooty, tight-lipped & righteously indignant about her brother having "lived" and written "poetry" and yet morally obliged to see to its publication though always with an eye to making some money out of it'. The critic Vivian Smith is right when he says that Ethel is 'as good as anything similar' in Patrick White, Hal Porter, or

Humphries. As synthetic artefacts, Ethel's letters are as fascinating as Ern's poems and, in their image of a gormless philistine, acid satire.

If Ern Malley's work aspires to the condition of poetry, Ethel's letters aspire to fiction. They were largely composed by Harold Stewart though McAuley also worked on them and McAuley's wife Norma recalled contributing some detail. She would join the hoaxers for lunch in the Melbourne Botanical Gardens opposite the Victoria Barracks, while they worked out the details of Ern's life. 'At the time I thought it was unlikely that anyone would believe such a story,' she recalls. 'It was great fun working out all the details. I'm afraid I did get into it occasionally, making up the story and trying to make it believable.' Stewart remembers:

The letters required much more literary skill and much more time and trouble than – having been written over several weeks – than did the actual poems themselves. Not only did we have to create the character of Ethel Malley, the middle-aged, middle-brow, middle-class young lady of no great education, who had come upon these supposed poems of her imaginary brother, but also we had to create his character through her letters, and as he would have appeared to her, and so that required very delicate dislocations of grammar and spelling.

Ethel paints a vivid picture of her poor brother's career: his dates of birth and death, the schools he attended and fled, the places he worked, even the cemetery she put him to rest in – how could any grieving sister fail to mention that? But this biography is a house of cards waiting for a puff of wind. Some of the detail was fictitious: there was no Palmer's Garage on Taverner's Hill and, while Rookwood exists, no Ern Malley was ever reduced to ashes there. Other detail is hearsay or conveniently beyond verification. Ern's rejection from the army gives his early death a context but means there were no military records to be checked. The doctor's inexplicable refusal to operate eliminated hospital records. Since he was born in England his birth certificate was unavailable. The demise of his parents meant all other intimate witnesses of his life were silenced. For the key period of Malley's life, his exile in Melbourne where he wrote his poetry, Ethel resorts to information that can't be corroborated: 'some-one I knew met him . . .' That single room in South Melbourne may ring true but offers a sleuth next to nothing. As it happened, Harold Stewart had a room, at the time, in South Melbourne – and the hoaxers did lift details from their own lives to draw their composite portrait. Like Ern, Stewart often visited the Melbourne Public Library on Swanston Street, about a mile from the barracks, partly because his job in the army required this, and partly to pursue his own intellectual interests. The reduction of Ern Malley's library to a single book – Thorstein Veblen's *Theory of the Leisure Class*, signalling the poet's left-wing bona fides – was Jim McAuley's joke. 'Another one of the books on James's desk,' Harold Stewart recalled. 'He was reading that at the moment. I've never read it, I must say. Not my cup of tea at all . . . Veblen was a very fashionable name of the period.'

Almost the craftiest thing about Ethel's letter is the way she disguises her own paucity of information by disapproving of the way Ern lived his life. She judges him by petty standards ('I have always thought he was very foolish not to have got his Intermediate') and is miffed at the way he excludes her ('I had no idea how bad he really was'). She cannot conceal her misgivings: 'He was terribly irritable and hard to do anything for . . . I did my best to persuade him but he went.' There are gaping holes in the story ('After that I did not see much of him or hear from him', 'I wrote to him but he did not reply for a long time', 'I did not hear from him again until the beginning of this year'). Ethel can hardly hide the fact that *her* biography is a fake, a travesty skint for evidence. She admits as much, sad and bewildered, overcome by a failure of expression, though we know just what she means: 'I am sorry I can't tell you much more about Ern, but as I said before he kept very much to himself. He was always a little strange and moody and I don't think he had a very happy life, though he didn't show it.'

Ethel's artlessness was cunningly registered: she would, for instance, say something and then in the next sentence show she did not understand what she had just said. Harris was certain of the order in which Ern wanted his poems published because Ethel pointed out that the manuscript was paginated – in the breath before she lamented the absence of any publishing instructions. It was also part of the joke for the hoaxers, po-faced, to use Ethel to express their own views about their handiwork – 'I had no idea they might be good enough to publish overseas' – or their glee at the success of the hoax: 'I am very glad to know that you think they are so good.' And Ethel has a gift for vagueness: of what kind were mother's relations, for instance? What were those 'other things' Ern was 'good at'? The surface of her prose is a minefield yielding tiny explosions, like the fact that Ern shares his birthday with an actual prodigy, Albert Einstein.

Ethel did her duty, and gave her recalcitrant brother to the world and fame. But her account shows how traumatic their relationship was. Ethel can't hide the fact that she was the hated voice of authority, the surrogate mother Ern could not abide and had to escape. He clearly didn't mind stringing her along – through a third party he supplies some disinformation about selling insurance and then comes up with that feeble furphy about repairing watches.* He knew she was a sucker for any limp phrase: 'doing other work on the side'. Back in Sydney, and dying, Ern did his best to resist her inquisition, being 'nervy and irritable'. The letter doesn't quite suggest that Ern committed suicide ('The crisis came suddenly') but it sometimes reads like Ethel's signed confession too.

If this sounds improbable, Ern was not likely to have died of Graves' disease either, an illness identified in the nineteenth century by the Irish physician R. J. Graves. This disease of the thyroid gland, also known as exophthalmic goitre is, like Ern, of

---

*In 1959, in *The End of Modernity*, a savage rejection of the heresies of modernism, James McAuley wrote that those poets are happiest 'who have a trade whose exercise gives satisfaction but which does not make excessive demands on the higher personal energies. I mean something like watch-repairing.'

unknown origin, though women are more often afflicted than men, 'in the proportion of 8 to 1, or even higher'. Graves' disease makes the patient go bug-eyed. 'A startled or frightened expression is thus given to the countenance', reports *Black's Medical Dictionary*.

Palpitation of the heart is the most constant symptom. Sleeplessness, irritability, disorders of digestion, diarrhoea, uterine derangements, muscular tremors, and an unusual readiness to perspire freely are common accompaniments. All the bodily activities are carried on at high pressure, and there is consequent wasting of the fatty and muscular tissues, with increasing thinness . . . Exophthalmic goitre is not often a directly fatal malady, but the nervousness, palpitation and muscular weakness may render the patient unfit for even the slightest exertion.

It sounds like the perfect illness for an agonized, moribund romantic, yet Graves' disease is easily treated with an iodine compound. Ethel reported that Ern kept going by 'dosing himself' with the stuff. 'We just got it out of a medical dictionary,' Stewart recalls. 'The Graves part was so appropriate we couldn't resist it, even though nobody dies of the disease. Wouldn't you have thought that would have alerted them?'

He was twenty-five years and four months old when he died. McAuley and Stewart did not randomly hit on this span of years. Keats was exactly this age when his final breath bubbled out of him in Rome in 1821. 'Yet we are as the double almond concealed in one shell,' Malley hinted, himself a double almond in a shell, in his 'Colloquy with John Keats'. His early death puts him in eminent romantic company of course. Laforgue and Trakl made it to twenty-seven, Shelley to thirty. Ben Jonson declared that Donne had 'written all his best pieces ere he was 25 years old', a statement much truer of Ern Malley than it is of John Donne.

'I'd rather have an art of genuine humour than fake tragedy,' the Australian artist Donald Friend once said. Ern Malley is both. And Ethel is the perfect teller of his tale because she represents the reality he dedicated himself to oppose. We can see – and

Harris saw – in Ethel's description the poet she cannot describe. Her account is a series of dots which, linked, reveal the figure of the *poète maudit* in a philistine society, intent on achieving what Harris described as 'the perfection and integration' of his life's work, the sixteen poems he gave to the world.

By now the hoax was beginning to write itself. The pair decided Ethel's package should include Ern's 'Preface and Statement' – the final draft was scrawled out by McAuley – to parody the kind of credo they saw not only in *Angry Penguins* but English publications like *Horizon* or *Poetry London*. Ern became a master of the epigram: 'Every poem should be an autarchy.' This kind of thing was lifted from the writings of Herbert Read, who declared, for instance, in one of his columns for the *Listener*, arguing for anarchist self-government: 'Art is a product of autarky – that seems to be the lesson of history.' 'It shows the signs,' A. D. Hope commented to me in 1988, 'of somebody who'd been right in and out the other side and could use the language in that way. It's rather cleverly done. It's not simply parroting. It's a parody of that kind of thing but quite original in itself. That of course helped the thing to catch on.' The 'Preface and Statement' reeks of aloof cleverness: it testifies to Malley's seriousness, to his systematic vision. It reinforces his biography ('The writing was done over five years'), especially his premonition of dying ('What might not X have done if he had lived?'), though McAuley and Stewart also used statements of absolute fact to bamboozle Harris: 'There is no biographical data.'

Ern's Dürer postcard, a further elaboration, also intensified the illusion of a life. But its cryptically amorous inscription – 'The plot is sprung the Queen is took, / One night enjoyed the next forsook' – was in fact a clue for Harris (as McAuley told him, years later) that his leg was being pulled. Not by Lois, Shakespeare, McAuley or Stewart, the couplet misquotes Nahum Tate's libretto to Purcell's *Dido and Aeneas*, an opera probably first staged in 1689, three years before Tate assumed the position of Poet Laureate. It was a 'great favourite' of the hoaxers, which they knew by heart from listening to SP gramophone recordings.

(Harold Stewart even sang bass in the final chorus 'With drooping wings ye Cupids come' for his university choral society in 1936.) The challenge for Harris was to recognize the plundered couplet.* He might then have questioned the anomalous Ern's taste for opera and the meaning of the lines in this weird context.

The hoax was also a parlour game to fox the opponent with superior erudition or false clues; McAuley and Stewart exploited to the hilt 'the richly paradoxical character of Ern Malley, the motor mechanic without formal education who could beat Max Harris at his own game'. They seized on what they knew well, not minding whether they had misremembered or were getting it wrong. In such circumstances how could one get it wrong? But Harris, who did not think of his literary activities as a game and never underestimated Ern, read the surprises Ethel bestowed on him as fragments of a life. Not looking for a trick, he missed every warning of one.

As Harris's love of Malley accelerated, it seemed the joke could be elaborated at will. Harold Stewart decided their prodigious Penguin was an artist too. He made eleven small photo-collages from black-and-white photographs he cut out of old *National Geographic* magazines – the May 1929, January 1931 and May 1931 issues in particular – and pasted on to army-issue brown manila card. There was a twelfth, *Happy Landing*, which has gone missing. 'It was an airfield below with people waving to welcome the tail-fins of an aeroplane in the air above, preparing to make a landing – without the rest of the plane which must

*The couplet that foxed Harris weaves together two separate moments from Tate's libretto to *Dido and Aeneas*. First a snatch from the gloating song of 'The Sorceress' and her 'Inchanteresses', neo-classical descendants of the hags who spur Macbeth, after Aeneas has abandoned the queen and sailed for Italy: 'Our Plot has took, / The Queen forsook, ho, ho, ho.' The second line is from an earlier passage where Aeneas grumbles about having to leave Dido: 'How can so hard a Fate be took, / One Night enjoy'd, the next forsook.'

Casting Ern Malley as Aeneas, founder of cities, betrayer of queens, was a bit rich. It was a neat trick to keep the word 'took' but shift its sense from 'worked' and then 'endured' to one suggesting the stratagems of chess and sex. Harris, or Lois, says the couplet, was mated if not screwed.

have dropped off somewhere else in flight.' Was it a visual equivalent to the reception of Ern Malley's poems, and a comic gloss on 'Boult to Marina': 'Only a part of me shall triumph in this . . . The rest of me drops off into the night'?

Stewart showed the collages to McAuley, and there was talk of sending them to *Angry Penguins* 'as a later discovery of Ethel's, who found them under the newspaper lining at the bottom of Ern's old tin trunk'. Malley's poetry, 'gluings' of fake fragments, quotations, and snatches of translation, is a kind of collage. And when the two poets embalmed the corpse of Ern Malley, modern art was laid out on the mortician's table too. Lines were devised from titles and crypto-descriptions. 'The twin balconies are breasts' in 'Baroque Exterior' borrowed its surrealist flavour from Salvador Dali's *Les deux balcons*, painted in 1929. In 'Sweet William' the reference was to Blake, and the opening couplet, 'I have avoided your wide English eyes: / But now I am whirled in their vortex' allowed Malley – dying, bulbous-eyed, from Graves' disease – to identify with the visionary poet whose 'wide English eyes' the poets knew from the famous portrait by Thomas Phillips. The echo of Pound ('whirled in a vortex') and allusion to vorticism was grist to the mill. The poem's climactic Yeatsian progression,

> And I must go with stone feet
> Down the staircase of flesh
> To where in a shuddering embrace
> My toppling opposites commit
> The obscene, the unforgivable rape

alluded not to *Don Giovanni* as Max Harris guessed, but to the dropsical female figures in the series of paintings Picasso produced at Fontainebleau in 1921. 'You know, the lady by the stream with those enormous ferro-concrete feet,' Stewart explained. 'The staircase of flesh' derived from Duchamp's *Nude Descending a Staircase* and the 'toppling opposites' were Ern's version of yin and yang from the Tao, courtesy of Harold Stewart. Yin and yang also gave the poem its post-coital resolution: 'My white swan of quietness lies / Sanctified on my black swan's breast.'

Salvador Dali may have been one catalyst for the production of the collages. When he visited the *Herald* exhibition in 1939, Stewart caught sight of Dali's painting 'L'Homme Fleur', which had already outraged many viewers:

I'd never seen a Dali before, though I'd seen the limp watches in reproduction. Here was a painting with the most exquisitely painted watches, and so I went up and looked closely at the canvas. They'd been cut out of a Sears Roebuck catalogue and stuck on the canvas. Dali was a brilliant technician, he could draw, he could paint – like Picasso, he was brilliantly talented – but if you exploit and abuse your talent and are deliberately dishonest with the public, I think you've forfeited your artistic integrity.*

Stewart's direct model was a hoax invented by the painter Donald Friend a few years earlier. On 16 November 1943, Stewart wrote to Friend to find out more about this earlier hoax, and in the process hinted at the 'practical joke' he was perpetrating on 'an unfortunate poet'. He wanted, Stewart said, to assemble a history of hoaxes. Friend obliged with a detailed account. Invited by the *Christian Science Monitor* to produce an article about early Australian art, he decided to mock 'American snobbism, which dotes so madly, without real appreciation, on the primitives, colonial spoons, ancestor worship and Hollywood heraldry'. Friend invented a phoney antipodean Rousseau, a convict painter named Michael Collins, the son of a poor Irish 'peat-and-potato-eating' farmer, who was transported in the early nineteenth century after being caught poaching pheasants in Tipperary. Collins, according to the life Friend gave him, served

*Stewart's collages mocked forms of art that scarcely existed in Australia. In 1940 Sidney Nolan displayed a few collages at his first solo exhibition in his studio at 320 Russell Street, Melbourne. He took nineteenth-century steel engravings of old master paintings, and cut squares and rectangles out of them which he pasted back in unexpected positions. The single image then shatters like a mirror into many images which the eye cannot keep in focus. Borrowing from Dali, Nolan called the collages 'paranoiac'. Stewart, however, was not aware of these experiments.

his term and became a part-time painter who did 'a few commissioned portraits for the local landed gentry'.

Friend manufactured his primitive by making a collage from two postcards depicting Sydney Cove in about 1810 which he chanced on in Jim Tyrell's bookshop in George Street, Sydney. To this backdrop he glued a 'reproduction of an American primitive portrait of a little boy', a photograph of the *Vogue* 'poodle of the year', a couple of frigates floating in the Cove, and a group of Aborigines around a campfire. Friend had his creation photographed and despatched it, along with the fake biography, to his editor at the *Monitor* who 'adored' it. 'That,' said Stewart, 'gave me the idea . . . I got to work with scissors and paste and some old *National Geographic* magazines.'

Stewart's collages have much in common with the elliptical wit of Max Ernst, one of the inventors of the form. Around 1920 Ernst made a number of photo-collages using images he found leafing through catalogues, encyclopaedias, books of natural history and science. Several years later he collaborated with Paul Éluard in the production of two books of poetry illustrated by collage. These were the precursors of Ernst's famous series of collage 'novels', those sometimes amusing, sometimes impenetrable, sometimes terrifying sequences of images constructed mainly from woodcut illustrations to nineteenth-century penny novellas. In his early photo-collages – like *The Hat Makes the Man* or *The Swan is Very Peaceful* – Ernst exploited the pedestrian detail of the cut-outs he was pasting to create new images that were jokey and disturbing. It was an hallucinatory art constructed from ordinary elements: 'the coupling of two realities, irreconcilable in appearance, upon a plane which apparently does not suit them', as Ernst described it. Max Ernst may be thought the patron saint of Ern Malley the artist: Ernst is, of course, an anagram of St Ern, and Max a reverberant name in this context.

Ern Malley's artworks are more neatly deracinated creations than the poems, assembled like Ernst's collages with meticulous finesse. They lack the thundering anarchy of the poetry but they have Ern's comic insolence and intellectual affection for the bizarre. *Malice in Underland* juxtaposes a Pollyanna type with letterbox for head against a mountain wearing a worker's cap on the brim of which soars a diminutive hero, his left hand aloft, his palm spread wide in inspired acknowledgement. Lower left lurks a staircase and draughtsboard; in the centre a girl's beribboned hair; lower right a banner with Chinese script advertising boots. In *The Mad Hattery* a sequence of Dali-esque hats sprouting mouths, eyes, noses and ears floats above an old dray. (The 'Chacha Hat Merchant of St Thomas' whom the *National Geographic* photographer snapped has been neatly omitted.) *Chicago* presents a man in a three-piece pin-stripe suit against an aerial shot of the city. Firecrackers fizz around the man's teacup head.

Other collages are exact visual puns. Like a riddle by Magritte, *Proteus Rising from the Sea* shows the back of a man's head, sporting a boater, atop an island emerging from a level sea. In *Wordsworth Country* a hand stretches from top right to pour cream from a jug on to a waterfall (Stock Gill Force in the Lake District) which cascades down into lush foliage. The picturesque turns absurd. In *The White Citadel* a commanding view of snow-lined Alps is foregrounded by an outsized hand struggling over a crag towards – a grandfather clock. Documented travel, the subject of the *National Geographic*, becomes preposterous. A car free-floats in space, bearing an elephant aloft. A skier plummets to dry earth as if from a plane, past a statue of noble proportions, and a cluster of eggs. ('The man shown in mid-air covered 148 feet in this leap,' the *National Geographic* disclosed.) And the directorate's work in anthropology, geography and scientific discovery is sent up too. In *The Creation of Antarctic Light* a penguin – of course – stares with solemn intensity at systems of delicate glassed-in instruments, Riefler clocks, in fact housed in Elgin, Illinois, that 'with the aid of stars keep practically perfect time'. Out of the clocks to charm or choke the penguin stretches a pair of tattooed hands.

Harris and *Angry Penguins* were under assault on another

front at the same time. Like his friends McAuley and Stewart, Alec Hope held the view that the magazine was 'a lot of nonsense, if you know what I mean. It was a new critical standard and so on – I thought it was rather phoney.' He recalled that 'some remarks attributed to Harris and Reed reached me via friends describing what I wrote as academic stuff, so I decided to pull their leg a bit'. He sat down to produce his own hoax. By a process of free association Hope then wrote ten poems – 'deliberately phoney constructions . . . on the surrealist plan' – in two sittings of an hour each. He intended

to send them to *Angry Penguins* and then blow the gaff later on. My two friends McAuley and Stewart at that time were in the Army Research Centre in Melbourne. I was in constant correspondence with them and I mentioned this project of mine and immediately got I think a telegram and a follow-up letter saying 'hold your hand, we've got something much better under way'. Of course they said they'd keep me posted so more or less from the beginning I was fully aware of what was going on and the methods they'd adopted.

How extraordinary that Hope planned to foist his own hoax on Harris at the *same time* that the *same idea* occurred to his friends. The *Zeitgeist* is not often so focused.

In December 1943, while still corresponding with Ethel Malley, Harris published his only novel, *The Vegetative Eye*. Its title was taken from the visionary writings of William Blake. In spite of Harris's enormous hopes for its success, the novel would have sunk without a trace had a rival editor not sent it into hostile territory for review. 'Yes, I'd love to do *The Vegetative Eye* – or do it over,' Hope wrote to Clem Christesen, editor of *Meanjin*, on 6 March 1944, licking his lips at the prospect of carving up a book he hadn't yet seen. 'I may be a bit rude to Comrade Maxie but I won't involve you in any libel action.' Do it over he did, in a notorious review entitled 'Confessions of a Zombi'.

Hope wielded a venomous pen. In 1941 he had attacked the Jindyworobaks as 'The Boy Scout School of Poetry' with 'the rich incoherence of the type of mind that thinks almost entirely in abstract nouns'. (This was the one point Hope and Harris agreed on: 'I never thought to find myself on the same side of the fence with Maxie Harris and the schizo boys,' Hope wrote to Christesen, 'but there you are.') He thought poorly of most Australian writers ('of whom I know so little and by whom for the most part I am profoundly bored or irritated') though he admired the work of his friends McAuley and Stewart, describing the latter as 'excellent – the only really exact critic of poetry in Australia'. Hope was sceptical about the promotion of general views of culture, especially the Australian variety, and looked askance at *Meanjin*'s literary nationalism. 'You do publish quite a lot of criticism that is [a] pure waste of time,' he told Christesen. 'All these general articles about Kulchur, in the first place! They go the round in their treadmill of generalisation and dogmatic inaccuracy with a monotonous sameness.' But Hope supported *Meanjin* as the best periodical of a bad bunch, and implored Christesen to be wary of the 'flapdoodle critics who abound in this country at present'.

Did Hope decide to use his piece to cuff Harris about the ears after McAuley and Stewart beat him to the punch with Ern Malley? Years later he admitted that he wrote 'this piece of tomfoolery' to pay Harris out for his scornful opinion of Hope's work. Whatever the case, 'Comrade Maxie' was in for it. Hope submitted his review of *The Vegetative Eye* a few weeks later, on 27 March, and wrote to Christesen: 'Here is Maxie's head on a charger. Afraid it's a bit long but I couldn't resist the openings. I didn't say half the things that could have been said. I expect Max will write me a long chatty letter after he reads it'.

Hope's review, 'Confessions of a Zombi', was murderous. He derided the way Harris whored after writers in vogue, and declared that while 'nearly all the characters in the book turn out to be Mr. Max Harris . . . the book owes very little to Mr. Max Harris. It reads like a guide to all the more fashionable literary enthusiasms of the last thirty years.' Hope warmed to his task: 'Baudelaire gave us an example of the artist as the analyst of his own moral sickness,' he wrote. 'Mr. Harris is morally sick and discusses his symptoms with the gusto of an old woman showing the vicar her ulcerated leg.' After a few words about Harris's immaturity, and the undergraduate air of the novel, he moved in for the kill:

The great names which inspire Mr. Harris with such enthusiasm are those of born writers. Mr. Harris himself writes like somebody who has heard about writing and thinks it would be fun to try his hand at it . . . The plain fact is that Mr. Harris cannot write. He is adept at the parody of various styles, and there are some amusing examples of this in *The Vegetative Eye*. But when he has to depend on himself he has no style at all. He is completely at the mercy of his language, and it is to be assumed that the language, finding him lost and helpless in the field of prose, has taken a malicious revenge on him for the abuses he has so often committed upon it in his verse.

Hope was not attacking a masterpiece as he did, years later, when he described Patrick White's *The Tree of Man* as 'pretentious and illiterate verbal sludge'. *The Vegetative Eye* was the work of a very young writer whose poetry, despite Hope's scorn, showed talent – but Harris's novel revealed how unformed his art really was. The book is so breathlessly eager to do everything at once that its language suffers from a kind of oxygen debt: 'The whispering innuendos of the train wheels scampering their pornographic secrets deep into the depths of the brain, so it seemed, lapped their presence oppressively about her dying thoughts. She closed her eyes.'

The trouble with *The Vegetative Eye* is that its enthusiasm for literary creation never finds a focus. Its 'modernism' is merely wishful, and the failure of the novel has a certain pathos: one tries to imagine the context Harris thought he was compensating for. Why did Hope bother with a book that never had a chance? At the end of his review he declared that Harris

cannot convince us that even with his vegetative eye he has ever been in contact with the external world at all. His Jeannies and Jacks and Hanses are not observed people transformed. They are just made up. They are not projections of Mr. Harris's imagination on real people he has met but projections of Mr. Harris upon himself. The result is that

Mr. Harris himself never comes to life either. It is all in the dream world. Had the writer's ability matched his conception we should have had the picture of a living man. As it is, we have a Zombi, a composite corpse, assembled from the undigested fragments of authors Mr. Harris has swallowed without chewing and animated by psychological Voodoo.

If, therefore, Mr. Harris should be inclined to be wounded by this article, I can safely assure him that no reference in it is intended to any living person.

Hope's assassination of the novel is part of the froth and wash generated by the hoax. He wrote his review with access to inside information which he knew Harris had failed to guess at. Like the hoax, which he understood as 'a serious piece of criticism', his piece was consummate satire. These sentences were written with one eye on that other 'composite corpse' whose fragments, assembled by his partners in crime, Hope knew that Harris had also swallowed without chewing. The image of the dead buffoon given power to walk and of literary composition as a process of 'undigested' association is compelling. If that final fake disclaimer means Hope thought the novel a dead duck, doesn't it also conjure up McAuley and Stewart's straw man? At its climax the review turned into a portrait of Ern Malley, the non-person. Hope would have scorned *The Vegetative Eye* even in the absence of Ern Malley – but, in the absence of his own hoax on *Angry Penguins*, Ern Malley gave him a way of talking about the book, a parodic image he made the most of. Thus the hoax began to exert its influence on the terms of Australian literary trade. Hope had no trouble making the connection to Christesen: 'The best touch from my point of view is his coupling Ern Malley and Himself as author of the Vegetative Eye. The conclusion that if one is phoney so is the other is irresistible.'

By January 1944, all the elements of the hoax were in place. The war, which had brought McAuley and Stewart together in Melbourne, was about to separate them again. On 20 February 1944, not long after Ethel's final letter, James McAuley's work with the directorate took him on an extended trip to New Guinea, where Australian forces were still encountering Japanese resistance. This was the first time he had been out of Australia. Harold Stewart, meanwhile, had been on army business in Sydney where – without McAuley's knowledge – he sought out his old friend Tess van Sommers. She was doing 'donkey work' in the office of the mass-circulation tabloid the *Sunday Sun*, waiting to win her cadetship. 'I can't remember where, but he came to me in a state of great excitement. He told me that he and Jimmy McAuley had set out to play a joke on Max Harris. He was bubbling with joy.' Stewart spelt out the story of the late garage hand from the western suburbs whose sister Ethel was in fruitful correspondence with the editor of *Angry Penguins*. Stewart swore her to secrecy but gave her permission to break the story. 'When you are a journalist you can have this as your scoop,' she remembers Stewart telling her. 'He was very proud of the fact that he knew the word "scoop".'

Stewart's generosity was also expedient: with van Sommers the hoaxers had a contact in the press 'who could be trusted to understand the affair, in literary terms, and who could shove the story in the right direction'. At their meeting he gave her 'a sheaf of their failures'. These were the drafts of Ern Malley's poems. 'I can still see the marks, pale brown tea stains, a semi-literate looking hand in pencil, rather a big hand on ruled paper. If I had kept them they would probably now be indecipherable. They were only in a light pencil.' As van Sommers stared at them, Stewart bubbled away about their secret. It was a 'wonderful jape', he was saying, and they 'were going to absolutely slay Max Harris'.

6 Malley Who?

The Ern Malley issue of *Angry Penguins* began to circulate. In the first week of June, Harris took delivery of 200 copies by train from Melbourne, which he set about distributing to Adelaide bookshops. He was keen for publicity to bolster sales and sought out likely reviewers. An obvious choice was Brian Elliott, who taught literature at Adelaide University and was sympathetic to modern poetry. Harris had taken one of his courses a few years earlier: he was a clever student, Elliott remembered, but 'not a jumped-up type. He just sat there and took notes – like the Devil.' Elliott knew of talk that Harris had something special in store, 'a new Australian poet' whose work 'would surprise everybody'. On Friday, 9 June 1944 he bumped into him at the university office. 'Here's a present for you,' said Harris and thrust him a copy of *Angry Penguins* from the pile under his arm.

Even before Elliott finished reading Ern Malley's first poem, 'Durer: Innsbruck, 1495', he 'began to smell a rat. It puzzled me so I took the thing home – and the rat got more and more noisome.' In the following days he digested the issue with increasing wonderment. Ern Malley's poems dazzled him. Elliott felt they had to be phoney but came to the wrong conclusion. He decided that *Harris had written Ern Malley as a joke against himself*: 'I thought that he'd come to his senses and was satirizing all the foolish things that he'd been doing.' This suggestion was put to Harris who denied it vehemently. Elliott backed his judgement and wrote a teaser for *On Dit*, the Adelaide University newspaper, which appeared on Friday, 16 June 1944. *On Dit* put the story on page one:

LOCAL LECTURER CRIES 'HOAX'
IS MALLEY, MALLEY OR MALLEY, HARRIS
– OR WHO?

. . . Mr. Elliott and other academics seem to think that the poems published as the work of the hitherto unknown, now deceased, poet Ern Malley, in 'Angry Penguins' are really by Mr. Harris, that Mr. Harris is hoaxing the whole literary world or that Mr. Harris is being hoaxed by some mysterious person. Superficially Malley's work and opinions could be taken as belonging to Mr. Harris – they are in true 'Penguins' style . . . One must remember, however, that despite the mystery (or hoax?) the poetry is generally recognized (even by Mr. Elliott) as being very good . . .

Mr. Harris sincerely insists that HE is not hoaxing anyone – there is nothing to gain from doing so; but on close examination Malley has left clues of literary knowledge, which, to the learned and initiated, indicate Adelaide as the source of the poems, and if not Harris, then a close friend of his – who then, is this Malley, real or fictional?

Thus began the ballyhoo of Malley Who? This first public reaction to the hoax, with its plausible errors, set the terms for much of the debate. For a week or so the Malley poems were whatever you wanted to think they were – and by the writers of your choice. Like the Sybil, they gave a compelling if cloudy response to any question asked of them. If you wanted to gape at the remarkable new writer Harris believed in, there he was, the black swan of trespass on alien waters. If you were looking for gobbledegook, that bunch of keys Malley carried with him were jingling like fate in his omphagic ear. A trick mirror, the poems confirmed every prejudice of the 'learned and initiated', a status attained by glancing at *Angry Penguins*. The money for now was on Harris and Adelaide: but they were only the first of the front runners.

How to explain the breathless pursuit of the author(s) of Ern Malley? A diversion from the tedium of slogging out the war in a country no longer under threat of invasion? An opportunity for the philistines to ridicule poetry all round? Both: the hunt for Malley, which astonished the hoaxers themselves, helped confirm the status of poetry as a parlour game by providing a real game called 'find the poet'. If poetry was kind of code and modernist poetry a code doubly difficult to crack, then playing sleuth was the most natural thing in the world. The lack of an author was far more sensational than any revolutionary agenda in the poetry itself, and the frantic scrabbling of students, journalists and littérateurs to ferret out Ern Malley more truly indicates how bleak the cultural weather was than does any recalcitrant hostility to the 'new'. Poetry was worth the sport when the odds suggested it was not poetry at all.

Elliott's piece for *On Dit* was an anti-review, a pastiche of *The Darkening Ecliptic*, an acrostic imputing that Ern Malley was fabricated by Harris:

Batrachic Ode

Malley! orphicular wraith, whose diapason
Astral is cotyledon to no plucked guitar,
Xoanon in my antique land, Aum's avatar —

How have you anger of the maculate seas,
Accessory the chain and anchor and all the
Rose exfoliate leaf by petal warm
Renounced invulvate with the grave disease?
Ischiatic, corpulent, dog-toothed with sunken knees
Scabrous – this check have you cashed,
    O furciform
Homunculus, hail! You deft epitome
Of Tamburlaine and Twankydil's apt dwarf!
And yet on Taverner's Hill no syndrome
Xists I warrant of your polymorph

Dear Mr. Editor – I promised to review the new 'Angry Penguins' for you. The task is beyond my humble capacity. I ask you to forgive me. Some splendid poems . . . are bound to be eclipsed in the 'Darkening Ecliptic' by Ernest Lalor Malley. This sequence of poems, some of which I understand, fires me to passionate admiration. I send you above my testimony; I can do no more. It is a trifle malarial, but I trust it will not sting too septically. I am now engaged upon a systematic search for a pair of park gates with iron birds, because those symbols are obvious; but alas, I cannot find them.

Yours apologetically,

B.R.E.

PS – Malley is the goods. Nothing better has been written since the 'Vegetable Pie'.

Elliott did well to apologize for the fake rhyme in the final stanza of his ode and his 'passionate admiration' for the sequence was equivocal. The 'Vegetable Pie'? That was J. I. M. Stewart's pet name for *The Vegetative Eye*. 'Tamburlaine' and 'a trifle malarial'? A nod at Malley's mosquito poem 'Culture as Exhibit' which triumphantly paraphrased Marlowe's Faustus: 'Now/ Have I found you, my Anopheles'. 'The grave disease'? Elliott discovered without much trouble that Malley's affliction rarely sent sufferers to that fine and private place. The park gates with iron birds that 'looked disapproval' were to be found – but only in 'Night Piece', the sixth poem in the sequence: 'The symbols were evident', it said. And Taverner's Hill where Ern worked as a mechanic? Elliott could not track the name down, but the place exists all right, a small pocket of land bounded by the inner Sydney suburbs Leichardt and Petersham on Parramatta Road, west of the city – the site, it just so happens, of Fort Street High School where Ern Malley's polymorph first began to write.

The only person who saw that Ern Malley was a hoax was hoaxed himself. Identifying Ern with Max, Elliott followed Harris's own logic. Harris thought he had shown the world how to read Ern Malley's work. Elliott's insight turned this into wrenching comedy. He blew the whistle and set in motion the mad quest for Malley which, like the pursuit of Cinna in *Julius Caesar*, could end only in the death of the poet.

In the meantime, Elliott had put the wind up Harris. As soon as he knew about the story in *On Dit*, Harris hired a private detective in Sydney named Bannister to watch Ethel Malley's address. Bannister ran his business out of an office on the ground floor of Newlands House, in Elizabeth Street in the city. Find out if Ern Malley ever lived in Dalmar Street, Harris told him. Bannister was not terribly sure of his brief. In the beginning he cased the wrong joint and in the early afternoon of 15 June wired Harris to tell him that someone called Millard lived at number 14, and had been living there for the past ten years. He asked people walking up and down the street, and knocked on doors, but no one had heard of Ethel Malley. Bannister searched the electoral roll and found there was no E. Malley listed living in Croydon. He concluded she must have another address, and wired Harris to this effect, who wired back telling him to find out who lived at number 40. Harris was worried by now and telegrammed Reed on the morning of 16 June: 'STRONG CHANCE MALLEY FRAUD HAVE DETECTIVE AGENCY INVEST-IGATING'. Bannister meantime, in thorough confusion, assumed this must be just another divorce job. He staked out the little house with the rose bush in the front yard, and kept Harris on tenterhooks, letting him know who came and went from the house, and how many times the lights were turned on and off. But who lived there? Bannister finally knocked on the door that night. There was no answer. He went next door, and discovered the family at number 40 was called Stewart. At eight the next morning he paid another visit. A middle-aged woman answered the door. The only person, she said, who could tell him anything about Ern Malley was in hospital and could not be contacted. This information was sent to Harris.

By mid-June 1944, when *Angry Penguins* started to make its troubled way into the world, seven months after the Ern Malley poems were written, the hoaxers had been separated again. McAuley was back in Melbourne at the directorate after three months in the jungles of New Guinea, some of it spent with Australian soldiers on patrol mopping up Japanese resistance – but Stewart, who had fallen seriously ill the previous year with suspected meningitis, was now recuperating from surgery to remove an abscess in 113 Military Hospital in Concord, a suburb of Sydney. They were both tickled pink by the presence of *Angry Penguins*. 'It is a sheer joy,' Stewart wrote to Donald Friend, 'all those lovely baby garments which Maxie knitted for his found-ling child!' Their fabulous secret was safe, they thought. McAuley and Stewart knew nothing at this stage of Elliott's detective work, and had plans for the hoax which required the Ern Malley show to run as long as possible.

In the same week that *On Dit* was preparing to publish Elliott's squib and Harris was sending Bannister into the streets of Croydon, Tess van Sommers was walking down Martin Place in the heart of Sydney during her lunch hour. As she passed a magazine stand, she idly scanned the publications on display but then stopped in her tracks. 'My eye fell on this frightful Sidney Nolan painting and *Angry Penguins* and Ern Malley.' She had not seen Stewart since their meeting but 'it all came back to me then. I suddenly realized this was Harold's hoax come home to roost.' Van Sommers was electrified by the sight of *Angry Penguins*. In her excitement she assumed that because the issue had now appeared she was free to publicize the truth about its contents in the *Sunday Sun*. Her scoop lay before her eyes.

I hastily sacrificed 3/6, or whatever it was, and rushed back to the office. The first person I encountered was a highly cultivated little man named Julian Russell who was a music critic, and I said to him 'This is a hoax!' He instantly grasped the significance. Now the star of the paper in those days was a man named Colin Simpson, a very experienced journalist, and he took the story over.

The fact that van Sommers was not yet a ticketed journalist meant she could not write the story as Stewart intended, and her seniors, smelling blood, elbowed her aside. ('I was twenty-three or twenty-four, and pretty wet behind the ears. They forcibly took over. They said, "You cannot do this story. It's too big. It's world class".') Simpson was one of the leading journalists in the country, who would later make a name for himself as a travel writer. He also wrote the occasional poem himself. In mid 1944, Simpson was editor of *Fact*, the magazine supplement to the *Sunday Sun*. He was 'in a state of frightful excitement as everyone was' and kept saying 'we must get hold of these men, we must get hold of these men'. He traced the hoaxers and a hook-up was arranged on the 'two way switch'. Simpson, McAuley, and Stewart spoke together. But neither hoaxer would divulge information to anyone except van Sommers. She was led forward and put on the telephone and relayed what they said to Simpson, who took notes.

McAuley was furious with van Sommers and exploded at her down the line from the directorate, 'We won't get Read now!' 'Jimmy never really forgave me for blowing the gaff,' she recalls. 'He was somehow going to engineer Herbert Read into this controversy. He felt that Read would inevitably come down on the side of Max Harris, that Read was really the superior sinner as the leader of a school of poetry which was ill-founded.' In November 1944 McAuley admitted, 'It was the egregious Herbert that we set as our mark, hoping to keep the thing going long enough to reach him, and knowing he would be a dead sucker for any gross rubbish that came his way. He is, at least in the publicity sense, "bigger" than the locals, and would give the thing less of an air of taking lollies from children.'

The two poets were now under pressure. Read, it seemed, was off the hook, and Ern Malley's collages, which might have interested him, were headed for mothballs. They were no longer in control of the timing of the hoax and were taken aback by the manic interest Ern was arousing. It was agreed during the phone conversation that *Fact* would run a teaser on Sunday, 18 June, and give the full account a week later. The delay would give McAuley and Stewart time to prepare a joint statement, but it would also have the effect of heightening to fever pitch any speculation about who wrote the poems.

Simpson had no idea the hoax was unravelling in Adelaide. He knew his strategy of running the story over two weeks was risky – it could only work if he gave Harris as little time as possible to do his own investigating. Harris would not be able to see the hoaxers' statement prior to publication. He would not have the right to reply in *Fact*. He would have to respond *on the spot*, without the opportunity to consider his position, or prepare a statement. Simpson decided to wait until his deadline was upon him, and then call the Penguins in the dead of night. He phoned John Reed after midnight on Friday, 16 June to elicit Harris's number, and boasted that his paper was ready to reveal 'the biggest literary hoax Australia had ever known' though he would tell Reed nothing except that two men had written the poems. Then he phoned Harris who was dislodged from

a Nembutal-stupefied sleep at 2 in the morning . . . I gave the statement as the major business but some silly bugger at the other end kept asking me ludicrous questions which made it difficult for me to hold back irritation, e.g.

Q Now your own poetry. Has it any meaning?
A If it hasn't I've been fooling myself for ten years.
Q What would you say if the authors of Malley said their intentions were wholly satirical?
A The history of literature is paved with intentions producing contradictory results.
Q Would you still say the poetry was good?
A Yes.

Harris knew nothing about Tess van Sommers and wrongly suspected Elliott was Simpson's source. He outlined events to Reed:

On Thursday Elliott issued the hoax challenge. I made no reply apart from the statement that he was wrong – I was not the author . . . The immediate job I thought was to gain possession of the facts . . .

I hired a private detective agency in Sydney to interview 40 Dalmar Street Croydon. The attitude of its 50 yr old Householder named 'Stewart' was inexcusable, but she admitted the emanation of the hoax from there. Either the guilty parties knew the game was up and tipped off the press, or far more likely Brian Elliott, who claimed to have set inquiries in action, contacted the Sydney press. The whole attitude of the Sydney chap indicates that he is working from the assumptions of Elliott. He knows no more than we do because he asked me innumerable times whether or not I was the author of the hoax.

He asked whether we at any time suspected a hoax. To this

question I simply told the truth. Of course we did. Numbers of people pointed out that possibility, but we consider it not our job to act as a detective agency towards our contributors, but to sincerely evaluate the material sent to us. The possibility of a hoax was not relevant, but the quality of literature within a possible hoax was.

I don't know how your attitude towards the poetry stands now over there. What has Nolan to say? But I feel myself largely responsible for the situation, & while agreeing that policy should be determined according to the combined tactic evolved over there, that if there is any attempt to humiliate or belittle anybody I should take the rap. I feel sure that you will stick & that the whole situation will bring us all closer together, but perhaps I was by far the least cautious, & you in effect warned me about lack of restraint in the introduction, so take it for understood that I will act as the Aunt Sally if occasion arises rather than the firm. This may sound pretty heroic but it is probably good policy also that an individual be onslaughted than the name of the firm. I rather think that they will have great difficulty in finding the author (especially if it were Harold or JIM Stewart) & the mystery will survive a fair while.

What is our legal position re misrepresentation?

. . . Above all – don't get depressed as you sounded last night. For one thing, it's establishing Penguins all over the country. For another it cements inner faith in our own sincerity, & for myself I feel it will produce a deepening & even more honestly naked quality in my own poetry.

The day after *On Dit* appeared, 17 June, Malley was picked up by the *Mail* in Adelaide, which reported a hot rumour, fuelled by Bannister's information, that the poems had been written by J. I. M. Stewart. His qualifications amounted to an interest in modern poetry and the detective novels he wrote as Michael Innes. Stewart played these rumours with a straight bat, saying 'that he had heard of Ern Malley and of Max Harris, but he did not wish to comment on either of them'. In Sydney, Bannister now went to the offices of *Fact* where he grilled Simpson and van Sommers – both of whom were tight-lipped. On 18 June, *Fact* put Ern Malley on its front page. Beneath the heading 'Ern Malley, the great poet or the greatest hoax?' were these remarks:

FACT, which has no high opinion of the Ern Malley 'poems', investigated the Ern Malley life story in *Angry Penguins*, found:
- There is no Palmer's Garage, Taverner's Hill, nor has there been one to the knowledge of the Leichhardt police, whose station is near by.
- No insurance salesman named Ernest Malley has ever been employed in Victoria by the National Mutual Life Assurance.
- Nobody named Malley has been cremated at Rookwood in the past 10 years.
- No Miss Ethel Malley is known at the address in a Sydney suburb from which the writings were sent to *Angry Penguins*.

There was a sub-heading, 'Harris says – ,' and:

Phoned in Adelaide, Max Harris told FACT he had not written the Ern Malley poems and if the Ern Malley whom he had believed to be the author did not write them he did not know who did.

Co-editors of *Angry Penguins* Max Harris and John Reed (Harris is an Adelaide University student of economics, Reed a Melbourne solicitor) made this joint statement:

'Whoever wrote the Ern Malley poems was a fine poet. When we received them we felt there were modes of expression and words reminiscent of other poets (for example, of T. S. Eliot), but it is not surprising when the idioms of contemporary poets overlap.

'We were satisfied with the intrinsic merits of the verse.

'However, the personal life and philosophy of the poet is always a factor of deep significance and we will willingly give you all possible help to clear up the mystery.'

Asked if he had ever suspected the poems of being a hoax, Harris said:

'There was some such suggestion but it is not our job to inquire into credentials but to valuate the work as poetry.

'Anyone who says that they are not poems of remarkable value, or that they lack deep and serious meaning, is cutting the throat of a very fine talent in making such a statement.

'It is not a rational probability that the writings of Ern Malley do not possess intrinsic merit, in the light of the critical responses we received on the work from the American poet in the US forces, Harry Roskolenko, and many others.'

Asked what would be his reaction if it could be proven that the writings of 'Ern Malley' were nothing but obscurantist nonsense

intended to test his critical judgement, Max Harris replied: 'I hope not –
otherwise I've been fooling myself for a long time.'

Asked what would be his reaction if the poems were written with the
intention of parodying his (Harris's) own style of writing, Harris said:
'It would be very flattering! It would need to be a very high talent to be
thus parodied in the first place.'

Asked if he understood the poems, Harris said that, in general, their
meaning was clear to him, and although Malley had a remarkable
vocabulary which sometimes created 'images' that could be obscure, he
had found no discomfort in understanding any of the 'symbols'.

Mr Harris was asked the meaning of the following Ern Malley lines:

> There have been interpolations, false syndromes
> Like a rivet through the hand
> Such deliberate suppressions of crisis as
> Footscray

He said he thought the lines had a 'fairly patent meaning'. The 'rivet
through the hand' was a reference to Christ which was also in the
associative word 'crisis'. After the 'universality' of 'suppressions of
crisis' there was a 'local image' in 'Footscray'.

Harris did well, considering when the statement was made, but
he might have done better to reply to Simpson in the manner of
T. S. Eliot when asked the meaning of the line in *Ash-Wednesday*,
'Lady, three white leopards sat under a juniper-tree'. 'I mean,'
Eliot said, ' "Lady, three white leopards sat under a juniper-
tree".' Footscray – a working-class suburb in Melbourne – is
certainly a local image but of what Harris did not say. The place
name was there to signal Ern's revolutionary instincts but also to
seem absurd and bathetic in this 'visionary' context. (It is still
possible to raise a laugh in Australia by inserting a local name
into a song everybody has heard of: 'By the time I get to Wagga
Wagga, she'll be rising . . .') Simpson was toying with his victim:
why did he keep asking Harris if he had written the poems? And
what was the expression on his face when Harris offered him 'all
possible help to clear up the mystery'? The newspaper article
concluded:

FACT knows:
- Max Harris did not write the Ern Malley poems.
- Professor (Michael Innes) Stewart did not write them.
- The actual authorship.

A statement is being prepared for FACT next week which will clear up the 'mystery', motives and merit of 'Ern Malley' and his poems.

Simpson's strategy was working so far. The story had taken off like a fire in a wind, but with all this Malley mania it hardly seemed possible the identity of the hoaxers could be concealed for much longer. On Monday, 19 June the *News* reported in Adelaide – in spite of the statements in *Fact* – that student bookmakers were offering odds of 6 to 4 that the Jury Professor of English Language and Literature at Adelaide University had written the poems of Ern Malley. The following day, after the odds had eased to 30 to 1, Stewart denied to the *News* he was the author:

'I have no relatives in Australia,' he said, 'and unlike some of my colleagues, who seem to own pie shops and garages and things in Sydney, I have no property there.'

With the evidence of this clue, students at the Adelaide University now suspect that the author of the poems may be Douglas Stewart, a Sydney poet and author of the recently produced verse play for radio, 'Ned Kelly'.

Another Sydney poet, Harold Stewart, also figures in the betting.

In the meantime, Roy Leaney, the editor of *On Dit*, wired Murray Sayle, the editor of *Honi Soit*, enlisting his aid to investigate Ethel Malley's address. Stewart had been a familiar face around the *Honi Soit* office: Sayle and his staff drew a rapid conclusion once they were given Ethel Malley's address. Sayle's reply from Sydney was published in Adelaide in the *News* on Wednesday, 21 June after it had arrived that morning:

Local poet Harold Stewart lives at 40 Dalmar Street, Croydon. Internal and other evidence gathered. We strongly believe he is author.

It was a long week of unknowing for the Penguins who could only speculate about the real Ern Malley. 'Everything points to

Adrian for a certainty and Michael as a good possibility,' Reed suggested to Harris on 19 June, meaning Adrian Lawlor and Michael Keon, another writer on the edge of the Penguin circle. 'Latest Malley news: the whole thing was concocted by 4 or 5 people one afternoon with the aid of numerous glasses of beer,' Reed suggested to Harris on 21 June. 'This improbable story comes from someone who is evidently partly in the know: his information in turn comes from "someone from the Sydney university who was recently in Melbourne but has now returned." Can't get past that.' Two 'soldier poets' were mixed up in it all, Reed suggested to Harris on 23 June. 'This apparently points to Stewart and Macauley [sic], but in spite of all these clues we stick to Adrian as an almost 100% certainty.' On 3 July, a week or so *after* full disclosure, Reed suggested to Harris: 'I heard an indirect story this morning that someone had told someone else that there was an Ern Malley and that this person had taught him when he was a boy. Maybe the story isn't finished yet.' (There was not one but several Ern Malleys. The *Directory of Victoria* for 1944 listed two of them, quietly going about their lives in the suburbs of Melbourne.)

'The symbols were evident' that week. At the Hoyts Rex in Adelaide, Tyrone Power and Maureen O'Hara could be seen in *The Black Swan*. The feature at Sydney's Lyceum cinema was *Undercover*, starring Leslie Howard. Greater Union was screening Charles Laughton's phoney version of an ageing digger in *The Man from Down Under*. At the Majestic, in Melbourne, Abbott and Costello's *Hold That Ghost* was in its fifth week. What's more, a short-sighted Pomeranian dog answering to the ill-chosen name of Dodo vanished from the Victoria Barracks, where her job was to smell out rats, which overran Australian cities during the war. According to the *Sydney Morning Herald* of 29 June 1944 there were over a million rats in that city – 'as big as cats and bursting with fat from garbage on vacant land', the paper announced, plagued by internal rhyme. In Adelaide 'rats could be seen at dusk in seething masses on rubbish dumps', the *News* declared on 15 June. Dodo's disappearance from the barracks in Melbourne suggested something weird was up. Was this an act of imaginative sympathy, a canine rhyme with events at their moment of crisis? 'I think we are in rats' alley / Where the dead men lost their bones', T. S. Eliot intoned in *The Waste Land*. By late June, perhaps, Dodo was somewhere similar, in rats' alley where dead men lost their poems.

There are no rats in Ern Malley's poetry, though animals abound, among them a swan (black), a kestrel describing a mind, a hawk, an ichthys made out of alabaster, another swan (white) a rabbit or at least the foot of a rabbit, the feet of a caterpillar, a brooding bird of unspecified species which the evening as it settles down is said to resemble, frogs, an undetermined number of iron birds sitting on the gates of a park, a lion being killed by Samson, some disturbed swallows, some mad wasps, elephants, a cobra, a shark grinning wisely, mosquitoes (referred to by their scientific name *Anopheles*) on location in their breeding grounds of swamps, marshes, borrow-pits and other areas of stagnant water, striped fish, ibises with long shanks, an eyeless worm, a carolling magpie, a bleeding iguana, the Goat, the Crab, the Lion, all zodiacal, ectoplasm, a thirsty dromedary, a peacock, a bed-bug, a cockroach, and a careful spider. So many birds, but not a penguin in sight and not the whiff of a rat.

Booksellers capitalized on the hoax in that long week of un-knowing. The magazine was walking off the shelves. In Adelaide the Argonaut Book Shop on North Terrace sold 112 copies. On Saturday, 24 June this advertisement appeared in the *Age*:

CHESHIRE'S BOOKSELLERS

NEW AND WANTED BOOKS ARRIVING BY EVERY MAIL

ANGRY PENGUINS, Australia's leading forum of the Contemporary Arts, 1944 Autumn Number, containing the Ern Malley verses, authorship of which is at present a mystery. Price 5/-. Postage 4d.

Such prominence for a highbrow literary magazine was a by-product of the war, and the book famine it produced. Imported novels were especially hard to come by and, since Australian fiction was thin on the ground, that meant a general scarcity of

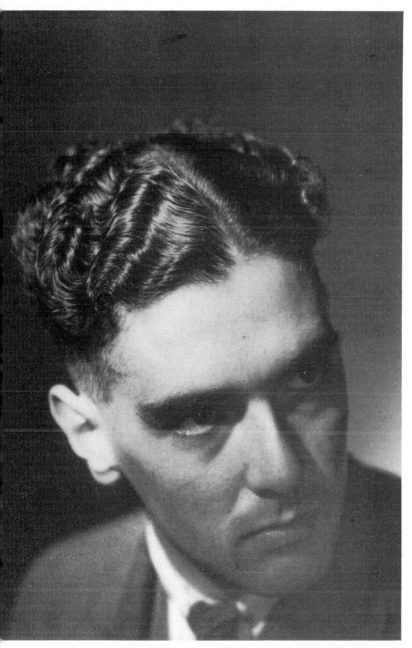

1 Max Harris, the young romantic poet, in the early forties

2 Max Harris, *enfant terrible*, hurled into the Torrens on a sunlit
winter's day in Adelaide in 1941
3 Harris in the Tarax Bar in Swanston Street, Melbourne, in 1942
4 A. D. Hope – 'I may be a bit rude to Comrade Maxie'

5 Ern Malley's polymorph at Fort Street High School in Sydney in
1934. James McAuley is second from the right in the second row;
Harold Stewart is seated in the front on the right

6 Harold Stewart in military hospital, the week Ern Malley's identity was revealed

7 James McAuley in the early forties, before the army conscripted him

8 Alf Conlon, with crewcut, horn-rimmed spectacles and pipe, in
Sydney in 1937
9 Sidney Nolan swimming in the Yarra at Heide in the early forties
10 John Reed, co-editor of *Angry Penguins*

11 Sunday Reed at Heide
12 Alister Kershaw, author of 'The Denunciad' and suspected of
writing the Ern Malley poems
13 Albert Tucker, self-portrait, taken in 1940

No

So Long

The wind masters the waves
As the waves the sea
And all of it ~~whole~~ entire
And none of it to me.

I had thought it was finished
~~that it is no use~~ And now it is useless
Like the writing on graves
Empty of future

Renew the ~~sign~~

the sign
At the moment of

14 Ern Malley's 'So Long' – 'a heart-rending unfinished poem in MSS
blotted with the dying poet's tears'

<u>Preface and Statement</u>

These poems are complete. There are no scoriae or unfulfilled intentions. Every note and revision has been destroyed. There is no biographical data.

*

These poems are complete in themselves. They have a domestic economy of their own and if they face outwards to the reader that is because they have first faced inwards to themselves. Every poem should be an autarchy.

*

The writing was done over five years. Certain changes of mental allegiance and superficial method took place. That is all that needs to be said on the subject of schools and influences.

*

To discover the hidden fealty of certain arrangements of sound in a line and certain concatenations of the analytic emotions, is the "secret" of style.

*

When thought, at a certain level, and with a certain intention, discovers itself to be poetry it discovers also that duty does after all exist: the duty of a public act. That duty is wholly performed by letting the pen to paper. To read what has thus been done is another thing again, and implies another order of loyalty

*

Simplicity in our time is arrived at by an ambages. There is, at this moment, no such thing as a simple poem if what is meant by that is a point-to-point straight-line relation of images. If I said that this was so because on the level where the world is genuine mental occurrences, I should be accused of mysticism. Yet it is so.

*

15 Ern Malley's 'Preface and Statement' for *The Darkening Ecliptic*

2.

...one who say: What might I not X have done if he had lived demonstrate their different way of living from the poet's way. It is a kind of truth, which I have tried to express, to say in return: All one can do in one's span of time is to uncover a net of objective allegiances. The rest is not one's concern.

16 Albrecht Dürer, 'Innsbruck 1494–1497', watercolour on paper

40 Dalmar St.,
Croydon
N. S. W.
14th January 4

Dear Mr. Harris,

I am sorry I couldn't reply to your last before, but what with Xmas and the New Year I just haven't had a moment to myself.

I never imagined when I sent the poems that you would have so high an opinion of Ern. I suppose it is because Ern was just one of the family but I find it hard to think of him as a great man. It is very kind of you to publish his poetry, but as I said earlier I don't want any money from it. So long as it is published I feel I have done all I can.

Enclosed please find the postcard you asked for though I don't think it will help you much. I'm rather surprised the National Mutual did not have some record of him but

17 The last letter Ethel Malley wrote to Max Harris

then he was only a casual salesman. I'm quite
certain that was the firm I was told he was with
I hardly like to say this and I know I can rely
on you to treat it as <u>strictly</u> <u>confidential</u> but
I have an idea that Ern might have got into some
sort of trouble in Melbourne and gone under another name. I only mention this because if you
come across anything he would not want to be
known I know I can rely on you not to
make it public. I am sure you will agree it
would not be fair to his memory.

Would you please send me anything you
publish about Ern as I would like to keep it. How
long do you think it would take for the book to
come out?

I must close now, hoping you will let me
know if there is anything else I can do
    With best regards,
        yours sincerely

            Ethel Malley.   P.T.O.

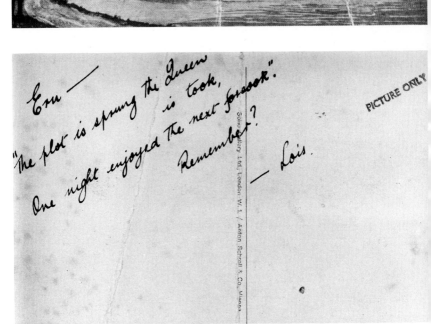

18 The 'coloured postcard' Ethel sent on to Harris, showing traces of the drawing pin that had fixed it to Ern's wall – 'the writing on the back seems to be personal'

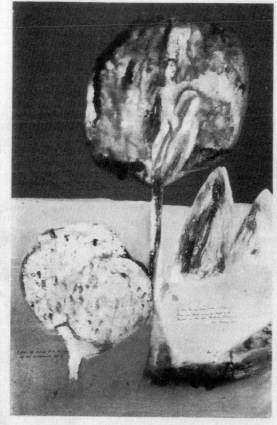

Angry Penguins

1944 Autumn Number
to Commemorate
the
Australian
Poet
Ern Malley

"*I said to my love (who is living)*
Dear we shall never be that verb
Perched on the sole Arabian Tree"

"*(Here the peacock blinks the eyes*
of his multipennate tail.)"

Painting by Sidney Nolan.

19 When *Angry Penguins* introduced Ern Malley to the world in 1944,
its cover featured Sidney Nolan's 'The Sole Arabian Tree', a painting
inspired by Malley's poetry

Office of Origin.   No. of Words.   Time of Lodgment.

URGENT X 167 SYDNEY SUB 48 12-55 P

REED AND HARRIS BROOKMAN BUILDINGS
GRENFELL ST ADELAIDE

ETHEL MALLEY NOT KNOWN AT 14 DALMAR ST CROYDON STOP MILLARD
LIVING AT THAT ADDRESS TEN YEARS NAME MALLEY NOT KNOWN IN
STREET SEARCHED ELECTORAL ROLL NAME MALLEY NOT IN CROYDON
STOP ADDRESS MUST BE HOAX WIRE FURTHER INSTRUCTIONS ... BANNISTER
(14)

Office of Origin.   No. of Words.   Time of Lodgment.

N 294 ADELAIDE STOCK EXCHANGE 19 11-30 A

JOHN REED
360 COLLINS STREET MELBOURNE

STRONG CHANCE MALLEY FRAUD HAVE DETECTIVE AGENCY INVESTIGATING
WILL YOU PHONE AFTER NINE
(360 MALLEY FRAUD)

20 Bannister, the Sydney private eye, wires Harris on 15 June 1944
21 Harris telegrams Reed on 16 June 1944

"ERN MALLEY"
McAULEY ———— STEWART

22 Ern Malley revealed to the readers of *Fact* on 25 June 1944

23 Cartoonists, like Gil Brown who drew for the *Sun* in Sydney, dismissed the Angry Penguins as adolescent tyros

"He is going to be one of those 'Angry Penguins,' I think dear"

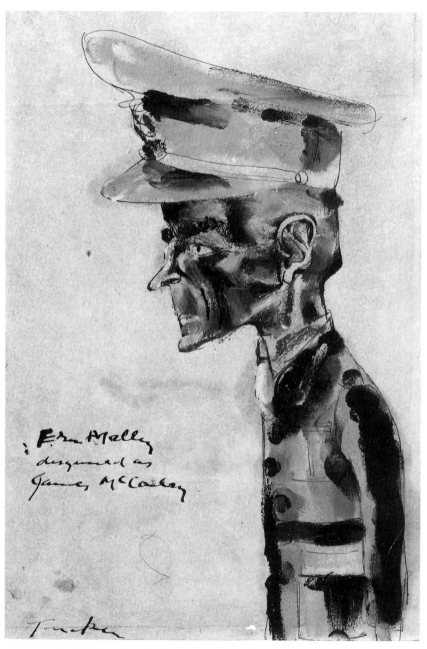

24 Ern Malley disguised as James McAuley, Albert Tucker, *c.* 1945,
pen, gouache on paper, 26.5 × 17.3 cm

25 'These things are real': Max Harris with Ern and Ethel Malley in
March 1988

HANDS ACROSS THE SEA

26–36 The Ern Malley collages by Harold Stewart, a series of black and white photo-collages, paper and glue on brown manilla card, mounted on card 22.9 × 35.4 cm

OUTWARD BOUND

SOLO FLIGHT

27, 28

CHICAGO

MALICE IN UNDERLAND

29, 30

WORDSWORTH COUNTRY

31

THE WHITE CITADEL

ROCOCO INTERIOR

THE MAD HATTERY

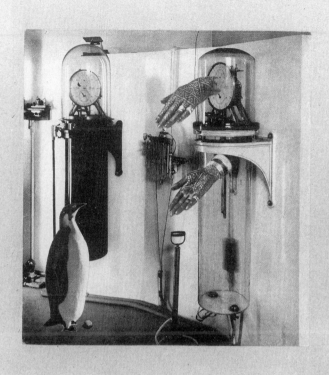

THE CREATION OF ANTARCTIC LIGHT

PROTEUS RISING FROM THE SEA

36

reading matter. After five years of war, tastes were changing too. On 30 June, as the Ern Malley issue was selling out of every store that carried it, the *Sydney Morning Herald* announced 'an unprecedented rush for the classics. Trollope, Thackeray, Thomas Hughes with his "Tom Brown's Schooldays", Smollett, Hardy, George Eliot, the Brontes, Dickens, Dumas and Jane Austen are selling as never before.' Little magazines like *Angry Penguins*, whose editors saw their work as a genuine part of the war effort, loomed large in these circumstances. 'When you finish with *Angry Penguins* why not send it on to a friend in the Forces?' the back cover of the journal suggested. In such a context of heightened visibility, amid a taste for Trollope and Tom Brown, Ern Malley, cause himself for conflict, was the perfect diversion from real battles.

He continued to divert Alec Hope that week, who wrote, Puck-like in his merriment, to Clem Christesen on 22 June, careful not to give the game away:

I suppose by now you have heard of the super-hoax played on Maxie Harris. Two pals of mine invented Ern Malley and led Max right up a tree. After you've read the last A. P. 'Ern Malley Special Number' and reflect that it was all done by two of the conventional poets whom Max particularly despises, you will indulge a few moments' serious reflection on the humble danger in which the editor of a literary journal lives and then you will sit back on your heels and indulge in a good horse laugh. I've been sitting on the bank for the last six months watching Maxie played for sucker – but of course sworn to secrecy. Apparently all the surreal boys in Maxie's backroom fell for it too and Harry Roskolenko has been sucked in too – makes you think don't it! We nearly captured the Federal Attorney General in the net as well. What a lot of hate there's going to be in Adelaide from now on! How Max will roll those great big bedroom eyes as one of the conspirators remarked. How Angry was my Penguin! Do review it in your next number – it's the finest literary hoax since Bacon wrote Shakespeare.*

*Geoffrey Dutton chanced on this letter when he was writing his history of Australian literary modernism, *Snow on the Saltbush* (Viking, Ringwood, 1984,

The letter was signed 'yore luvin frend, Jim the Penman'. It was no doubt his glee which led Hope to over-reach himself with that final gibe – there was never much doubt that the author of *Hamlet* could write. Hope wrote again three days later: 'I am rather pleased by the whole thing because, amusing as the hoax is itself, Stewart and McAuley have conducted it in a way which raises it above the level of a mere hoax and makes it a serious piece of criticism . . . The Ern Malley poems are complete artifacts and it will be very difficult for Max to unsay what he has said about them.'

Malley also exercised the mind of Brian Elliott that week, who had kinder things to say about Harris, and wrote without the benefit of inside information. There is no better testament to the impact of the hoax on a minuscule literary world than the breathless account Elliott sent to Christesen on the eve of the full disclosure.

Max has taken my part of the business in the best possible spirit and has become very friendly and is, I am satisfied, quite genuine. It has been the most tremendous chastener for him! Hit him on all his weak spots, and he's far too intelligent to miss the point of it after the exposure is made – Though why he should have been so gullible before I don't quite know. It has been rather a revelation of his character & nature, I think, & I must say I like him even so much more than I did, for the way he has behaved in what must have been an extremely mortifying situation. He has kept his temper admirably.

155ff) and thought he had at last found evidence that the Ern Malley poems took much longer to write than the hoaxers had admitted. 'The hoax had been planned and discussed between Hope, McAuley and Stewart for at least six months,' Dutton wrote. The letter provides no evidence of this. Ethel first wrote to Harris on 28 October 1943. Harris was in possession of all the poems by November. Ethel's final letter was written in January 1944. The rest – Hope's six months of 'watching Maxie played for sucker' – was spent waiting for the issue to appear. In the end it was published in mid-June 1944. Dutton's mistake is also pointed out by Brian Matthews ('Literature and Conflict', *The New Literary History of Australia*, Penguin, Ringwood, 1988, 303ff).

Actually I am still very puzzled about a number of things. One of them – why Harris was sucked in at all – is only a minor affair.

The local press has assumed because the address in Sydney from which the poems originated is H. Stewart's, that he is the author. I haven't seen much of his verse, but from what I have I don't think it is likely. What seems plain as a pikestaff to me is the fact that the stuff has been carefully (I should say diabolically) designed to fit in with Max's idiom of ideas – images, symbolistic method, literary references, etc. In view of the erudite nature of the material and also the laconic shamelessness of the pretence (there are several very clear nods and winks which anybody but blind Max shd. have seen), I took it that the whole thing was a bare-faced hoax of some kind . . . Curiously, if Max and I had been a little thicker beforehand it might never have happened. Everybody else about the University, it appears, knew about these amazing new poems but me – if I had seen them before all the publicity would perhaps have been spared him! (I own to a certain gleeful satisfaction!) Why they were perpetrated in the first place I don't quite know, but I should think purely as a joke. It must have been a somewhat malicious joke, but not really ill-natured. What's more, they must have cost a great deal of very exacting labour. Not only did the writer have to do something very erudite, but it had to be Max's own particular erudition – Marlowe, Pericles, Dante, Villon, Wyndham Lewis (wrong try, Max hasn't read him) & various others (rather too much T.S.E. but (carefully) no Hopkinese).

The labour of getting these things together must have been extraordinary – but think of the preliminary close study of Max's own writings! – His immaturity of ideas, his habit of imagery (not too closely imitated – if it was his I took it to be a new style being tried out) and some of his own particular mythological humbug – the Egyptian stuff etc, which is bunk anywhere but very bunk in Max (& Malley).

The position for Max is that he has been caught – hook, line and sinker . . . I don't think anything could have happened so salutary – so completely prophylactic! I fancy we may watch the Angry Penguins with interest now. They must grow circumspect or perish – and perish they will, unless they mature considerably. This issue is selling marvellously – but what of the rest? Time may bring some remarkable changes.

As parody, the Malley sequence is remarkably painstaking. Actually, although the tongue is lodged conspicuously in the cheek all the way through, they really are quite remarkable as literary craftsmanship, I think. Some bits are first rate. The Anopheles poem is a masterpiece. The twin night pieces are lovely and not so slight as they look. There is something most unique about the whole thing – a sort of quizzical, amused, philosophic banter with an almost Rabelaisian relish for the joke behind it all. I wish I *did* know who wrote it – it may be composite . . . End of tether

While Hope and Elliott wrote, the smoke thinned. On Friday, 23 June, *On Dit* blew Harold Stewart's cover on its front page. The editor, spellbound like everybody else in the country by the 'Pyjama Girl' trial, dubbed the hoax the 'Pyjama Boy Mystery'.* The other, professorial Stewart made his final denial of authorship: 'I hope it is no aspersion upon a body of men,' he said, 'to suggest that some of their number are associated with the automotive industry, and I would myself rather be supposed to own a pie shop than to have written the Malley verses.' On 24 June 1944, the *Daily Telegraph* in Sydney scooped *Fact* by naming both Stewart and James McAuley. 'Stewart at present is in a military hospital in Sydney,' the article confided. 'Interviewed yesterday he would not deny having written the poems.'

*In September 1934, the burned and battered body of a young woman wearing lemon-and-white crêpe pyjamas embroidered with a dragon motif had been discovered in a culvert near the border dividing New South Wales from Victoria. Exhaustive police investigations failed to identify the 'pyjama girl' or her killer, and the body was placed in a formalin bath at Sydney University. Her identity obsessed the country. Almost a decade later, after fresh evidence emerged, the ruined face was made up, and the matted hair fashionably set. The pyjama girl was identified by various witnesses as Linda Agostini, and her Italian husband Tony, a waiter-cum-journalist, was arrested and tried in Melbourne in mid-June 1944. He was convicted of manslaughter.

7 A Serious Literary Experiment

Alf Conlon burst through the door of L Block at the barracks. 'Here it is,' he shouted, 'here it is!' He was clutching a copy of 25 June's *Fact* in which he read:

Ern Malley, Poet of Debunk: full story from the two authors

Last week FACT said it would clear up the 'mystery', motives and merit of the 'Poems of Ern Malley'. This week it does so.

The Works of Ern Malley were deliberately concocted, without intention of poetic meaning or merit, as an experiment to debunk what was regarded as a pretentious kind of modern verse-writing.

● The 'Works of Ern Malley' were written, in collaboration, by two Australian poets, JAMES McAULEY and HAROLD STEWART.

Conlon skimmed the thumbnail biographies to get to the main event, the hoaxers' statement:

We decided to carry out a serious literary experiment. There was no feeling of personal malice directed against Mr. Max Harris (co-editor of *Angry Penguins*).

Nor was there any intention of having the matter publicised in the Press. It became known to FACT in an unforeseen manner. Some public statement is, therefore, necessary.

'Decay of meaning'

For some years now we have observed with distaste the gradual decay of meaning and craftsmanship in poetry.

Mr. Max Harris and other *Angry Penguins* writers represent an Australian outcrop of a literary fashion which has become prominent in England and America. The distinctive feature of the fashion, it seemed to us, was that it rendered its devotees insensible of absurdity and incapable of ordinary discrimination.

Our feeling was that by processes of critical self-delusion and mutual

137

admiration, the perpetrators of this humorless nonsense had managed to pass it off on would-be *intellectuals* and *Bohemians*, here and abroad, as *great poetry*.

Their work appeared to us to be a collection of garish images without coherent meaning and structure; as if one erected a coat of bright paint and called it a house.

However, it was possible that we had simply failed to penetrate to the inward substance of these productions. The only way of settling the matter was by experiment. It was, after all, fair enough. If Mr. Harris proved to have sufficient discrimination to reject the poems, then the tables would have been turned.

What we wished to find out was: Can those who write, and those who praise so lavishly, this kind of writing tell the real product from consciously and deliberately concocted nonsense?

We gave birth to *Ern Malley*. We represented Ern through his equally fictitious sister *Ethel Malley* as having been a garage mechanic, an insurance salesman, who wrote, but never published, the 'poems' found after his tragic end at the age of 25 by his sister, who sent them to *Angry Penguins* for an opinion on their worth.

'One afternoon'

We produced the whole of Ern Malley's tragic life-work in one afternoon, with the aid of a chance collection of books which happened to be on our desk: the Concise Oxford Dictionary, a Collected Shakespeare, Dictionary of Quotations &c.

We opened books at random, choosing a word or phrase haphazardly. We made lists of these and wove them into nonsensical sentences.

We misquoted and made false allusions. We deliberately perpetrated bad verse, and selected awkward rhymes from a Ripman's Rhyming Dictionary.

The alleged quotation from Lenin in one of the poems, *'The emotions are not skilled workers'*, is quite phoney.

The first three lines of the poem *Culture as Exhibit* were lifted, as a quotation, straight from an American report on the drainage of breeding-grounds of mosquitoes.

The last line in the last poem (printed in *Angry Penguins* as: *'I have split the infinite . . .'* &c.) read in the manuscript: *'I have split the infinitive. Beyond is anything.'*

Our rules of composition were not difficult:

1. There must be no coherent theme, at most, only confused and inconsistent hints at a meaning held out as a bait to the reader.
2. No care was taken with verse technique, except occasionally to accentuate its general sloppiness by deliberate crudities.
3. In style, the poems were to imitate, not Mr. Harris in particular, but the whole literary fashion as we knew it from the works of Dylan Thomas, Henry Treece and others.

Having completed the poems, we wrote a very pretentious and meaningless *Preface and Statement* which purported to explain the aesthetic theory on which they were based. Then we elaborated the details of the alleged poet's life. This took more time than the composition of his *Works*.

'Hypnotism'

Mr. Harris and Mr. John Reed (co-editors of *Angry Penguins*), Mr. Brian Elliott (Lecturer in Australian Literature at Adelaide University), Mr. Harry Roskolenko (the American poet in the US Forces, who had some *Ern Malley* poems published in New York in an anthology of Australian verse he collected), and others, accepted these poems as having considerable merit.

However, that fact does not, as it might seem to do, prove a complete lack of intelligence. It proves something far more interesting.

If proves that a literary fashion can become so hypnotically powerful that it can suspend the operation of critical intelligence in quite a large number of people.

We feel that the experiment could have been equally successful in England. Apparently, it was in America, to the extent that a publisher was taken in.

Such a literary movement as the one we aimed at debunking – it began with the *Dadaist* movement in France during the last war, which gave birth to the *Surrealist* movement, which was followed in England by the *New Apocalypse* school, whose Australian counterparts are the *Angry Penguins* – this cultism resembles, on a small scale, the progress of certain European political parties.

An efficient publicity apparatus is switched on to beat the big drum and drown opposition. Doubters are shamed to silence by the fear of appearing stupid or (worse crime!) *reactionary*. If anyone raises his voice in protest, he is mobbed with shrill invective. The faithful, meanwhile, to keep their spirits up, shout encouragements and slogans, and gather in groups so as to have no time to think.

For the Ern Malley 'poems' there cannot be, as a last resort, any valid *Surrealist* claim that even if they have no literary value (which it has been said they *do* possess) they are at least *psychological documents*. They are not even that.

They are the conscious product of *two* minds, intentionally interrupting each other's trains of free association, and altering and revising them after they are written down. So they have not even a psychological value.

● And, as we have already explained conclusively, the *Writings of Ern Malley* are utterly devoid of literary merit as poetry.

James McAuley,
Harold Stewart.

Conlon, along with 250,000 other readers of the *Sunday Sun*, found its magazine supplement *Fact*, 'the up-to-the-minute Australian news-review', wedged between the sports and the comics: 'Ginger Meggs', 'Popeye', 'Speed Gordon'. The first three pages of *Fact* were given to snippets of news about the war from all over the world, and the last page reserved for tit-bits of sport, odd anecdotes, gobbets of Australiana. Here the Ern Malley story took pride of place. The hoaxers' statement, by far the longest article on the page, was illustrated by postage stamp snapshots of the co-conspirators bridged by the words ERN MALLEY, thus giving the hydra a name. There was no denying the seriousness of what McAuley and Stewart had to say, but *Fact* did not make for strenuous reading, and the edition for 25 June 1944 was no exception.

On the same page as Ern Malley was a lurid portrait of Tony Agostini, on trial for his life for the murder of the 'Pyjama Girl'. *Fact* was fascinated by this 'slight figure in a gabardine raincoat with something of the professional stoop of a waiter taking an order'. The case called for a touch of Hollywood. As Agostini sat in the pulpit-like enclosure at the back of the courtroom, only his head could be seen with its 'pale' eyes that were also 'mild, imperturbable, gazelle-like'. A court veteran thought him 'the calmest man I've ever seen facing a murder charge'. Another story with the riddling title 'He threw the game away and won' described how a 33-year-old Philadelphian coffin salesman called Alfred (Doc) Manuszak hurled a golf ball around a course in New Jersey to win a bet: 'On the wicked 603-yard fifteenth hole he threw smack into a 150-yard wide lake. He shed his clothes and fetched it, taking an 11 for the par-5 hole.' That was one way to forget the war. Or you could distract yourself from the pangs of rationing by reading about the prisoner in Sydney's Long Bay Gaol who requested his food parcel include 'two cartons of jam, two cartons of cheese, four cartons of biscuits, three dozen bottles of tomato soup and of chicken soup, butter, fruit, cake, sugar (18lb), 12 jars of paste, a dozen blocks of chocolate'. Anyone familiar with the title of Ern's Works could note that Wednesday, 21 June 1944 was the shortest day of the year, 9 hours and 54 minutes long, caused by the 'obliquity of the ecliptic'. Most touching of all was little Elza Jerram of Sycamore Street, Malvern, the eleven-year-old daughter of a railwayman, stricken with infantile paralysis, unable to move her useless arms but able to thread a needle with her toes. 'Sometimes, unthinkingly, I ask her to pass me something, perhaps a saucepan,' Elza's mother told *Fact*. 'I get a shock when she hands it to me (if you can use such a term) with her toes.'

Shocks, of a mild degradable kind, were *Fact*'s business. McAuley and Stewart had not anticipated how well Ern would make model copy for pap. In the event, publication in *Fact* maximized the titillation of the hoax and stymied debate. How does one take issue with a paralysed child, a man who throws golfballs into lakes, or a poet of debunk? It would be trivial to argue with such trivia. Besides, the name of the magazine suggested its contents were beyond debate. Ern Malley was a fact. He was a phoney just as Doc Manuszak was a coffin salesman. *Fact* solved the mystery of Ern in the same way it explained that the shortest day was due to the earth tilting 'on its axis to the angle ($23\frac{1}{2}$ degrees) where the sun was farthest away from the southern parts of the globe's surface' or assessed the value of that bulimic food parcel at '£13/3/10'.

The publication of McAuley's and Stewart's stern statement in *Fact* brought the goofy side of the hoax into sharp relief. Ern becomes a passing freak, the lifeless wonder who anticipates Andy Warhol's dictum that everybody will become famous for fifteen minutes and revolutionizes it: even Warhol never imagined non-persons might hog the spotlight. And Ern fulfils a principle that poetry merits publicity when it generates gossip about its own strangeness – in this case at the moment when, supplanted by the story of its composition, it ceases to exist.

The statement was not hatched in the easiest circumstances. Stewart wrote a draft from his hospital bed in Sydney. McAuley produced his account in Melbourne: about a thousand words long, it formed the basis of the published statement, but much of the anecdotal detail about how the poems were written came from Stewart's slightly longer version. The two documents were edited together by Colin Simpson, and Stewart approved the final text after consulting with McAuley by phone. Simpson spliced paragraphs together, omitted a few sections, and did some minor copy-editing. Several paragraphs in *Fact*, identifying the source of 'Culture as Exhibit' and revealing the quotation from Lenin to be fake, are not in either draft; these were added by Stewart at Simpson's request. McAuley had his version of things ready by Monday, 19 June, and sent it to van Sommers with a letter advising restraint:

I think the enclosed statement covers the ground adequately. It is a temptation to work off on Max all the bright cracks one can think of, but it is far better to take a quiet and almost deprecating tone. I leave it to Harold to emend as he sees fit but I strongly urge him to master the impulse to poke malicious faces. The thing was a dignified 'experiment', not a hoax; no malice was intended – it was all in the cause of enlightenment!

Tess, I submit the statement on the understanding that it will be published *entire and in one piece* in the form that it leaves Harold's hands. If your paper wants to play around with it Harold can simply withhold it, deny everything and shut up. I'm still a little curious to know just what the course of events was after Brian

Elliott's review, and at what point you took a hand.

However, 'all shall be well and all manner of thing shall be well' as that terrible old fellow T. S. Eliot recently said.

Beneath this was a postscript: 'If Harold still doubts the virtue of taking a quiet tone tell him to think how much hotter coals of fire it heaps on Maxie's head. Politeness is the deadlier weapon.' That 'terrible old fellow' was in fact quoting Dame Julian of Norwich, but McAuley wanted to hose down the fire he had lit. Those 'bright cracks' he warns against had already kindled the hoax itself. To argue for 'a quite tone', intended to heap 'much hotter coals of fire . . . on Maxie's head' is disingenuous: it suggests that the dignity of the 'experiment' was in direct proportion to the number of blisters sustained by Harris. The reluctance to poke faces is magnanimous in itself, but there is also something defensive in McAuley's attempt to absolve himself of the mischievous side of the deception. His disinfectant is the term 'experiment'. Stewart used the word 'hoax' in his draft but this was cut from the final version. 'Experiment', with its implications of judicious inquiry, of 'scientific' disinterest, became essential to the hoaxers' story. It also parodied one of the key terms in the modernist lexicon, since the Ern Malley 'experiment' equated 'experimental' writing with drivel. But if Ern Malley really was *an experiment to debunk* the poetry of the pretentious Penguins, it was not hard to tell the monkey from the scientists. The phrase suggests the hoaxers knew the result they were after. The dice after all were loaded: if Harris had written 'Dear Ethel Malley, Unfortunately your brother could not write to save his life . . .', who would have been the wiser?

The term 'experiment' stuck. *Fact* ran the word 'hoax' in its headline on 18 June but banished it from the full disclosure. '*Meanjin*'s reaction to the "affaire Malley",' Clem Christesen wrote, in an editorial vetted by A. D. Hope before publication, 'is that McAuley and Stewart have not perpetrated a hoax so much as carried out a serious literary experiment . . . in the nature of a laboratory test, an aesthetic co-ordinate system, a mariner's "shooting a sight" to get a bearing when ordinary navigation methods fail'. The confusion of images suggests that Christesen did not really know what to think about Ern Malley. His nervousness is understandable. On 25 June, enclosing the *Fact* statement for Christesen's perusal, Hope warned him: 'keep your spirits up and your head down. The bullets fly close to the ground these days.'

McAuley's draft was lofty and revisionist, while Stewart remained puckish and unrepentant, closer to the spirit of the hoax itself. Not all the differences between the documents were ironed out in the editing. It was assembled in haste, and not rewritten. Harold Stewart agrees their statement was 'unsatisfactory, since it was cobbled up by letters and phone calls and really wasn't well-considered'. For instance, he led off with, 'For some years now we have observed with distaste the gradual decay of meaning and craftsmanship in poetry', which hardly suggests an even-handed approach. McAuley wanted to be seen to have an open mind. 'It was possible that we had simply failed to penetrate to the inward substance of these productions,' he wrote. 'Perhaps it was we and not the authors who were at fault. The only way of settling the matter was by experiment. It was, after all, fair enough. If Mr Harris proved to have sufficient discrimination to reject the poems, then the tables would have been turned.' Both points of view made it into *Fact*, but Stewart is the better witness here. Ern Malley was the product of a set of convictions, developed over a period of years – not an attempt by the hoaxers to work out in public what they thought of modern poetry. If Harris had rejected the poems, McAuley would not have changed his mind about the kinds of writing he had come to despise.

The passages Simpson, or Stewart, omitted tended to be inflammatory. Stewart attacked the international promotion of modernism: 'they have *made it pay*! – witness firms like Faber and Faber who have taken these fledgling pterodactyls under their patronizing wing and published their works – if such writing requires any work'. He scornfully celebrated the creation of Ern:

His was a wholly posthumous existence. In a manner of speaking he was still-born, since he seems to have been cremated several months before his birth. Of course we never for one moment expected someone as intelligent as we then believed Max Harris to be, to fall for so elementary a gag. To our great surprise he did, and further leg-pulling was irresistible, particularly as legally we were committing no criminal offence.

McAuley's draft was toned down too. He stressed the incoherence of Malley's poetry: 'There must not even be connected "free association". With two of us working together, it was easy to derange even the sequence of fantasy.' He gave this account of the fake biography: 'We make no apology for having surrounded the poems with an unreal story. Unless a poet is dead he cannot get a hearing. The quality of the poems is the only thing in question: who the author is makes no difference to their value.' The last sentence is what the ruffled Penguins were trying to say in their defence, and yet it is preceded by lame justification for the elaboration of Malley's biography: 'unless a poet is dead he cannot get a hearing'. Well, not quite. After all, McAuley also remarked: 'An efficient publicity apparatus is switched on to beat the big drum and drown opposition.'

The story of Ern Malley's life is inseparable from the poems because both are synthetic. Hoaxes work, as Hugh Kenner has shown, by counterfeiting not only products but their origins. Was Harris being challenged to see through the poetry or the story surrounding the poetry? Both, the hoaxers would say – but if there was any merit in Ern Malley's verse, as Brian Elliott suggested a month or two after the disclosure, then the test was 'confused by the presence of real poetic values to offset the absurdity of the story'.

McAuley also declared:

One thing that we regret very much is that the Ern Malley issue of Angry Penguins should also contain a boost for Mr William Dobell, a painter whose work we both admire. Mr Dobell has already suffered the spite and silliness of one set of bad artists and their friends; it is a pity that he should now have the embarrassment of being praised by others with whom he has nothing in common. That, however, is an unavoidable and common hardship which sincere artists have to bear. Many good writers and painters have produced work which at first sight appeared strange and wilfully obscure. Always the busy non-entities on the look-out for a new 'thrill' have seized upon it, and surrounded it with ignorant adulation. But time sweeps them into oblivion, and the work remains to win the gradual appreciation of the discriminating. Mr Dobell's work will survive the temporary embarrassment of being in any way connected with the sort of feeble painting which decorates the front cover of Angry Penguins.*

The 'spite and silliness' suffered by William Dobell arose from the infamous Archibald Prize litigation of 1944. The previous year Dobell had won the £500 prize for a portrait judged annually by the trustees of the Art Gallery of New South Wales. A group of academic artists – whose pictures the judges rejected – then alleged that Dobell's highly mannered painting of fellow artist Joshua Smith was not a portrait but a caricature, and therefore ineligible for the prize as defined in J. F. Archibald's will. The fight, like Ern Malley, was between traditionalists on the one hand and the moderns on the other, with these key differences: the painters attacking Dobell were talentless hacks, and Dobell defended himself by saying, 'I am not a modern painter; neither am I breaking new ground. I have studied the old masters intimately, and based my paintings on Rembrandt, Corot, and others.' The case, an attempt to use the courts to settle questions of aesthetics, was viciously fought. A doctor, for example, testified on behalf of the litigants that Dobell's portrait

---

*McAuley's remarks are puzzling: 'at first sight . . . strange and wilfully obscure' sounds like a potential defence of Ern Malley. And John Reed's 'boost' for Dobell in Angry Penguins was not flattering: 'Dobell is really the answer to the prayer of those who instinctively realize the bankruptcy of the academician, but equally instinctively fear the revolutionary power of the truly creative artist'. He added that the 'master technician' was now 'falling into that ghastly error of endlessly repeating himself'.

resembled an image of a three-month-old corpse! The action failed – the judge confirmed the picture's likeness to the sitter – and Dobell kept the prize.

The most startling thing about the hoaxers' published statement is how different it is from the hoax. At the moment of revelation McAuley and Stewart lost their sense of humour. The confession seems to be by men different from the culprits. The 'wonderful jape', became 'a serious literary experiment'. They 'were going to absolutely slay Max Harris' but there was 'no feeling of personal malice' directed against him. Brian Elliott remarked on this at the time: 'I felt the newspaper statement to be an anticlimax: because it reduces the genuine Aristophanic hilarity of the parody to a kind of sour academic philistinism.' The distance between the three voices of the hoax – Ern's swirling histrionics, Ethel's stodgy gossip, and the devastating rhetoric of the statement – shows how brilliantly articulated the strategy was, and just how much McAuley and Stewart conceived of their joke as a position to argue from. The *Fact* statement is formidable and very confident, but there are hints of overkill: the final sentence comes like the slam of a door to end the argument.

There is overkill too in the political references penned by McAuley which seem to have the teaching of John Anderson behind them, and anticipate the kind of cold war slanging McAuley practised in the fifties. His inference that the urgings of Harris and his cohorts form a parallel with a totalitarian rhetoric, of the left or the right, wildly overestimates the influence of *Angry Penguins*. The magazine was despised by the right and constantly abused by communists who loathed the liberalism of its aesthetics, but this is really beside the point. Nine hundred copies of a highbrow journal hardly add up to Nuremberg or Red Square and McAuley cannot really have imagined that *Angry Penguins* represented a threat to freedom of expression. Surely the *absence* of *Angry Penguins* would have been the greater threat: however uneven and self-regarding the magazine, there was nothing like it in the country.

The statement in *Fact* acquired an unassailable authority, precisely because it was by the authors of Ern Malley. For the majority of people who took in the hoax, it was the only explanation of how the poems work. There has never been another account to match it. And yet the statement is inadequate in several respects, despite the hoaxers' sincerity. The assertion that Malley lacks all literary value will not do because it does not consider the poems as parody. A satire in perfect tune with the mannerisms of its target, the sequence is a technically dazzling imitation, and a literary attack as coherent and intelligent as, say, *Shamela*, Henry Fielding's comic put-down of Richardson's *Pamela*.

The assertion that 'There must be no coherent theme, at most, only confused and inconsistent hints at a meaning held out as a bait to the reader' is also not equal to the experience of reading the poems. The hoaxers' declaration that Malley's works were a collection of 'nonsensical sentences' will not hold water. However delicious or patent some of the non sequiturs in Ern Malley, he was never just that. Look at the delightful cunning which connects the end of 'Sybilline' – 'The figure that strode hell swinging / His head by the hair / On Princess Street?' – with the opening of the next poem, 'Night Piece': 'The swung torch scatters seeds / In the umbelliferous dark'. Had McAuley and Stewart, blindfolded, taken a verse from the Bible, a sentence from a newspaper, a line from Shakespeare, a fragment from a popular novel and so on, shuffled the lot and sent Harris the results, this would have accorded better with their own description of their method. It would also have brought them much nearer to the model of the surrealist's 'exquisite corpse', than that random act of collaboration it might seem their statement describes. But McAuley and Stewart were only pretending to be surrealist: they needed the best parts of their conscious minds to capture the semblance of the unconscious at work. They admitted as much: the poems, they said, were 'the conscious product of two minds, intentionally interrupting each other's trains of free association, and altering and revising them'.

Interrupting Malley's deranged stream of consciousness enabled the hoaxers to make sense when they wanted to. Elaborations of the idea that Malley himself is bogus, a trick, 'the incomplete circle and straight drop / Of a question mark', occur regularly enough to become one of the themes of the poetry. 'Now we find, too late / That these distractions were clues / To a transposed version / Of our too rigid state. / It is an ancient forgotten ruse / And a natural diversion.' The lines give the game away, at least to readers now. The poems are illusions, they say, and we will learn too late that we were seduced by an image of ourselves, because our point of view was too narrow. It's neatly done, and without such passages Brian Elliott would never have picked the hoax.

The figure of Ern Malley palpably unifies the poems. If the lines only amounted to 'confused and inconsistent hints at a meaning' it would never have been possible for Harris to extrapolate his sentimental image of a moribund genius who seemed to understand the kind of poetry he wanted to write: 'New images distort / Our creeping disjunct minds to incredible patterns.' From the outset the poetry constructs a voice readable as that of a young man who believes in his vocation as a poet, recoiling from a broken love affair, a martyr dreaming up his own art of dying. The scenario may be hand-me-down, but it exists. The confused lines, the poetic 'mistakes', the zestful gaucheries all make Malley's troubled, labile presence more credible. McAuley and Stewart discounted this because they did not take Malley seriously for a second. But the poetry conjures him up. 'One moment of daylight let me have,' says Malley, knowing he is not long for this world, 'Like a white arm thrust / Out of the dark and self-denying wave'. 'Among the water-lilies / A splash – white foam in the dark!', the haphazard armorist recalls, spinning out the image and thinking perhaps of that girl he was fond of in Melbourne. 'And you lay sobbing then / Upon my trembling intuitive arm.'

Finding himself to be a dromedary, in the twenty-fifth year of his age, Malley pulls out all the stops for his last poem and declares, 'I am content at last to be / The sole clerk of my metamorphoses':

> In the year 1943
> I resigned to the living all collateral images
> Reserving to myself a man's
> Inalienable right to be sad
> At his own funeral.

Such detail ('twenty-fifth year', '1943'), read against Ethel's 'unreal story', is no more irrational or random than the absurdity of Ern's self-recognition as a camel weeping at his own obsequies. 'Petit Testament' is funny because it is so sad, sad because it is so funny. The poem reads like a summary of the entire sequence itself and the bold clarity of Ern's *ave atque vale* is striking. It dramatizes the maunderings of an overwrought youth watching his life flit before his eyes. Malley is aware of the 'problems' his poetry raises: he despairs 'of ever / Making my obsessions intelligible'; he recounts his romantic failure 'Scrubbing my few dingy words to brightness'; he recalls his squalid life where 'the cockroach / Inhabits the crack and the careful spider / Spins his aphorisms in the corner'. This fractured destiny is elevated into a political allegory, a cipher for the trauma of war:

> I have heard them shout in the streets
> The chiliasms of the Socialist Reich
> And in the magazines I have read
> The Popular Front-to-Back.
> But where I have lived
> Spain weeps in the gutters of Footscray
> Guernica is the ticking of the clock
> The nightmare has become real, not as belief
> But in the scrub-typhus of Mubo.

When Sidney Nolan read these lines he thought they were 'rather terrific', though he was taken aback by the sardonic view of the left they begin with. The politics might not cohere but the sensation of reading the transcription of a life is powerful. If Ern

Malley approaches a realized consciousness in this poem it is –
hilariously, poignantly – because, having told the story of his
days, he confronts the fact that he is a fiction, filled with defiance
in his lament for his own non-being:

> It is something to be at last speaking
> Though in this No-Man's-language appropriate
> Only to No-Man's-Land.
> Set this down too:
> I have pursued rhyme, image, and metre,
> Known all the clefts in which the foot may stick,
> Stumbled often, stammered,
> But in time the fading voice grows wise
> And seizing the co-ordinates of all existence
> Traces the inevitable graph
> And in conclusion:
> There is a moment when the pelvis
> Explodes like a grenade. I
> Who have lived in the shadow that each act
> Casts on the next act now emerge
> As loyal as the thistle that in session
> Puffs its full seed upon the indicative air.
> I have split the infinitive. Beyond is anything.

Ern Malley is the solecism that came to life, the split infinitive that
made it into print. Anything *was* beyond. However *right* McAuley
and Stewart were in the thrust of their statement, however
accurate the criticism the hoax delivered, however chastening its
effect on the pretensions of their contemporaries, they had, by the
time their statement was released, lost control of their automaton.
His fate now lay in the public domain. Few writers receive press so
adulatory and then so hostile. Ern Malley thrived.

Dixunt: McAuley and Stewart withdrew while the noise ampli-
fied around the scene of the crime. On the eve of the disclosure
Harris was shown a copy of the hoaxers' statement and his reply
appeared the same weekend in the *Mail* (24 June) in Adelaide:

If 50 million monkeys with 50 million typewriters tapped for that number of years, one of them would produce a Shakespeare sonnet. It is to be hoped that Lieutenant McAuley and Corporal Stewart have not produced such a phenomenon.

Not their claims of exposure, but time tells the story, and time will explain the fact that the myth is sometimes greater than its creator.

Even now it is becoming clear that the history of the last generation has been written powerfully and sensitively by the T. S. Eliots and the Audens.

Their work – and it is towards it the attack is fundamentally directed – is so deeply rooted in the consciousness of thinking men today that they are impregnable.

I hope this proves true of the bulk of contemporary artists.

These two people are relatively unknown in Australian journals. I hope they will one day themselves grow larger than their highly commendable myth.

On 27 June, Reed sketched out to Harris what would become the *Angry Penguins* response: that McAuley and Stewart, released from inhibition by their extraordinary method of composition, wrote much better than they knew. He and Nolan, Reed wrote, had decided to aim for:

the substantiation of the poems from internal and subjective sources focussed around the unconscious impact on the writers (McA & S) of the creative stream of the age, which in this case has, unknown to them, broken through their inhibitions and repressions. The position however is very extraordinary and Sunday is by no means happy that this is the solution of it. She has steadily adopted the attitude that once the hoax is disclosed, the poetry and the whole Malley set up undergoes some change and she can no longer feel the same about the poems. What that change is she is not quite sure, but she is equally not sure that our evaluation of the position is correct. It is certainly something new that good poetry is created out of deliberate boguery. Elliott of course dismisses the authors' claims that their intention was nonsensical and if this contention is right, it would presumably bring the poetry into some such category as satire and that places it on a different footing; but it seems quite obvious from their statement – unless they are arrant liars as well as hoaxers – that their intentions are clear enough. If so we are reduced to the deep, complex and entirely revolutionary hypothesis I have suggested, namely that these men have absorbed without knowing it the vital culture of the last hundred years (not 'beginning with Dada' as they stated), but have been inhibited by reason of some personal complexes from utilizing it in their 'serious' writing, and have only been released when writing in a way which imposes no obligations on them.

While the editors tried to formulate a response, Ern Malley was everywhere, a fool's head upon a platter. There were not enough copies of *Angry Penguins* to go around, though in Sydney the *Sun* drily noted on 27 June that there was 'no demand for earlier issues of the periodical'. The press guffawed, lectured and moralized. *Fact* was culled again and again for the same details: the poems were patched up in an afternoon, they wove together nonsensical sentences, they included lines from an American report on the drainage of breeding grounds of mosquitoes.

The hoaxers, who took no joy from the butchering of Harris's self-respect 'to make a newspaper holiday', must have blushed at some of it and were finally, Stewart recalls, 'disgusted by the way the press handled the whole thing. We felt poor old Max had been victimized publishing our dreadful obscene works.' The *Bulletin* of 5 July gave 'earnest thanks' to the 'Diggers' whom it described as 'joint debunkers of Bosh and Blah and Blather'. The *Argus* reported that the hoaxers had been awarded the degree of 'Doctor of Science of Oxometry' by the Sydney University Oxometrical Society, the emblem of which was a bull. The *Sun* published a cartoon by Gil Brown in which two penguins natter against a glacial backdrop. Their adolescent offspring is stomping away in disgust. 'He is going to be one of those "Angry Penguins," I think, dear,' says one to the other.

In Melbourne the *Herald* carried a story about the 'great literary leg-pull' on 1 July and two days later the angry editors of *Angry Penguins* replied that 'Ern Malley was a fine poet but the two soldiers who created him are not', promising to treat the matter fully in the next issue of their magazine. The *Herald* editorial found the 'moral' of the tale was 'to have a humble confidence in one's own judgement. That much derided phrase, "I may not know much about art, but I know what I like" is good sense after all . . . it is the job of the artist or the writer to say what he has to say in line, colour or language which the people can understand.' In Adelaide the *Advertiser* wrote approvingly on 4 July of the two 'cheerful and healthy minded young' hoaxers who 'blew to smithereens the irritating pretensions and incomprehensible philosophy of a school of so-called "modern poetry"'. Bernard O'Dowd, the bush nationalist poet by now in his dotage – McAuley especially despised him and later wrote off his work as a *cloaca maxima* – hoped that Ern Malley would 'dissipate the too prevalent charlatanism, cheap-jackery, vulgarity and verbose omniscience infesting poetic and critical organisms in Australia today'. Letters to the editor were published, the kind which thinks 'poetry should express simple thoughts in simple language, so that even school children can appreciate it'. On 8 July the *Herald* published *Angry Penguins'* challenge to the hoaxers to submit six poems for publication alongside six poems by Ern Malley: 'We have heard a lot about the Malley "hoax" while the actual literary merit of the poems has been almost entirely ignored, though it is obvious that this is the only basis on which they can be judged.' Two days later, to no one's surprise, McAuley and Stewart refused the invitation.

The newspapers extended their hilarity at the hoax into a generalized contempt for new art. On 28 June the *Age* reported the Contemporary Art Society exhibition in Sydney by disclosing that 'for two days one of the exhibits was hung upside down without attracting undue attention. The picture was that of a reclining nude.' This stampede to enfranchise anyone at all who found new art insulting had its comic moments. The *Sydney Sun* of 2 July reported that 'two Diggers on leave' visited the exhibition and inspected a painting described as 'a jumble of bright colours and large white square blobs that had long stems with red lips'. One of the Diggers 'twisted his head, knelt down and almost stood on his hands. "It's got me beat, Bill," was his comment when his equilibrium was restored.'

Then the debate turned rabid. The Penguins were attacked by enemies who loathed each other but shared ground on Ern Malley, the communists and the Catholics. On 29 June the *Tribune* applauded the hoaxers' diagnosis that 'artistic decadence of the Max Harris brand is a feature of all capitalist countries at the present time' and put in a plug for propaganda: 'real art has generally been in touch with real life, taking the struggles of the people for material and working it up with skilled craftsmanship into something that is beautiful and inspiring.' In a shot at John Reed, the card-carrying artist Noel Counihan thought the hoax confirmed 'the complete cultural bankruptcy of the decadent Right Wing of the Contemporary Arts Society'. Though he did not trust the hoaxers, Counihan was led by Ern's dubious politics ('Why is Lenin dragged in with a fictitious and absurd quote?') to agree that the poems had 'no literary value at all'. Another painter, Vic O'Connor, put it more strongly in the *Communist Review*: 'Only the complete lack of talent, common sense and critical standards of the editors, and their blind obedience to an art ideology which exalts obscurantism and fantasy above meaning and profundity made possible the success of this unscrupulous attack on experimentation and cultural development.' In a letter he wrote soon afterwards, O'Connor dismissed the hoaxers as 'decadent Australian Anderson products and mediocrities'. Ern Malley took the shape of a fascist conspiracy: the bogus tag from Lenin was, O'Connor had heard, in fact 'taken from a speech by Goebbels'.

The *Advocate*, Melbourne's weekly Catholic newspaper, stomped into the debate on 5 July with an article by Niall Brennan. Harris had launched an attack on 'Adelaide (City of Churches)'; he was guilty of 'gaseous self-adulation' and of fostering 'the greatest piece of literary charlatanry Australia has ever seen'; his magazine *Angry Penguins* had the support of 'every neuro decadent in the country'. In a startling image Brennan declared that Ern Malley's poems were published with 'a dignity of layout that is like an archiepiscopal procession', a remark that suggests a bleak view of archiepiscopal processions.

Brennan saved his best for last: 'You cannot afford to ignore typhus, and we cannot afford to ignore Harris and his gaggle of penguins. They have attacked the intellectual foundations of Australia by a direct assault upon truth and beauty and it is to be hoped that the counter attack of Messrs. Stewart and McAuley may well have fatal results for this mental disease which brandishes its sores and boasts of its health.'

The following week the *Advocate* took another swipe at Harris and his school, whom the Catholic journalist P. I. O'Leary described as 'our contemporary masters of the unintelligible . . . Not for nothing were they coeval with the Black-out. For they are the Bards of the Black-out.' McAuley and Stewart he praised as 'self-elected missioners of sweetness and light'. *Freedom*, another Catholic publication, broadened the attack on 26 July by linking *Angry Penguins* with the argument against contraception: 'A civilization that has outlawed large families, and pities or insults maternity . . . even when it clearly means national suicide, deserves only literature like *Angry Penguins*.'

As Harris took a pasting in almost every newspaper in Australia, he found an ally 12,000 miles away in London. When Herbert Read's copy of *Angry Penguins* arrived, he was intrigued by Ern Malley's poems, and mentioned the hoax to Sean Jennett, the typographer and poet, who in turn showed them to T. S. Eliot: news filtered through to the Penguins in Australia that Eliot was 'extremely interested, but that this was not for publication in any way'. If Eliot was coy, Read's bold response was to cable Harris:

I TOO WOULD HAVE BEEN DECEIVED BY ERN MALLEY BUT HOAXER HOISTED BY OWN PETARD HAS TOUCHED OFF UNCONSCIOUS SOURCES INSPIRATION WORK TOO SOPHISTI-CATED BUT HAS ELEMENTS GENUINE POETRY

A few days later he forwarded an explanatory letter:

I read the poems in an objective spirit, and though I find them very uneven, often obscure and sometimes absurd, yet allowing as I would normally do for some adolescent crudity, the general effect is undoubtedly poetic, and poetic on an unusual level of achievement. There is not only an effective use of vivid metaphor, a subtle sense of rhythmic variation, but even a metaphysical unity which cannot be the result of unintelligent deception . . .

Read's theory was that the hoaxer

must inevitably use processes akin to, if not identical with, the processes which produced the original work of art. If his model is something conventional, the parody may be all the more difficult to make, for it is easy to detect. But if, as in the present case, the type of art parodied is itself unconventional, experimental, then the parodist has exceptional freedom, and because of this freedom, *can end by deceiving himself.* (The case is similar in painting: it would be much easier to fake a Picasso, for example than an Ingres, and in the process of making a fake Picasso, the faker *might*, if he had the native sensibility, create an original work of art.) . . .

It comes to this: if a man of sensibility, in a mood of despair or hatred, or even from a perverted sense of humour, sets out to fake works of imagination, then *if he is to be convincing*, he must use the poetic faculties. If he uses the faculties to good effect, he ends up by deceiving himself. So the faker of Ern Malley. He calls himself 'the black swan of trespass on alien waters' and that is a fine poetic phrase.* So is 'hawk at the wraith of remembered emotions' and many other tropes and images in these poems. Others are merely sophisticated or silly.

'The elephant motifs contorted on admonitory walls'

'Move in a calm immortal frieze
On the mausoleum of my incestuous
And self-fructifying death.'

'I have mistrusted your apodictic strength', etc

*Harold Stewart glossed Read's praise for this line in a letter to me on 11 May 1990: 'Ern was an *Australian* poet and knew perfectly well that our black swans were *not* trespassing on alien waters, but swimming around in their native habitat on the Swan river! It would take a *white* swan to trespass on the alien waters of Australia, and that is just the misreading that Read and everyone since has given the line, assuming that the poet was living in the northern hemisphere, where a black swan would be an intruding outsider. Correctly read, the line is a self-contradictory one, as Jim and I intended.'

This kind of rhetoric is modern Ossian, but like Ossian, can understandably deceive the best of critics. So much for Ern Malley.

Whether the faker of Picasso has an easier time of it than the faker of Ingres seems open to question, since in either case the task is to conceive of the original as a system of contours to be mimicked: and anything can be mimicked. But in 1944 Picasso's *oeuvre* was unfinished business, and who could tell what that sorcerer of forms might not get up to (even faking Ingres?). This is really what Read means: Ern Malley was a leap into the unknown, since he was imitating a kind of poetry which itself claimed to leap into the unknown.

Harris and Reed took tremendous heart from Read's words. They wanted to release a press statement on the strength of it, but eventually decided to save his letter up for the next issue of *Angry Penguins*. Adrian Lawlor was very impressed that the Penguins had drawn support from 'the leading authority on literature and the expressive arts in the English-speaking world, if not the world at large'. Hoist with their own petard became Harris's position too. But other theories began to circulate. In Sydney, John Anderson, who thought the true poet a 'heretic' and the sign of poetry 'the arrival of "new perceptions"', entered the debate. Harris had shown a 'certain weakness of judgement', but Anderson criticized the hoaxers for 'making the populace the judge in aesthetic matters', and for thinking their *intentions* in fabricating the poems of more significance than the poems themselves. Malley contained 'the element of *protest* which is absent from the ordinary work of these two writers', he said. The kind of natural outsider Anderson approved, Malley was 'free of the customary associations' and enabled one 'to see the arbitrariness of orthodox beliefs and attitudes'.

The Melbourne critic Colin Badger put a different spin on things with an unsigned article 'The Strange Case of Ern Malley' that appeared in the *Age* on 4 November 1944. Badger thought the poems were 'good stuff for those who like the modern manner' and added:

Whatever the deficiencies of Mr. Max Harris as critic and poet, it is very difficult indeed to feel that he erred in his estimate of these poems. That many who have not read them should doubt this is to be expected, and that those whose taste in literature was formed and fixed by what they were taught at school should mock is also to be expected. But with whatever doubts and hesitancies, honest criticism will endorse Mr. Harris's judgement, and we will undoubtedly hear more of this matter.

If poems the hoaxers asserted were 'bad' are 'good', how can this be accounted for? Badger's solution was to treat the statement in *Fact* as a strategy:

Either the writers wrote better than they knew – which seems to be the view now adopted by Mr. Harris – and improbably, setting out to produce sheer nonsense, produced instead a series of fine poems which they themselves failed to recognise as such, or – and the mind boggles at this suggestion – the hoax is of another kind than they have said, more subtle, more intricate. Can it be that they have deliberately chosen to put a test of literary sensibility to the public in this daring way? The test is simply this. Even when you are told that good verse is a hoax, told in the most authoritative way that it is 'bad', can you still recognise it for what it is? That, indeed, has intriguing possibilities in it, though it suggests a really breathtaking ingenuity.

Yet it is not impossible, not perhaps even improbable. The idea that competent writers produce first-rate verse in a fit of absence of mind, not knowing it to be good, is altogether too absurd to be considered. Once satisfied then that this verse is good – and that is a point about which it is genuinely difficult to see how criticism can differ – the alternative hypothesis seems the only one possible, and until more is known about this exceedingly puzzling affair it may perhaps be allowed to stand.

Writing well and then denying it, the hoaxers played a trick on Harris, the public, and the idea of literary reputation itself. They showed that the 'value' of poetry depends not just on what is said about it but by whom. This is the same truth Oscar Wilde perceived as he listened from the dock, 'sickened with horror', to the prosecutor Lockwood's denunciation of him which sounded 'like a thing out of Tacitus, like a passage in Dante, like one of

Savonarola's indictments of the Popes at Rome'. Then Wilde thought, '*How splendid it would be, if I was saying all this about myself!*' and saw 'that what is said of a man is nothing. The point is, who says it.'

If Badger was right, then McAuley and Stewart were actually in secret agreement with Harris about the poetry. McAuley's reaction was to credit Badger with an 'ingenious hypothesis' before adding, 'ingenuity, however, may not be what is required here'. Badger's theory really seems to be an attempt to account for the deafening lowbrow cheering of the hoax. The public was hostile to modern poetry – or all poetry – partly because it did not know how to tell good from bad. The hoax titillated those who resented this fact by proving that those supposedly in the know, like Harris, were having trouble too.

The sport of enjoying bad poetry was recent. It had been popularized in 1930 by D. B. Wyndham Lewis and Charles Lee who assembled *The Stuffed Owl*, an oft-reprinted anthology of poetry its writers had once thought good enough to publish but which it was easy to show, just by quoting it, was dreadful. Lewis and Lee left contemporary poetry out of their book but the sensibility informing it was emphatically modern. Part of the frisson of *The Stuffed Owl* was the fun of watching noble names like Tennyson slipping on a banana skin:

> So past the strong heroic soul away.
> And when they buried him, the little port
> Had seldom seen a costlier funeral.

The novelty of *The Stuffed Owl* was that it allowed readers to tell when words had failed and to revel in the *clunk* they made. Its connoisseurship of good Bad Verse, to which Lewis and Lee attributed an 'eerie supernal beauty' hints at a genial contempt for the art itself. It turns every poet into a potential buffoon. The Ern Malley hoaxers absorbed the lesson of *The Stuffed Owl* by providing an actual buffoon and constructing verse some readers would think good enough to publish but which they could then prove was bad.

Herbert Read's solution to the Ern Malley problem, which Badger thought untenable – that poets can write well when they think they are writing badly – is complicated by the hoaxers' subsequent concession that the poems were seeded with enough good lines to lure Harris but that this did not invalidate the hoax since the odd good line does not make a good poem. This is a reasonable point but it begs the question of what makes a good line, especially in poetry where a sensibility trained on *The Stuffed Owl* would think the worst lines the most fun:

> It was a night when the planets
> Were wreathed in dying garlands.
> It seemed we had substituted
> The abattoirs for the guillotine.
> I shall not forget how you invented
> Then, the conventions of faithfulness.

How are we to read the opening of Ern Malley's 'Perspective Lovesong'? It begins amid collapsed cosmic grandeur, but turns enigmatic in that remotely absurd middle couplet which looks as though it means something. The final two lines are like a wan version of Catullus, though this cocky lament does not lack confidence:

> It seemed that we were submerged
> Under a reef of coral to tantalize
> The wise-grinning shark. The waters flashed
> With Blue Angels and Moorish Idols.
> And if I mistook your dark hair for weed
> Was it not floating upon my tides?

That last conceit with its flip Marlovian sexiness shows a fingertips control, but now we trip on some Bad Verse, the kind of Technicolor confession panting adolescents write:

> I have remembered the chiaroscuro
> Of your naked breasts and loins.
> For you were wholly an admonition

That said: 'From bright to dark
Is a brief longing. To hasten is now
To delay.' But I could not obey.

'Wholly an admonition' is babu, hardly English. But wait:
'From bright to dark / Is a brief longing. To hasten is now / To
delay' is a different order of invention. It really does sound like
Catullus, an idea those inverted commas help along. The climax
comes with Malley's apostrophe to his beloved:

Princess, you lived in Princess St.,
Where the urchins pick their nose in the sun
With the left hand. You thought
That paying the price would give you admission
To the sad autumn of my Valhalla.
But I, too, invented faithfulness.

This is funny, bathetic, grand, moody and cynical. What made
the poetry in *The Stuffed Owl* comic was that it was meant to be
grave and sonorous: 'Spade! With which Wilkinson hath tilled
his lands'. Wordsworth didn't know that was a giggle – which
made it one. Decorum has turned farcical. Ern Malley was never
decorous. Instead, he detonates poetic effects that might move
heaven and earth, knowing from the start that *his* owl was well
and truly stuffed.

What Ern Malley didn't know was that from a position of total
obscurity he had by now become an international press sensation. 'Australian Plaudits Go To Fictitious Poet', the *New York
Times* announced on 3 July, 'Drainage Report Gems Culled In
Hoax Called Tremendous'. Next day the paper ran an editorial
approving of the 'good joke' and confiding that the 'Orphic or
Cryptic School of Poetry is now full of pupils. Some puzzled
readers have even suspected these enigmatists of deliberately
spoofing the public . . . Let the good work go on.' On 17 July
Time went for the screwball angle, deciding the hoax was 'as
fantastic as a duck-billed platypus' and that *Angry Penguins* was
a 'long-haired little review'. *Newsweek* ran a note the same week

headed 'Such Power! Such Feeling!' and scoffed at Ern Malley as the 'epitome of Australia's striving for culture'. In 'The Talk of the Town' the *New Yorker* drily remarked of the 'Great Australian Literary Hoax' that, if taken seriously, it 'spoils anyone for modern poetry for the rest of his life' and the 'sensitive reader . . . quickly has to give the stuff up and go back to Tennyson, who is at least beyond suspicion'. The *Nation* remarked that Ern Malley parodied the writings of Max Harris but made more sense.

The press shouted hooray on the other side of the Atlantic too. *John O' London's Weekly* of 14 July opined that Malley was written 'as a comic imposture and no good verse was ever written as a comic imposture'. The poems had 'no merit but meaningless-ness' and that the object of Malley was 'to warn readers . . . never to pretend to enjoy balderdash merely because other people have solemnly praised it'. The *News Chronicle* sent a reporter around to interview the Apocalyptic poet Henry Treece but he sensed a trap and refused to comment. The *Spectator* rehearsed the plot, praised the spoofers and concluded, 'These men have not lived in vain.'

PART III The Trial

8 Persona Non Grata

Max Harris remained in Adelaide in the days after the hoax became a byword. He wavered between despair and feeling brave about everything, but he lashed out to Reed about 'the malicious vapourings of the thwarted literary virgins, J McA and HS'. Reed surmised that Harris was 'disposed to dismiss the whole thing and concentrate on the creative impetus' it supplied him with. This was not exactly true. 'I've said all I desire to say about the poems,' Harris wrote, 'and see no need to retract any of it. The hoaxed part of it, the Malley myth, I take in good part entirely . . . I cannot now say much about Malley tactics except I hope they're vigorous . . . I'm probably too busy licking my wounds to trust my impulses.' Later, making 'the utmost concession to the most rigid critical judgement', he remarked on 'a certain gawkiness' in some of the poems. He liked Ethel 'no end' and thought she was 'a finely conceived Jane Austen character'.

The hammer blows kept coming, and there was nowhere for Harris to shelter. At the end of June the new *Meanjin* came out with Hope's mauling of *The Vegetative Eye*. Harris was not amused: 'Another of the clan, the daddy of reaction,' he wrote to Reed on 1 July, 'has published a review . . . of utter injustice'. The piece was considered a great success, even by those sympathetic to Harris. 'Hope on V. Eye very nice,' Brian Elliott remarked. 'Max quite defensive which is a sign of success.' Harris had always revelled in going on the attack and now that he was being savaged himself the urge to lash out became irresistible. On the rebound, five days after the hoax broke, Harris did a hatchet job on the performance of an amateur theatre company in Adelaide. He swaggered into his badly proofed notice, and even quoted Ern Malley in flooring an actor whose voice lacked 'the fluidity and emotive control to ever be of dramatic use. (I have split the infinitive.)' His principal target was an amateur actress, a solicitor by profession, named Patricia Hackett:

Alack, and alas, and alaska! We have now seen Miss Hackett as a Biblical dame, Virgin Mary, a Moon Woman, Salome, a Grey Sword, Queen Elizabeth, and a Renaissance Wife. It remains only for her to play a Life of Stalin, Dinghillef [sic], and Little Nell.

Harris closed his piece by scoffing at the 'panther passions of the Hackett demi-monde'. It was a big mistake. He intended to suggest Hackett hovered between establishment and arty circles, not knowing that 'demi-mondaine' is a euphemism for whore.

Patricia Hackett came from the top drawer of colonial society. She was the daughter of Sir John Winthrop Hackett, an Irish Protestant out of Trinity College, Dublin, who had emigrated to Australia in 1875 at the age of twenty-seven. He became editor of the *West Australian*, a member of the Legislative Council, and prime mover in the foundation of the University of Western Australia. Sir John was 'not robust but highly strung. Aloof and imperious, with a strong sense of duty, he could yet charm with his melodious Irish voice.' Pat Hackett's mother, Deborah, was fiery and of independent mind, a great beauty with 'dark blue eyes and raven hair' who outlived three husbands, prospected for minerals in the remote deserts of Western Australia, and cut a formidable figure in the best drawing rooms of Perth, Adelaide and Melbourne.

Pat Hackett, who inherited her father's nervous, lofty disposition, and her mother's grasp of style, had a passion for drama. She converted the cellar of her house 'Nepenthe' in the Adelaide suburb of Hackney into a tiny playhouse where she staged for select audiences performances of classics like *Medea* or *Antony and Cleopatra* with herself in the leading roles. A slender, elegant, sharp-featured woman, she was not to be fooled with. Once, she summoned a journalist – a man named Sidney Downer, Cambridged-educated, and a member of the family that owned the *Advertiser* – from the gallery of the South Australian Parliament after he had written that she was 'not happily cast as the leading woman' in a production of Geza Silberer's *Caprice*. When he came within range she flung at him an open bottle of ink which connected above his eye and drenched his clothes. 'I took a bottle of ink to Parliament House to use the same weapon against a man that he had used against me,' said Miss Hackett. 'There was no altercation. The ink was thrown. He picked up the bottle from the floor and said, "Your ink, I think." I replied, "I think you have most of it", and left.' After everyone from the Premier down had expressed outrage at this violation of parliamentary decorum, Miss Hackett protested, 'I did not wish to make any disturbance whatsoever. It is regrettable that the inked person should have found it necessary to make a public showing of his inkiness.' She was convicted a week later of assault and fined £20, a hefty sum.

Hackett was furious with Harris. This insult would not be allowed to stand. He heard of her intention to sue for libel in the first week of July and decided to duck: an erratum notice was inserted into the next issue of *On Dit*, explaining the previous edition 'was not proofed, and innumerable errors crept into the type setting. In the theatre review "ideal" was an inaccuracy for "but nearer ideal". And "panther" for "pathetic". "Demi-monde" was actually "beau monde".'

Hackett didn't buy it. Three days later a writ for libel was issued out of the Supreme Court of South Australia by Charles Lempriere Abbott, King's Counsel, Member of the South Australian Legislative Assembly, whom Hackett had instructed to proceed against Harris. A red-faced, corpulent man, rather Falstaffian in appearance though certainly not in temperament, Abbott (whose nephew had helped dunk Harris in the Torrens three years earlier) was a traditionalist of the old school. He loathed modern art and in July 1942 was so offended by an exhibition of new work in Adelaide, sponsored by John Reed's Contemporary Art Society, that he twice raised the matter, amid parliamentary debate about fuel shortages and wartime austerity measures, of these 'peculiar pictures'. He was an ardent mason, eventually becoming Grand Master of the South Australian Grand Lodge, a passionate monarchist, and occasional scribbler of after-dinner verse. In court he was appalled by the poor expression of witnesses: constructions such as 'I seen' could elicit the retort, 'And where did you go to school?' The law at the time in South Australia permitted the use of the lash for certain violent and sexual crimes – when he became a judge in the Criminal Court Abbott made full use of these powers. His nickname, uttered out of earshot, was 'flogger'. He was elected to parliament as the member for Burnside in 1933, and by 1944 was Minister for Education and Attorney-General of South Australia.* From this elevated position he took aim at Harris.

Reed initially dismissed the whole episode as a joke and told Harris on 12 July to find himself a good lawyer: 'Quite possibly the whole thing can be got out of by an apology worded in such a way as to cover yourself as well as her. It is obviously not worth getting into an action if you can avoid it by any conceivable means. I don't expect you are enjoying it over much and these sorts of things are a nervous drain.' By now he was writing to Harris almost every day. On 19 July he said:

I haven't yet seen the article and don't know all the facts, but from what you have told me, I should have thought your position was not too bad and that your correction before the writ was issued would have made the Libel only a technical one at most, which would carry merely nominal damages and the probability of Hackett having to pay her own costs. You spoke on the phone of a lot of underlying dirty work which you were going to tell me about, but so far, haven't done so.

Reed underestimated Adelaide and the implacable Hackett. No news from Harris was bad news. Harris had now met Abbott at his chambers. He described the meeting as 'a remarkable experience' where he encountered 'hysterical, malicious abuse plus

---

*In 1946 Abbott became a judge on the Supreme Court of South Australia. He was eventually knighted.

gloating'. 'We can if necessary fight this matter through the
Supreme Court until the point of your bankruptcy,' he reported
Abbott told him, a threat he took to heart since he complained to
Reed: 'A charming prospect for a Minister for Education driving
a student to bankruptcy.' At the meeting Harris agreed to an
apology to be written by Abbott and published in newspapers
nominated by Hackett, at Harris's expense. In Melbourne on 21
July, John Reed picked up his copy of the *Herald*, and was
stunned to find on page three a statement by Harris acknow-
ledging he had committed 'a gross and malicious libel of Miss
Patricia Hackett which I now deeply and most sincerely deplore'.
Harris admitted his 'untruthful' erratum notice was intended 'to
shield myself from the legal consequences of my libel'. He
'sincerely and humbly apologized to Miss Hackett' and was
'grateful' to her for declining damages. Reed did not know, but
the apology also featured prominently in *On Dit* and the
Advertiser.

Reed was aghast at this new vivisection of Harris, and hurt
that he did not confide in him: 'It does not seem enough to say
that you are tired, very true though that may be, because we are
deeply involved in this with you,' he told Harris. 'You should
have disclosed to me right at the very outset the whole truth of
the business . . . I might then have been able to have been of some
real help to you – I would certainly have come over to Adelaide if
necessary.' Harris replied sadly to Reed about

certain inescapable things I do, perhaps immaturities, lacks of
balance in myself, which it is unfair for you people to have to suffer.
When my actions affect us all then I am heavily to blame . . . The
'libellous' article so-called was objectionable only on the basis of that
one word . . . I appear as a disproportionately menacing figure to
these people.

Self-contained and tightly organized, Adelaide was really a big
country town. Everybody knew who their enemies were. The
establishment had a pious regard for upright behaviour; now,
with *Angry Penguins*, the city had its own bohemia to cope with,

and Harris was *persona non grata*. Among those dedicated to the preservation of public order was the official responsible for police prosecutions, the Crown Solicitor, a man who signed the letters he wrote to the *Advocate* and the *Advertiser* A. J. Hannan, KC, but whom everybody knew as Tacky. A close friend of Attorney-General Abbott, Hannan was a devout Catholic, the holder of a Papal Knighthood, and a fierce anti-communist. He was also an influential member of Catholic Action, a vigorous lay movement dedicated to protect society from its sleazy elements, and instil Christian thinking into the community. Hannan subscribed to the *Advocate* where he read about the 'decadent perverts' who wrote for *Angry Penguins*. In fact he wrote to the paper on 12 July 1944, the same day Patrick O'Leary described Ern Malley as 'an imp of verbal darkness', complaining that current economic thinking in Australia had 'as little Christian principle as if it had been formulated by the Government of Turkey'.

Hannan took a dim view of what he saw as the shallow modern world, the collapse of solid values. Culture had ceased to be decent, to be 'culture'. He once lamented in an after-dinner speech the passing of the three-volume Victorian novel, and said that Adelaide did not deserve to be called 'The Athens of Australia' as it sometimes was. This was no city for rhapsodes, he said, filling out the metaphor. If someone 'were caught in Adelaide reciting an English version of "The Shield of Achilles",' he remarked, 'or declaiming Milton's Address to Light from *Paradise Lost*, he would almost certainly be dealt with under the City Council's By-Laws and might finish up in the Enfield Receiving Home'.

On 21 July, Tacky Hannan clipped Harris's apology to Pat Hackett from the *Advertiser* and pasted it to a blank sheet of paper. Harris's problems were not over yet.

When things go wrong they all go wrong. Malley, McAuley, Stewart, Hope, Hackett and Abbott fell on Harris like cluster bombs. And now Sidney Nolan, a fully fledged Angry Penguin and a full partner in all their enterprises, was in trouble in

Melbourne. Rattled by loneliness, boredom, and the prospect of death in combat, his tolerance of the army was exhausted. His unit had moved in February 1944 from the Wimmera to the Watsonia Barracks in Melbourne, not far from Heidelberg and the Reeds, who tried to look after him. In the midst of Malley, on 23 June, he fell ill with a pulse below fifty and a temperature below ninety-six. 'It is the culmination of too much strain which may lead anywhere,' Reed reported. By 5 July, Nolan was in camp hospital but

the doctor who is sympathetic if not very bright is going to try to get him to a psychiatrist at the Heidelberg Hospital. It *may* mean a discharge but may equally well mean being sent back to his unit. But there is no other course open. N is really a very sick man and pretty near to having had as much as he can take: he finally did get so sick he had to go to bed – no pulse no temperature & couldn't keep awake and couldn't eat and vomited whenever he tried to. Even then they made a valiant effort to decide he had a stomach ulcer!

By 11 July he had

battled his way through to a psychiatrist & at least pinned him down to an hour's talk. The psych says he will do what he can but he can't work miracles & has his own personal responsibility to consider. If Nolan would only cut off his ear they would be quite happy. The M.O. said 'you are all right now & I don't see how you can be discharged – I give you another 12 months'! At any rate Nolan has made up his own mind he is not going back to the Army.

This day or the next Nolan leapt the camp fence and deserted. For a while he lay low at Heide, recovering his strength. A criminal now, on the run from the military police, Nolan vanished. He shed his official identity and, while Reed organized fake papers for him, thought about Ern Malley whose significance he was sure of. On 14 July he wrote to Malcolm Good, a member of the Communist Party, to account for the way the Angry Penguins embraced Ern Malley.

John Reed was influenced by Max's judgement, perhaps reinforced by myself. It is asking a great deal of us isn't it to, in effect, betray the very experience we function by. The hoax has caused us to question many fundamentals in ourselves, naturally it has had a sharp and bewildering impact, but I must insist the way out of it is also a human one . . . Doubless Macauley [sic] and Stewart intended to do all they said, but I think you will agree that previous history is packed full of examples of men who were overwhelmed by a reality they helped to build . . . the authors have built the poems with the language of this immediate time, which seems natural enough, and have then distorted the implications of doing so. Which seems foolish.

> But no one warned that the mind repeats
> In its ignorance the vision of others.

Is that not an accurate and lovely description of the mysterious way in which art has persisted? What has hoax got to do with it? Poetry such as that may be somebody's poison but it is not mine. It deepens my insight not the reverse. Again, from 'Documentary Film':

> Footscray:
> The slant sun now descending
> Upon the montage of the desecrate womb
> Opened like a drain.

Is that true or not true? It seems like a fair and above board description of Footscray. It is hardly a matter of aesthetics even. I have worked in these suburbs, knowing the people in them and have felt such evenings. But because of two poets who assert it is all a hoax anyway, I forget about Footscray?

> I have remembered the chiaroscuro
> Of your naked breasts and loins.

As a painter this presents me with an image that refers me to the perfect fluidity of Rembrandt. What do I do then, choke out these valid memories and images because the poets hoaxed me these too? And so on. They have even hoaxed the 'scrub-typhus of Mubo'.

I have quoted only a few lines, but enough I hope to make clear that my reaction to Malley derives its acceptance [from] a quite serious and genuine belief that the poems deal in experiences that are accessible to me & many of them talking a more instinctively familiar language than I have yet found in Australia.

This was a personal defence of Malley by a working-class boy who wanted to go his own way free of Party strictures, and Malley gave him a focus. 'I learnt to paint in precisely the same way as any other worker would have to do. Look around him, use his eyes, fight for the opportunity to strengthen his vision,' he remarked to Good, with a nod towards Malley's 'Preface and Statement': 'The relationship of the artist to the people is by no means (as things stand) a simple straight-line relationship.'

Ethel Malley, seer without a mind, foresaw everything. Six months before Sidney Nolan went AWOL she wrote to Harris: 'I hardly like to say this and I know I can rely on you to treat it as *strictly confidential* but I have an idea that Ern might have got into some sort of trouble in Melbourne and gone under another name.' Nolan's desertion made this fiction prescient. Almost the instant McAuley and Stewart dropped their masks, Nolan donned his. He emerged from hiding as Robin Murray – and with papers to prove it. Under this phoney identity, he produced many of the Wimmera paintings, the St Kilda paintings and, most famously, the series based on the infamous Ned Kelly, the iron-helmeted outlaw. 'Without Ern Malley there wouldn't have been any Ned Kelly,' he later remarked. 'It made me take the risk of putting against the Australian bush an utterly strange object.' In 1948 Nolan took advantage of an amnesty and was dishonour-ably discharged from the army.

As an old man, a famous painter and a knight of the realm, Nolan recalled that, 'your heightened perception, which you got as a birthright from not being educated or born into a structured society, gave you the insight or the freedom to do what you thought fit'. Nolan did not desert from the army because he conscientiously objected to war. 'I didn't think it was wrong to go to the wars, and lots of my friends were at the wars,' he remembered.

I just wasn't interested whether the Japanese came or whether they didn't come. If they didn't come now they would come in fifty years time. I just took it for granted that these kinds of things could happen, that you would change your identity according to circumstances. What was your identity or who did it belong to? Did it belong to the Australian Army or did it belong to poetry or did it belong to your father or mother?

These were questions Nolan had been mulling for some time. In December 1942 he did a painting called *Head of a Soldier*. It is an image of a warped, misshapen head, the bruised and bloodied face dominated by glazed Picassoid eyes, grotesque mouth and lolling tongue. The soldier wears an army issue slouch hat but has no rank, no identity. So compelling is the stylization of insanity that the staring vacant head becomes like a mask, excessive and cartoonish. The painting was used on the cover of Reg Ellery's *The Psychiatric Aspects of Modern Warfare* which Reed & Harris published in 1945, a study of the trauma of massed battle under unprecedented conditions. Ellery was a left-wing Freudian, reputed to have the largest private library in Melbourne, with over 10,000 volumes. Like everybody else he was remarkably productive during the war. He wrote a study of schizophrenia, and several starry-eyed accounts of life in the Soviet Union, one of which sold 30,000 copies, an impressive figure in Australia in 1944. His opening sentences in *The Psychiatric Aspects of Modern Warfare* were like a gloss on the painting on its cover: 'This books deals not with lunacy but with war. The two subjects have more in common than their names suggest. They are almost exclusively human phenomena, and both are rooted in irrationality.' To emphasize the point he illustrated the book with drawings from Goya's *The Disasters of War*.

Head of a Soldier was to persist in Nolan's mind. In 1973 he began work on a series of paintings and calligraphic drawings based on the Ern Malley poems. He wanted to show that Malley 'did make sense by doing a drawing of each four lines to try to prove to McAuley and Stewart that the thing did have a logic and a meaning like other forms of poetry, and it wasn't nonsense'. Among these works was his celebrated portrait of Malley himself, a brutal garish death's head, bloody and bespectacled.

Ern Malley turns out to be a direct descendant of *Head of a Soldier*. Here too is the slouch hat, the streaky face, the lolling tongue, the army shirt stripped of insignia. But what in 1942 was an almost comic dislocation of form becomes in the later painting gruesome and confrontational. The face flares with a peacock's tail of blood. The obscene tongue dangles in mockery. The eyes behind the glasses are blind splodges of blue. Cadaver teeth push through the mouth. Not much else in Nolan's arsenal of work is so aggressive and contemptuous.

Nolan's Malley is an outcast, a grotesque leering rebel who can never be brought into the fold. Why depict him like this? Why echo the earlier work? In part to evoke the period, and because the hoax was produced by two poets in uniform. In part to suggest Ern Malley's berserk, anarchic qualities. But this painting is autobiographical. Nolan gave each work in the 1973 Ern Malley series a subtitle lifted from the poems. He picked the epigraph to the portrait of Malley from 'Boult to Marina', and, thirty years later, directly linked his fugitive exit from military life with the hoax. Nolan's desertion answered Boult's question – 'What would you have me do? Go to the wars?' – in a word.

Amid these crises, Reed and Harris continued to work on the next issue of *Angry Penguins* which was to present a symposium of diverse opinions on the hoax. Not everyone from whom they solicited pieces liked Ern Malley but the idea was to suggest ways in which the poetry could be discussed seriously. Alec Chisholm, Dean of the Faculty of Arts and Professor of French at Melbourne University, thought some of Ern Malley was 'really good poetry', and doubted the poems could have been written in an afternoon. 'Trying to write pidgin poetry and feign poetic drunkenness,' he said, the hoaxers 'lapsed into poetry more often than they intended'. Brian Elliott was of the view that McAuley and Stewart were 'blind to the brilliance of their execution . . . Their intention was manifestly serious, and so have the results been.' Albert Tucker saw in Ern Malley 'acts of recognition which depend on feeling and intuition rather than intellectual apprehension' and noted that 'highly civilized artists have also produced some of their finest work under conditions where willed, intellectual control of meaning and conscious adherence to any aesthetic standard has been suspended by drug, sleep, trance, illness or the simple acceptance of images and meanings which occur involuntarily'.* H. M. Green, historian of Australian literature, thought the hoax 'was justified and timely, as an attack upon a perversion of poetry that has spread to three continents and misled a number of talented young men, of whom Mr Harris is an outstanding Australian example'. His wife Dorothy, to whom McAuley wrote his letters from Bungendore, argued that most of Ern Malley was 'not poetry at all, but prose, and at times very poor prose'. Her only objection to the 'Ern Malley experiment' was 'the indiscriminate condemnation it has brought on modernist art'. For their part, Harris and Reed affirmed their belief in 'the substantial correctness' of their judgement.

Reed and Harris decided the best way to affirm their faith in Ern Malley was to reprint his poems in book form as well. The question was, did the Penguins have the right to do this? Harris had no doubts. 'I suggest 1,000 copies & to hell with the authors,' Harris wrote to Reed. 'Ethel told us we could use the poems as we wanted.' *The Darkening Ecliptic* was released in September 1944. Five hundred copies were exported, and the run sold out. Then Penguins also hit on another line of defence for their 'primitive' poet Ern Malley. By chance Albert Tucker stumbled on some paintings in a bike-shop window, and discovered they were by a man named 'Tipper', an eccentric famous for riding from Melbourne to Sydney on a penny-farthing. Tipper was also the first person – surely the last as well – to ride a 5″ bicycle while singing 'The Highlands and the Lowlands'. Reed described the pictures as 'really delightful, with the naive and

---

*Tucker recalls discussing the hoax with its two architects over a minestrone at the Latin Café in Bourke Street. He began to outline his views about Ern Malley but the conversation came to an abrupt end when McAuley, followed by Stewart, stood up and stormed out of the restaurant. After this, Tucker painted his gaunt, tight-lipped portrait, *Ern Malley disguised as James McAuley*.

bright colourful approach of the true primitive' and he chose one for the cover of *Angry Penguins* which showed Tipper

in the centre with a penny-farthing bicycle set in a bush scene, complete with little stream and house and a winding path that, to go up-hill, leaves the ground completely. Perspective is of course ignored, but there is a lovely over-all harmony with the little incidents and figures picked out with devoted attention. If this doesn't shake the troops, nothing will.

On 3 July, Reed told Harris that 'the Tipper (primitive painter) idea seems more essential than ever as a powerful challenge and vindication of our aesthetic judgement'. Harris agreed it showed the Penguins were 'full of fight, & not retracing our steps from the path of vigour & originality one iota. I absolutely and unreservedly commend any moves to present another genius.'

Tipper's work graced the cover of the December 1944 issue of *Angry Penguins*. Sales were quiet, Reed reported,

but yesterday Mullens put all the Tipper paintings in their front window and we are hoping this will boost things along. If it won't, then nothing will, as the crowds are gathering outside and there is plenty of curiosity. The window really looks quite spectacular with the five Tippers and a couple of dozen copies of Penguins ranged around them.

Not among the browsers was A. D. Hope, who retorted to Christesen: 'What did you mean by asking what I think of *Angry Penguins* now? Have they been hoaxed again? I don't see their publication unless someone lends me a copy. I suppose it's too much to hope that someone has turned up with documents to prove that their famous primitive painter is really a chap called William Dobell.'

On the afternoon of Tuesday, 1 August, Max Harris was at work on the new issue of *Angry Penguins* in the Reed & Harris office in the centre of Adelaide. There were also end-of-term exams approaching for which he would have to cram. At about 3.30 p.m. two policemen, one in uniform, the other plainclothed, came to the door. The man in uniform did the talking, a certain Detective Vogelesang. 'We are police officers,' he said. 'What is your name?'

'Max Harris,' said Harris.

'We would like to have a talk with you. Are you the editor of a magazine *Angry Penguins*?'

'Well not exactly,' explained Harris, 'for there is a committee of four, of which I am one. There is Mr John Reed in Melbourne, Mrs Sunday Reed, and Mr Sidney Nolan.'

'Are you and the committee responsible for the publication of the magazine?'

'Well, what happens is that the articles are submitted to us, and when they are finally approved the book is printed in Victoria.'

Vogelesang assured himself that Harris was one of the proprietors of *Angry Penguins*, and was responsible for its distribution in South Australia. Then:

'I understand that in the Autumn number there was an Ern Malley section that you were responsible for publishing.'

'Yes.'

'Did you cause it to be published?'

'Together with the other members of the committee.'

'Was it submitted to you for publication?'

'Yes.' Harris had answered every question in good faith. It was time for the police to declare themselves. 'What is this inquiry about?' he asked.

'It is in reference to the magazine *Angry Penguins*,' Vogelesang answered unhelpfully.

'What do you want to know?'

'We first want to know if we are speaking to someone responsible for its publication and distribution.'

Harris was unsettled by now. 'I don't know whether I ought to answer your questions,' he said.

'You can please yourself about that.'

'Is this on the record or off the record?'

Vogelesang put on an official manner. 'We have been instructed to make inquiries and we are making inquiries in connection with the provisions of the Police Act with respect to immoral or indecent publications,' he said.

Max Harris gaped.

9 Indecent, Immoral, Obscene

The *Angry Penguins* obscenity trial was listed for Tuesday, 5 September 1944 at 10 a.m. in the Adelaide Police Court, a modest two-storey sandstone edifice with shuttered windows, on Victoria Square, before Stipendiary Magistrate Mr L. C. Clarke. Clarke was rather English in appearance, a tall, thin, white-haired man in spectacles. His manner was dry and plain and he was not famous for his wit. The usual business of his court was to punish misdemeanours: public drunkenness, reckless driving, petty theft. Mr D. C. Williams, of the Crown Solicitor's Department, a tough and gritty barrister only a few years older than Harris, prosecuted. Eric Millhouse, who was well-reputed in Adelaide legal circles, appeared for the defence. Harris entered a plea of 'Not Guilty' to the alleged offence of 'Indecent Advertisements'.

He had been preparing his defence ever since Detective Vogelesang's unwelcome visit. Reed flew to Adelaide as soon as he heard about the possibility of a prosecution. He arrived on Thursday, 3 August and left the following Monday, after helping to arrange legal representation for Harris. While the Penguins anxiously waited for a summons to be issued, they planned their strategy. Harris tried without success to get the librarians at the university and the public library to give evidence, since both institutions made *Angry Penguins* 'available for tender minds, and apparently consider it does no harm'. It was not clear what Harris would be charged with: obscenity or – far more seriously – blasphemy, or both. When the summons did arrive on 25 August, Harris telegrammed Reed at noon: 'NO REFERENCE TO BLASPHEMY . . . FINGERS CROSSED'. A few days later Harris thought he might have found an Adelaide parson to give evidence for the Penguins, but then wired: 'PARSON HERE HAS RATTED IS SKIPPING TOWN'. He sought out other witnesses to appear for them. Reed would give evidence, of course. J. I. M. Stewart, Reg Ellery and Brian Elliott agreed to testify. In the lead-up to the trial, Professor Stewart was summoned to the registrar's office at the University of Adelaide. Here he found a judge of the South Australian Supreme Court waiting to advise him 'most strongly' not to testify in Harris's favour. Five decades later Stewart could not recall the name of the judge, but the Vice Chancellor, Sir Herbert Parsons, also sat on the Supreme Court. Whoever applied the pressure, Stewart stood his ground.

In a moment of pique Harris declared he was finished with Australia but Reed pulled him up short on the idea that the country was not a fit place to publish serious work. 'For goodness sake, don't let us have that,' he told him. A few days later Reed added: 'It is not any picnic, but on the other hand, we can't pretend that we never envisaged such a thing as this and the very role we play has made it fairly inevitable.' Harris warned that 'if a policy of persecution and moral gangsterism develops in the cultural field of this country, then the whole tendency will be to destroy the integral impulse to creativity'. He was 'fairly calm', he said, 'but overall the past few months are making a pretty deep and permanent impression on me'. He began to realize just how isolated and precarious his position was in the Athens of the South. If a vendetta was being waged against him, it was possible the police would not only prosecute *Angry Penguins* but his novel *The Vegetative Eye* as well. Bundles of unsold copies sat in Harris's office. What if the authorities came after these too? At the *Women's Weekly* Catherine Caris came up with a solution. In secret she and Harris carried his copies of *The Vegetative Eye* down Grenfell Street into her office and stashed them in the storeroom under back numbers of the *Weekly*. The police would never think of looking *there*.

Harris believed the case derived directly from the 'personal reactions' of the Crown Solicitor, Tacky Hannan, to himself and *Angry Penguins*. 'It is quite certain Catholic Action is the guiding force,' he wrote to Reed. Near the end of August 'a complaint' was laid against Harris under Section 108 of the South Australian Police Act, which alleged that in Adelaide, in June 1944, he sold certain 'indecent advertisements'. Hannan signed the letter to *Angry Penguins* identifying thirteen passages in the magazine the Crown found offensive, seven of them in Ern Malley, the rest in Harris's writing, and the work of other contributors, including Peter Cowan and Dal Stivens, and the poet Laurence Collinson.

Section 108 defined 'indecent advertisements' as 'printed matter of an indecent immoral or obscene nature'. It had been on the books since 1897, when expurgated editions of the classics, especially for consumption in classrooms, were common. There was no allowance for literary or artistic merit as a defence: the only materials the section exempted were 'bona fide medical works'. The chief legal test of obscenity applied by Australian, British and American courts in 1944 dated from the Victorian era. In *Regina v. Hicklin* (1868) Mr Justice Cockburn specified the test as 'whether the tendency of the matter charged as obscenity is to deprave and corrupt those whose minds are open to such immoral influences, and into whose hands a publication of this sort may fall'. Strictly applied, this meant that if the kids could flick through a copy of *Angry Penguins* on the coffee table or in a bookshop, then the magazine's claim to be a serious literary and artistic forum could not constitute a defence against obscenity.

When Harris was summonsed this was the first official attempt ever to suppress Australian poetry. But censorship was common in Australia. In the 1930s the Customs Department prohibited thousands of books from entering the country. The NSW Collector of Customs, in a crude affirmation of Hicklin, announced in 1930 that the department's test was 'whether the average householder would accept the book in question as reading matter for his family'. Among the proscribed authors were Joyce (*Ulysses* and *Dubliners*), Defoe (*Moll Flanders*), Huxley (*Brave New World*), Orwell (*Down and Out in Paris and London*), Hemingway (*A Farewell to Arms*), Dos Passos (*1919*) and Hermann Broch (*The Sleepwalkers*). By 1944 many of these books had been released but hundreds of others were still banned.

The *Angry Penguins* trial concluded a script which nobody without a sense of humour could have invented, and nobody with one could resist. If the Ern Malley poems were surreal, so was the situation. The trial confirmed all over again that the hoax had demolished its literary boundaries, and invaded the world. It made Ern Malley even more famous and legitimized the shrieks of approval that greeted the hoax. McAuley and Stewart had not for a second intended to trick Harris into the courts. They failed to realize that Ern Malley would hand out guns to philistines – and now the state was providing the bullets. The trial was a shambles, with none of the rapier wit of the hoax. The police evidence was risible, the Crown prosecutor a lowbrow bulldog, and the defence counsel out of his depth.

The trial was the hottest show in town. Nothing like this had ever happened in Adelaide before. On the morning of 5 September, the courtroom on Victoria Square was 'crowded as a picture theatre', and buzzing with anticipation. The national press was in attendance, and the trial was reported throughout the country. Many had come to watch the law in action as a form of spectator sport though not everybody there was friendly to Harris. He reported to Reed that there were 'hordes of Catholics' in the courtroom. A few Angry Penguins turned up to lend moral support: Geoff Dutton wore his air-force uniform to raise the tone among the bohemians.

First witness for the prosecution was Reg Carter, manager of the Argonaut Business Library in Adelaide, who had done a very brisk trade in the Ern Malley edition of *Angry Penguins*. Under questioning by Williams, he testified that he had ordered in four separate batches of the magazine for public sale. Cross-examined by Millhouse, Carter informed the court that in 'quite a number of modern books' the words 'loving', 'bugger' and 'bastard' could be found and seemed to offend nobody. This was a very inauspicious start for the Crown case. It had been Williams' idea to have the bookseller testify and his eyes 'popped' in disbelief as Carter stepped down.

The Crown then called its major witness, Detective Vogelesang, whose name translates into English as 'birdsong' but who was known around town as 'Dutchie'. Vogelesang was Nordic in appearance: he was a tall, well-built man with an open face, square jaw, fair hair and blue eyes. He stood up straight in his uniform and obtained the court's permission to recount from notes his questioning of the defendant on 1 August. That afternoon, the court learned, Jacobus Andries Vogelesang, Detective stationed at Adelaide, armed with a copy of *Angry Penguins* (Autumn number, 1944), had visited Maxwell Henley Harris, Student, of 20 Churchill Avenue, Glandore, in his office at Room 83, Second Floor, Brookman Buildings, Grenfell Street, Adelaide and for the attention of the defendant had opened the magazine to page 11, where Ern Malley's poem 'Sweet William' was printed.

'Are you acquainted with all the poems in the Ern Malley section?' asked Vogelesang.

'Yes,' said Harris.

Vogelesang waved a hand at the magazine where the poem was fully visible.

'What is the theme of that poem?' he asked, like a teacher prodding a student.

'I don't know what the author intended by that poem,' Harris replied. 'You had better ask him what he meant.'

Vogelesang was not about to tolerate any sophistry about literary intention. He had his own ideas about the theme of the poem and they had nothing to do with who wrote it. There was another thing too – if the gossip was true, finding the author might prove a slippery task. Harris was the man he wanted. 'What do *you* think it means?'

'I am not going to express an opinion.'

Vogelesang saw straight through this. 'That means you have an opinion but you are not prepared to express it.'

Harris paused. 'I would have to give it two or three hours

consideration before I could determine what it means,' he said.

Detective Vogelesang did not have that long. The kind of meaning he had in mind was easier to find. It was time to drop a hint. The magazine was spread open on its spine. 'Do you think it is suggestive of indecency?'

'I haven't got an opinion,' said Harris.

The suspect was being difficult. Detective Vogelesang turned the page and pointed with his policeman's finger at 'Boult to Marina'. He renewed the exegetical pressure. 'What do you think this poem is about?'

Harris looked at him. 'Do you know anything about the classical characters?' he asked.

A bluff, best ignored. 'What I want to know is what it means,' said Detective Vogelesang in a gruff voice. The scene of the crime lay still on the page.

'Pericles and Boult are both classical characters and, when you know what they stand for, you can understand the poem.'

'Do you think the poem is suggestive of indecency?' inquired Detective Vogelesang, sticking to his task.

'No more than Shakespeare or Chaucer or others.'

Vogelesang thrust into this opening. 'You admit then that there is a suggestion of indecency about the poem?'

'No I don't,' said Harris. 'If you are looking for that sort of thing, I can refer you to plenty of books and cheaper publications that you can fill your department with. Our publication is intended for cultured minds, who understand these things, and place ordinary thoughts on a higher level.'

Vogelesang was not about to place ordinary thoughts on a higher level. 'What does it mean when it says "Part of me remains, wench, Boult-upright / The rest of me drops off into the night"?'

'I can't help the interpretation that some people might place on it.'

'Do you think that some people could place an indecent interpretation on it?' Vogelesang could, but didn't want to say so.

'Some people could place an indecent interpretation on anything,' said Harris.

'Well, what is your opinion of the poem?'

'I haven't got one,' said Max Harris, learning fast.

They stumbled through 'Night Piece' and its alternative version. When Harris confessed he didn't have an opinion on either poem, Vogelesang thought it time for some straight talk and told the court he informed the defendant, 'I think they suggest sexual matters, and I consider they are immoral.' Harris had no opinion either about 'Perspective Lovesong' and 'Egyptian Register'. Detective Vogelesang did and fixated on the word 'genitals': 'The genitals refer to the sexual parts,' he remarked brightly. 'I think it unusual for the sexual parts to be referred to in poetry.'

Detective Vogelesang thought it unusual for the sexual parts to be referred to in prose as well. He was worried by the phrase 'You can stick the money' in Peter Cowan's story 'The Fence' and asked Harris, 'Do you think it might mean "stick it up your anus", or the word that is used more vulgarly?' He isolated this passage of dialogue between a woman and a man in Dal Stivens' story, 'You Call Me By My Proper Name':

'You men,' she said. 'You're all the same. You always reckon it must be another fellow when a girl says she don't want to see you any more. You're all the same, the lot of you. You only want one thing.'

'It ain't like you to talk this way.'

'What the hell do you know about me?' Vera said loudly. 'All you men only want one thing from a girl.'

'You like it,' he said.

The girl's face went red and her head went down. Her hair fell over her face and she said, softly: 'It's all right for men. It's different for girls.'

Harris didn't think this indecent or immoral but Vogelesang did. 'Have you considered its effect on, say, high school children?' he asked. The detective also alerted Harris to dangerous tendencies in his own poetry. Harris had published a poem called 'Birdsong' in the Autumn issue of *Angry Penguins* but

Vogelesang passed over it. About others he was troubled, including this passage from 'The Journey North' which he read aloud:

> New Year brought its concertinas in,
> the redundant festivities of piano and song
> for the flatchested women of the camp,
> whose genitals ached like very hell
> for the passionate copulation in satin
> and passivity by the lowtuned radio,
> waking to the morning aubade of trams.

'Does it mean that the woman's sexual parts are aching for an evening dress?'

Harris, perhaps in amazement, agreed.

'Don't you think that is immoral?' asked Detective Vogelesang. He finished reading from his notes, and Williams tendered the Ern Malley issue of *Angry Penguins* as an exhibit.

Vogelesang's evidence under cross-examination by Millhouse was a sensation. He brought the house down. Williams had already tried to silence the simpering gallery by remarking that he would like to have some of the audience in the witness box. 'They would look a lot sillier than they look at present,' he said in a loud voice. Now the circling guffaws elicited a warning from Clarke, the SM: 'I want to make it clear that this is not an entertainment and on any more outbursts of laughter the persons responsible will be ejected.'

Vogelesang had not volunteered for this job. He admitted under cross-examination from Millhouse that he had only read *Angry Penguins* in order to question Harris about it. His opinions about the immorality of the material were his own, he added. He declared he had heard the expression 'you can stick it' several times, but 'not among other members of the police force, never'. (Gales of laughter swirled around the courtroom.) 'I did regard it as part of a phrase, such as "stick it up your anus",' Vogelesang explained. 'It is frequently used, abbreviated. There are lots of endings to it, all meaning the one thing. I have heard other meanings to it. It was on account of my hearing other meanings to it that I attached a meaning to it. I think that meaning would apply to other people, even if they heard other things.'

Meanings budded, flowered and died. If Ern Malley was written to be misread, no one had misread him like this. In 'Sweet William' Vogelesang objected 'to the thing as a whole', he said. 'The last five lines of the first verse are suggestive of sexual intercourse and the second verse is suggestive of the person or whoever it is having yielded to the temptation of sexual intercourse.' Is this person a man or a woman, Millhouse asked. 'In the second verse I should think perhaps it is a man. I think it is a man or somebody who has yielded to sexual temptation.' Prodded further, Vogelesang admitted, 'I couldn't say if it is a man or woman. In the second verse, because it is related to the five lines of the first verse, it refers to sexual intercourse. In the second verse, "My white swan of quietness lies quiet in the black swan's breast", the person "I" is testifying how he yielded to the temptation.' Again he insisted, 'That has not been suggested to me by anyone, that is the meaning I attached to it.'

Millhouse took the detective through 'Boult to Marina'. Vogelesang had read *Pericles* but 'before I interviewed Mr Harris, I did not know who Boult was, nor who Marina was. I knew the play of *Pericles*. I have read it, but I did not associate Boult with it, nor Marina.' In this poem Vogelesang objected to the words 'Boult-upright' and 'You shall rest snug tonight and know what I mean.' 'I don't think it could mean Boult was an upright man,' he said. 'It offends my decency to suggest that a character means that he wants sexual intercourse. I think that is immoral. That governs my opinion with regard to all these matters, where intercourse is referred to, I take it as immoral, in the circumstances in which we find them here. I would consider under certain circumstances that it was indecent to talk about the sexual act, to discuss it with a friend, for example.'

Ern Malley had no friends. Perhaps his lonely existence drew him to write about parks at night, a subject that had Vogelesang fingering his truncheon. 'Apparently someone is shining a torch in the dark,' he said, 'visiting through the park gates. To my mind they were going there for some disapproved motive.' His clue was the iron birds with rusty beaks. 'The nature of the time they went there and the disapproval of the iron birds, make me say it is immoral. I have found that people who go into parks at night go there for immoral purposes,' Vogelesang told the court. 'My experience as a police officer might under certain circumstances tinge my appreciation of literature.'

'Perspective Lovesong' suggested 'that someone is inquiring for intercourse'. Vogelesang vouched for the independence of his interpretation. 'That was all out of my mind,' he said. 'No one has mentioned it to me.' Of the word 'genitals' from 'Egyptian Register', he observed, confusing object and referent, 'they don't fit into the rest of the poem.' And he regarded the word 'incestuous' as being indecent. 'I don't know what "incestuous" means,' Vogelesang added. 'I think there is a suggestion of indecency about it.' But not about 'concupiscence to foin' from 'Young Prince of Tyre' which Vogelesang had not read when he interviewed Harris and confessed he did not understand when he did.

'I object to any description of any female parts in poems,' said Vogelesang. He complained about the line 'from the mother's womb the child is scraped away' which he stumbled on in a poem by Laurence Collinson. 'I wouldn't object if someone said, "Mrs Brown had a curette". If you said in the street, "Mrs Brown had her womb scraped", I would regard that as immoral.'

Millhouse announced he had no further questions and Detective Vogelesang stepped down. It was an astonishing performance.*

Williams summarized in an attempt to bring the Crown case

*During a visit to Adelaide in mid 1989 I copied from the local directory the number of every Vogelesang in the city, and set about phoning them. The retired police officer, whom his wife retrieved from his vegetable patch, was not pleased to hear from me and poured scorn on the 'research' I earnestly tried to describe to him. 'You'd be surprised how many jokers get grants to do this sort of thing,' he scoffed. I persisted, tried various tacks, got nowhere and decided to lighten the tone. 'It sounds like you must have had some fun with the *Angry Penguins* thing.'

back to life after the mauling Vogelesang had given it. The poetry of Ern Malley offended public standards, he suggested, and its spurious authorship was somehow related to this. 'Rumour had it,' said Williams, 'that Ern Malley did not even exist.' It was not easy to tell if the poems were on trial for obscurity or indecency and the confusion of the two had already become central to the Crown's case in Vogelesang's evidence. 'In parts, the so-called literature in the publication is impossible to understand,' Williams told the magistrate. 'From an ordinary man's point of view one cannot comprehend some of the sentences and critic-isms. Reference to sex is dragged in by the heels by some authors and it did not always fit in with the matter in question. There are not many pages in the book that do not refer to sex in some form or other, but I do not claim that they are all indecent. It is true that in places it is difficult to understand what the references to sex do or mean to imply but in other places no doubt exists what the authors meant.'

The prosecution rested its case. The show had lasted three hours. At 1 p.m. the court was adjourned until 26 September.

Ninety minutes later Harris walked across Victoria Square beneath the baleful stare of the grimy monarch and wired a triumphant message to Reed from the post office, 'MILLHOUSE THRASHED DUMB DETECTIVE'. A day or so later he dismissed Vogelesang as 'terribly pure'. But Harris – whose wife Von recalled how the couple were hissed at and cat-called in the streets of Adelaide – admitted he was feeling 'rather queer' and complained to Reed of

an irrational fear of physical violence, of being followed, of a secret powerful enemy in anyone who stares at me – & the cumulative effect is that I am now very much stared at in a small town like this. I can stand the fight, the force of mind, but the notoriety is distracting me so that I'm having to pull myself together all the time. I'm taking

---

'Fun!' he exploded. 'Is that what you think it was!' I mumbled something about wanting to get all sides of the story. 'Look,' he said, refusing to mix metaphors, 'it's a closed book.' And, politely dismissing me, hung up the phone.

too much Nembutal for the sake of sleep. I have not mentioned these things to anyone else – I try to face them out in verse. You're a sort of deus-ex-machina of sanity.

The adjournment was to allow Millhouse to fit the defence of *Angry Penguins* around his schedule. On 11 September Harris reported that in reaction to the trauma of the case he was experiencing 'an intellectual burst' and was writing poetry 'at fever pitch'. Then, exactly one week later, the *Angry Penguins* defence was left in 'chaos and confusion' when Millhouse announced his timetable would not allow him to appear in court on 26 September after all. Two days later a replacement barrister was found, Mr E. Phillips, who called Harris as the first witness for the defence when the case resumed.

There was a minor victory, against the objections of the Crown, when Stewart, Ellery and Elliott were permitted to remain in court as expert witnesses. Harris was led through the contentious passages by Phillips and accounted for each in turn. Williams objected to almost every question.

'Sweet William', Harris testified, 'discusses entirely a man at conflict with himself, without reference to anything else beside his mental condition. He has been subject to some image of desire symbolized by the "English eyes" and he finds himself within a mental or almost schizophrenic conflict. The "stone feet down the staircase of flesh" is a reference or an associative image from Mozart's *Don Giovanni* where the stone statue walks, and it is used to symbolize the conflict between his emotions of desire and what he later calls "self-denial". These two emotions are in conflict with each other, and the idea of the different mental aspects of the man struggling to destroy him is obscene in that dictionary sense which refers to "obscene" as "repulsive"; and "rape" of course is used in its classical sense "rapio" to seize, and need not have any sexual connection at all.'

The point of 'Boult to Marina', Harris claimed, was that 'for the first time some sort of noble trait is evoked in Boult, for although as the poem claims he might have silken eyes to kiss, part of him preserves integrity. The rest is still as before or drops off into the night.' 'Perspective Lovesong' introduced 'biographical elements' into the series: 'Malley is treating the moment of plighting of troth between himself and his beloved,' said Harris, 'but having a sense of impending death, the moment contains within itself not the finality of lovers plighting their troth, associated with the guillotine, but the abattoirs, which is associated with the carcass. His premonition of death gives a sense of unreality to the scene, and it is as if they were under sea with the wise grinning shark, his premonition of death, confronting him.' Harris denied the prosecution's contortionist claim that 'Egyptian Register' dragged in 'the genitals by the heels'. The poem was 'a study of the magical qualities of nature', he said. Court was adjourned at 12.50 until 2.15 p.m.

After lunch Harris was cross-examined by the Crown.

'Do you consider yourself one of the greatest Australian writers?' opened Williams.

'I do not,' answered Harris. 'I wrote a book called *The Vegetative Eye*.'

'Do you consider that a great work?'

'I am not in the position, as being so near to it, I leave that to the critics.'

'Do you consider the poems of Ern Malley to be great literary work?'

'I consider them serious literary work.'

'Are they a major event in Australian literary history?'

'In certain respects. Their technique has not been developed before.'

This line of questioning had nothing to do with the alleged indecency of Ern Malley. Harris was getting his comeuppance, and the poems, it seemed, were on trial for the fact that they existed.

'Take a person, myself, whose only training in literature is up to English I at the university. Should I be able to understand the poems of Ern Malley?'

'Most English I students can.'

'That is to say, I suppose, that most people of ordinary intellect should be able to understand Ern Malley?'

'I don't think it reflects on their intellect, it is a matter of if you can understand it. If you are quite illiterate you couldn't understand them.'

'Do you think that a court should be able to understand Malley's poems without any assistance from you?'

'It may be able to, it may not, it depends on the court.'

'Then do you say that a person who cannot understand the Ern Malley poems is not necessarily a fool?'

'Quite.'

Ern Malley was a bastard son. Williams aired the delicate question of his parentage. There were no objections from Phillips.

'You believe now that no such person as Ern Malley exists, don't you?'

'Yes.'

'Whom do you now believe to be the author or authors of those poems?'

'As rumour has it, Mr McAuley and Mr Stewart.'

'And have you any belief as to the purpose which the authors had in mind in writing the Ern Malley poems?'

'They claimed to be hoaxing the members of a modernistic culturism.'

'Don't you believe that Ern Malley's poems were never intended to be serious work at all?'

'I have no opinion on their intentions. I only worry about their content as poems.'

'Assuming that the poems were written by the gentlemen you mentioned, and that they wrote them as a hoax and with no serious purpose in view, do you still say their work is significant?'

'Yes.'

'And you say that it doesn't matter if the significance is accidental or otherwise?'

'I don't know if the significance is accidental. I am concerned with the significance.'

'So that this is the position, is it not, that nothing would shake your faith as literary work in the Ern Malley poems?'

'No.'

Williams now sought to establish that the Ern Malley poems were meaningless gibberish. He took Shakespeare as his model of clarity in English verse: 'The majority of people in Australia would regard the poems as nothing but rubbish.'

'Yes, and Shakespeare.'

'But you don't claim that a person reading *Pericles, Prince of Tyre*, after reading it wouldn't know what he had read?'

'He would find initial difficulty in following it if he had not been trained in literature. The ordinary person could understand it given the necessary energy and intellectual effort which I doubt he would give it.'

'What about *Hamlet*, there are any amount of passages in that which the ordinary person can understand without difficulty.'

'Yes, there are many passages they can understand without difficulty.'

'Having finished reading *Hamlet*, the reader would at least have some idea of what it was about?'

'He would have a general outline in his mind, the ordinary reader, of the emotional tension of the play and a rough outline from stage directions and the context in which it takes place — although he may have no idea what is biting Hamlet.'

'*As You Like It* is a play which is frequently set for school children to study, isn't it?'

'Yes.'

'And school children would have no difficulty in understanding a good deal?'

'As a child I had difficulty in all Shakespeare's works, I found it necessary to take out annotations by the teacher, and have the meanings of the words explained.'

'You don't mean to say there are passages in *As You Like It* which are not intelligible to sensible children?'

'I concede that.'

'There is nothing in Ern Malley's poems which a child of ordinary intelligence could understand, is there?'

'I think any child of normal intelligence could understand "Night Piece". Given the same explanation that we got of Shakespeare, I would say they would have no difficulty in either of the "Night Pieces", neither would they in the first poem.'

'Are you serious in that?'

'I don't think it is any more difficult than *As You Like It*.'

'You understand me when I said that there was not any passage in *As You Like It* the ordinary child wouldn't have difficulty in understanding?'

'Yes. I will concede that certain words like "interloper" would need to be explained, and "cowled". You would have to go to a child psychologist, but all I can say is that it is a simple poem. "Night Piece" and "Durer: Innsbruck" are the only two instances in the Ern Malley poems which are simple. With gradations, some of the others are extremely difficult. In my opinion, "Egyptian Register" is the most difficult.'

'What is difficult about it?'

'I think it requires or suggests a high degree of sophisticated intellect and remote images in the mind of the author, and a complex attitude to man and nature.'

*

> OLIVER: This was not counterfeit. There
> is too great testimony in your complexion
> that it was a passion of earnest.
> ROSALIND: Counterfeit, I assure you.
>
> *As You Like It*, Act IV, Scene iii

Discussing Shakespeare put Ern Malley in lofty company, something McAuley and Stewart did when they consulted a Collected Works to write his poems, perhaps because Herbert Read had sponsored a revival of Shakespeare in the thirties and urged the surrealists to claim him 'as an ally'. Malley is pretty familiar with the Bard. With nice ironic timing he quotes from *The Merchant of Venice* at the close of 'Culture as Exhibit' ('See how the floor of

Heav'n is thick / Inlaid with patines of etcetera . . .') and he drops in a couple of lines from 'The Phoenix and the Turtle' at the right moment in 'Petit Testament'.

Malley is also obsessed by the late, minor play *Pericles*, an interloper in the canon. It was excluded from the 1623 folio and nobody knows just how much of it Shakespeare wrote. With its drivelling dumb-shows and sea-swell music, the 'apocryphal' *Pericles* may be Shakespeare's most Malleyesque moment, and Ern draws on it for two poems, 'Boult to Marina' and 'Young Prince of Tyre'. The trouble is that Ern heads straight for the scenes everyone is sure Shakespeare wrote – the encounters in the brothel between Boult and Marina. *Pericles* is stuffed with wretched Jacobean doggerel which might have tested Harris's ability to distinguish good verse from bad, but the hoaxers were drawn to the liveliest, saltiest language in the play.

'Boult to Marina' suggests, plausibly enough, that Boult's conversion to virtue in the play is fake by his own standards. 'Part of me remains, wench, Boult-upright / The rest of me drops off into the night' is too charming a construction for Shakespeare's Boult, but Ern, in the person of Boult, is punning on the Bawd's orders to him which read like the catalyst for the poem itself:

Boult take her away, use her at thy pleasure, crack the glass of her virginity and make the rest malleable.

Make the rest malleable indeed! Before his capitulation to Marina's shining light of goodness, Boult gets to bark out lines such as 'if she were a thornier piece of ground than she is, she shall be ploughed'. One way to fake Shakespeare is to copy him out ('What would you have me do? Go to the wars?') but the final stanza of 'Boult to Marina' is all Ern and constitutes – though it may take Boult's delivery up a notch or two – a dazzling bit of ventriloquy:

> Sainted and schismatic would you be?
> Four frowning bedposts
> Will be the cliffs of your wind-thrummelled sea

Lady of these coasts,
Blown lily, surplice and stole of Mytilene,
You shall rest snug to-night and know what I mean.

Snatches of 'Young Prince of Tyre' were copied from *Pericles* too. The rusty armour and the ill-advised 'concupiscence to foin' which stumped Vogelesang are, however, pastiche. There were some popular lines in this poem, written with Elizabethan confidence, which Ern didn't find in Shakespeare. Sidney Nolan thought 'The new men are cool as spreading fern' among the most beautiful Australian images he'd ever read, and described the whole passage as 'a beautiful example of the English language being renewed in Australia, while the older poets fall away'. Even the title of Ern's Works, *The Darkening Ecliptic*, sounds like Shakespeare, though it derives from Ern's original account of Boult bragging to Marina: 'So blowing this lily as trumpet with my lips / I assert my original glory in the dark eclipse.'*

Malley often breaks into 'Shakespearean' when he wants to talk about sex. Mostly this is the language of the comedies ('Milord / Had his hand upon that snowy globe / Milady Lucy's sinister breast . . . / Knowst not, my Lucia, that he / Who has

---

*The tag has a sexual tang worthy of any Elizabethan dramatist, but 'the darkening ecliptic' is not out of *Pericles*. Its source may be even more obscure: *Nepenthe*, a long, saturnine meditation by the nineteenth-century romantic poet George Darley, conjures up the familiar figure of the phoenix in its first canto:

Sudden above my head I heard
The cliff scream of the thunder-bird,
The rushing of his forest wings,
A hurricane when he swoops or springs,
And saw upon the darkening glade
Cloud-broad his sun-eclipsing shade.

I sent this passage in triumph to Harold Stewart, who had alerted me to Darley – but he assured me that he had never seen it before. 'I cannot answer for Jim, who may have read Darley and so concocted the title of Ern's works by conflating words from the last two lines,' he replied on 15 March 1989, 'but I have strong feelings that this was not so, and that Jim derived "ecliptic" from some scientific work on astronomy that he was reading at the time.'

caparisoned a nun dies / With his twankydillo at the ready?'), though sometimes his vision of women is tortured and full of terror, as if snatched from the tragedies ('Take it for a sign, insolent and superb / That at nightfall the woman who scarcely would / Now opens her cunning thighs to reveal the herb / Of content'). A few of his 'ribald interventions' are cynical barracks-room humour, though some have a sensual and psychological credibility – 'The body's a hillside, darling, moist / With bitter dews of regret' – in keeping with Ethel's account of the haughty, thwarted lover who 'had some sort of difference' with a girl in Melbourne. This was all lost on the prosecution.

Williams took Harris through 'Egyptian Register' line by line. Though it was never stated with such clarity, the Crown case seemed to be that where the poetry was not obscene it was unintelligible, and that was almost as bad. They teetered into the ridiculous: Williams sought to deny a paraphrasable content where he could detect nothing risqué, but was on the alert for meaning if the poetry looked naughty.

'Are you able to take either of the stanzas in the verse of "Egyptian Register" and tell the Court what it means?'

'I can communicate to you the kind of emotional impact that the stanzas in question will have. You start off with the man as it were examining the body.'

'Where do you get that from?'

'Because he takes in turn various parts of the body, hand, skull, spine, lungs, etc., and lets his associations play about the kind of emotions they suggest to him.'

'Where do you get that from? You can't point to any word or sentence about that, can you?'

'Each thing he takes up suggests to him, within the context of the larger idea he is developing, that of the inexplicability of human life, the exotic or mysterious qualities in these physical things.'

'Where does he say anything about the inexplicability of human life?'

'A dark purpose I would say would be inexplicable.'

'That is what you are relying on for what you have said about the inexplicable purpose of human life?'

'I merely gave you one instance. "The skull gathers darkness" assimilates from without itself those things which are inexplicable.'

'It wouldn't be possible that what you have just read is meaningless gibberish, would it?'

'No.'

'What else is there which indicates that the author is talking about the inexplicable things of life?'

'Another suggestion of vagueness and inexplicability is associated with the spine reference.'

'But what is there inexplicable about that except the language?'

'The spine contains part of the brain, and the author links it with the harsh and inquiring element of the brain which pierces or attempts to pierce the obscurity of life.'

'What is the harsh and inquiring element of a brain? Where do you get that from?'

'The spine.'

'What actual words are there referring to the harsh and inquiring elements of the brain?'

'I am conceding that it is difficult to put these things into intellectual terms but it is apparent that the general emotional suggestion is there.'

'When you use the phrase "putting into intellectual terms" do you mean putting it into terms which the ordinary person can understand?'

'Roughly, yes.'

'What do you mean by that?'

'It is rather like trying to write out what a Beethoven symphony contains: you can talk about storm *ad infinitum*. In other words you are putting it into intellectual terms. If you read out the terms, the same effect if not communicated to you as if you listen to the symphony.'

'Is there anything else which you want to refer to which to your mind suggests the inexplicable purposes of life?'

'No.'

'Take the first line, "The hand that burns resinous in the evening sky". What does "resinous" mean?'

'I don't know, I think it refers to "residence". I did not look it up in the dictionary. That is not that it can't be understood, that is bad studentship on my part. There might well be other words in Ern Malley's poems which I can't understand.'

'Is that because you are too lazy to look them up, or did not think it was necessary to get a satisfactory reaction from the poems?'

'Partly both. Even though I don't know what it means, it evokes an image in mind.'

They clawed their way to the end of the stanza: 'I suppose you contend that a person would have to be particularly nasty minded to suggest that the words "immense index" used in connection with the genitals might refer to a large phallus?'

'I agree.'

'In other words you would have to be deliberately looking for some nasty meaning before you could suggest it meant that?'

'I think so.'

'You don't think it would be possible for any fair-minded person to think that the author in using the word "index" was referring to a penis in the state of erection.'

'Only the mentally depraved, I should think.'

'Do you consider that the standard of decency for writers such as yourself is the same or different from the standard of decency in ordinary polite conversation?'

'Yes, Shakespeare says things you wouldn't say in your drawing room.'

This was not good enough for Williams. He repeated the question. 'Do you consider that the standard of decency for writers such as yourself is the same or different from the standard of decency in ordinary polite conversation?'

'It is different.'

'Why?'

'Because through centuries of tradition the writer's job has been to present human life to human life, and not to present drawing-room conversation.'

At 4.15 p.m. court was adjourned until the day after next. It was all taking a long time. Harris had spent the entire day in the box, and seemed to be ahead on points, even if some of his interpretations of the poetry were not altogether convincing. But the cross-examination had one unforeseen result: it conjured Ern Malley into renewed existence.

At the resumption John Reed took the stand and testified under cross-examination that the hoax poems were 'great'. Williams persisted with this line of questioning – without objection from Phillips – until the magistrate began to wonder if he had read the summons correctly. 'Does it matter whether the Ern Malley poems are great or not?' Clarke asked.

'I won't pursue that line any further,' said Williams, and sat down. He did not ask Reed one question about the alleged indecency of the material he published.

Reg Ellery, consulting psychiatrist at the Women's Hospital in Melbourne, was sworn in. It was difficult for him to say anything since Williams objected to every question. Finally he got in an answer to Phillips' inquiry about the effect the Ern Malley poems might have on the average individual.

'Bewilderment,' said Ellery, perhaps with the example of Detective Vogelesang in mind. 'The majority of persons are mentally lazy and would not interpret them. Those not mentally lazy would interpret them and come to conclusions along the lines of Mr Harris. There are others again whom I do not think would try to reach a specific interpretation but would be satisfied with an emotional satisfaction such as one gets from listening to music, because the various sentences in these poems so far as I can see are held together not by logic so much as association of ideas.'

Ellery also gave his opinion to Phillips that 'the sexual references in these poems were too involved in their meaning to have a direct sexual effect or appeal to the reader'. This was an oasis of common sense in the drought that had overtaken the case. Williams, sensing that his terrier tactics might get him nowhere here, informed the court he had no questions.

He recalled Harris instead. The temperature went up.

'Would you enlighten me on what an "unforgivable rape" is, as used in "Sweet William"?'

'All rape is unforgivable, the phrase *in vacuo* is a redundancy.'

'The man in the street, hearing the term "unforgivable rape", don't you think he would take it as having sexual connotation?'

'I don't know what the ordinary man in the street thinks.'

Williams had been waiting for this. 'You consider yourself above the ordinary man in the street, don't you?'

Phillips objected and the magistrate asked Williams to put the question another way.

'Do you consider you are not one who could be classified an ordinary common man?'

'I have been born one, so I assume I am.'

'You will notice that in the poem "Sweet William" the sixth line ends with the word "flesh"?'

'Yes.'

'The next line ends with the word "embrace"?'

'Yes.'

'Then the last line of the first stanza ends with "rape".'

'Yes.'

'Don't you think it reasonable in view of the recurrence of the words "flesh" and "embrace" before "rape" for one to assume that sexual rape is referred to?'

'It is difficult for parts of mental personality to indulge in sexual activity.'

'Please put that in another way.'

'The images of the mental conflict are depicted in "rape" and the symbol "staircase of flesh" can bear no connection with the last part of the sentence. Your use of the words "flesh", "embrace" and "rape" as an association of ideas is utterly arbitrary, having been torn from the general meaning of the sentence.'

'Doesn't all that amount to this, that you refuse to try and interpret literally, not in the sense that you won't, but that you don't believe it is the proper way to study "Sweet William"?'

'When the words "staircase of flesh" are used, I don't intend to interpret it as a staircase made of flesh.'

The court adjourned for lunch. Harris resumed the stand in the afternoon and Williams continued in the same niggling vein.

In the middle of a protracted exchange over 'Boult to Marina', he queried Harris's interpretation: 'How do you get that out of it?'

'I can't explain how I get things, Mr Williams.'

'You are unable to suggest to me why I don't come to the same conclusion.'

'I can't suggest your defects, Mr Williams.'

'You assume that you are a super-intelligent being.'

'I assume nothing.'

'You assume that I haven't got the intelligence or the background to understand this.'

'I assume you are not trying to understand it. I do not assume that if you try to understand it you would come to the same conclusion as myself.'

'Do you concede that if I tried to understand it I could come to some conclusion quite different from yours?'

'I can concede there might be minor differences of interpretation but substantially we would have the same emotional experience. Further than that one is unable to go in modern poetry.'

Williams was indefatigable. Harris became increasingly abrupt though he never ceased to co-operate with this absurd exercise in practical criticism. Line by line the two of them sparred their way through 'Boult to Marina', 'Night Piece', 'Perspective Lovesong' and 'Young Prince of Tyre'. If Harris was too inventive or defensive in his answers he was dealing with a prosecutor who made no attempt to disguise his contempt and paraded his refusal to digest what the defendant was saying. He was still in the box when the court adjourned for the day, and stepped back into it next day for Williams to quiz him about the remaining passages in *Angry Penguins* the Crown objected to. It was mid-morning before they completed what seemed an increasingly futile activity. Harris had spent the best part of two days giving evidence and had analysed the poems to death. The overwhelming impression given by the prosecution case was not that the poems had outraged the community by their obscenity but that the moment had come to address anxieties about their anomalous condition, their failure to have been written by Ern Malley, their failure to mean anything.

J. I. M. Stewart's testimony was heard with 'oppressive respect'. He declared that *Angry Penguins* was a 'serious literary journal'. He took an aesthete's view that some of the writing in the issue was 'indecent in the sense of offending against delicacy' but 'would not deprave or corrupt save in point of literary style'. He also repeated Judge Woolsey's famous remark about *Ulysses* being 'emetic rather than erotic' though he did not refer the court to his source. Nobody took any notice.

Brian Elliott's evidence was brief and in agreement with Stewart: there were passages which were 'distasteful to one's sense of literary delicacy without any moral judgement being involved'. The case was adjourned for addresses by counsel on 4 October. Reed and Ellery took a crowded overnight train back to Melbourne. Ellery sat up until dawn reading *The Vegetative Eye*.

'The test of indecent language,' argued Phillips on 4 October, 'was that it should be highly offensive to the recognized standard of propriety. The only way that you can find anything pornographic and lewd in these articles is by converting what is put forward as self-analysis as sexual emotions, and seeing what you can read into it, regardless of the context.' Phillips described *Angry Penguins* as a serious magazine, though he seemed to concede ground when he admitted it might be crude or vulgar in parts but that it did not intend to deprave or corrupt. The Crown had seized words out of context, he said, and attempted to create an atmosphere of cheapness. Here Phillips had his grandest moment. He glanced across at Williams and declared, 'I can only give the answer in the words which Dr Johnson used to the woman who protested against words which appeared in his dictionary – "Madam, you are looking for them".'

Williams was blunter. 'The so-called Ern Malley poems have deliberately been used for the purpose of referring to sex,' he contended. 'It is revolting to common sense to say that these Ern Malley poems in particular have any clear meaning at all. It is only in one case that I can follow the defendant's explanation. The approach of Harris to this sort of rubbish, a man who said that minds have to be attuned to higher things, is shown by the fact that he could not tell me the meaning of one of the words he was questioned about.' Williams described the end of 'Egyptian Register' as 'a sting. If it means what I think it does it is clearly indecent. People can't be allowed to go around writing that sort of thing.' He referred to various passages as 'twaddle', 'meaning-less nonsense', 'revolting and crude in the highest degree, deliberate pieces of smut' which 'must arouse the most lascivious thoughts in the minds of those open to the influence of impure thoughts and ideas'.

Judgement was reserved. Harris telegrammed Reed: 'DEFENCE WEAK WILLIAMS VICIOUS OUTLOOK BLACK'.

Reed remained optimistic even though he felt the evidence the Penguins had given in their defence was 'confused', and he was disappointed with Phillips' 'dithering'. Harris held out no hope, and wrote a press release assuming they would lose. A few weeks later, on Friday, 20 October, the bespectacled Clarke delivered his twenty-page judgement. He interpreted 'indecent' as a 'milder and wider term' than 'obscene' which defined language 'highly offensive to the recognised standards of common propriety'. 'Immoral' he took simply to mean 'not moral'. He took Hicklin as the test for 'obscene'. Clarke accepted that standards of decency were not absolute and commented that 'the public is so used to somewhat gross literary aphrodisiacs that a work must be rather more daring than could have been published fifty years ago in order to unbalance the susceptible'. But it did not follow that 'writers can fix their own standard of decency without regard to the standard of the reasonable man of his time'.

Clarke was troubled, though, that the section did not allow literary merit as a defence, and thought it might be possible to prosecute certain plays by Shakespeare if their wording were interpreted literally. He got around this by citing decisions in favour of material that was prima facie obscene after the argument was successfully put that publication for the 'public good' was 'necessary or advantageous to religion, science, literature or art'. A prosecution under Section 108 might be defended in this way, Clarke suggested, and it 'would avoid the absurdity of a bookseller having to be convicted' because Shakespeare was on the shelves. This looked good for Harris – until the magistrate declared in the next breath that the passages complained of in *Angry Penguins* were certainly not advantageous to the pursuit of literature and art.

Clarke also addressed the question of the true authorship of the poems and decided it was not material. At the time of publication Harris 'firmly believed that the poems were Ern Malley's and that Ern Malley, whom he regarded as a great poet, was dead'. Thus, when it considered the matter, the court declined to rule that Ern Malley did not exist, though the magistrate was struck by 'the ludicrous aspect of a solemn and serious attempt to interpret seriously poems which may have been written in a far from serious spirit'.

Clarke analysed each of the troubling passages in turn. 'I do not attempt to set myself up as a literary expert,' wrote the magistrate in his discussion of 'Sweet William', 'but, in my opinion, the interpretation of this poem given by the defendant in evidence is sheer guesswork, and it seems to me impossible to give any satisfactory interpretation of the meaning of the poem as a whole. If the poem were intended to have a poetic meaning it seems to me that the poet has carefully disguised it so that no one but himself will know that meaning. To attempt to interpret this poem seems to me rather like attempting to unravel a crossword puzzle from a newspaper with the aid of only half the clues, and without the satisfaction of seeing the solution in the next issue.'

Clarke wanted it both ways: to deny 'satisfactory' meaning and then to interpret the poetry as he did in the next sentence: 'Although it is "my toppling opposites" which "commit the obscene, the unforgivable rape" after the person in the poem has or shall have proceeded "down the staircase of flesh" to where it happens, the image conjured up . . . "in a shuddering embrace" is the act of sexual rape, and even if "my toppling opposites" can refer to the emotions of self-denial and desire, in my opinion, the language used is poetically quite unjustifiable.' He found the poem to be neither obscene nor immoral, but indecent.

'Boult to Marina' was 'impossible to treat as a serious poem', the magistrate declared. ' "Boult-upright" is obviously a very poor pun . . . He is referring to his purpose of having sexual intercourse with her. "The rest of me drops off into the night" may well have an indecent meaning, but it is not absolutely clear . . . I have no doubt at all in finding that the first stanza is indecent.' Clarke found that neither of the 'Night Piece' poems were indecent, immoral or obscene, and he could not make sense of some of 'Perspective Lovesong' – though the third stanza gave 'the mental picture of a woman with naked breasts and loins' in which the poet was 'rather gloating of the recollection of the physical attributes of her nakedness . . . The rest of the poem to my mind does not need this from any poetic point of view. The passages are simply dragged in without apparent reason.' Guilty of indecency.

'Egyptian Register' was 'nonsense' which referred to the 'genitals' without justification, though the judge could not understand the phrase 'make an immense index to my cold remorse' and that saved it from constituting indecent language. In 'Young Prince of Tyre' the lines: 'Poor Thaisa has a red wound in the groin / That ill advises our concupiscence to foin' were pronounced to mean that 'Thaisa has her menstrual periods so as to make it inadvisable to have sexual intercourse'. The judge agreed with J. I. M. Stewart that the lines, though offensive to delicacy', would 'not be likely to deprave or corrupt save in point of literary style . . . Words can, however, be indecent without being likely to deprave or corrupt.' Harris was done for.

Ern Malley's lack of decorum and want of literary politeness convicted his publisher. Professor Stewart's use of the term 'indecent' in evidence did not help here, and Williams' dogged attack on the quality of the poetry proved to have been a shrewd tactic. Section 108 was far more restrictive than the Hicklin test which only defined 'obscene'. Denying a tendency to deprave or corrupt as Stewart and Phillips had sought to do would not get Harris off the hook. Hicklin was irrelevant. All the magistrate needed to be sure of was a lack of propriety. Clarke found none of the passages obscene or immoral but some indecent within the meaning of the term 'indecent advertisements'. Harris's contributions and Peter Cowan's 'The Fence' were found indecent too. 'There must therefore be a conviction,' Clarke wrote, and warned Harris that he displayed 'far too great a fondness for sexual references . . . I cannot but regard it as an unhealthy sign even from a literary point of view. Boldness in sexual reference is too often mistaken for brilliance. I think that the defendant should either acquire that art of delicacy in the handling of sexual topics which is so necessary in Literature, or avoid the topic altogether.'

Harris was fined £5 in lieu of six weeks' imprisonment. Costs of £21/11/– were awarded against him. He strode from the court and told reporters the Penguins would appeal all the way to High Court if necessary. *Angry Penguins* would continue being published but would not be available in South Australia. Then he walked past the triumphant, glowering Victoria once more and telegrammed to Reed: 'MAGISTRATE GAVE VICIOUS SUNDAY SCHOOL SPEECH'. Reed was shattered and reported a feeling of disgust. 'The guardians of our morals take liberties which are quite unpardonable,' he said, 'though one doesn't know whether to lay most blame on them or on the legislators or on the public which permits them to function in this way.' There was talk of establishing a Defence Fund, and the opinion of Ligertwood, a top Adelaide KC, was sought. His assessment was blunt. The law made no allowance for literary and artistic works; it was arguable a case could be brought against Shakespeare in South Australia and succeed. Clarke had interpreted the law correctly. The Penguins' best recourse would be to have the statute amended.*

The besieged Penguins had no contact with the inventors of Ern Malley either before or during the court case. McAuley and Stewart made no public comment on Harris's troubles. It is hard to see how the pair, given their opinions of Ern Malley's work, could have assisted the defence, though a cross-examination of what they understood as their motives and methods would have been fascinating. They were embarrassed and appalled by the actions of the police. Alec Hope expressed dismay at the 'Harris obscenity hunt'. The conviction was widely condemned by writers, artists and civil libertarians, including some who thought poorly of Harris and *Angry Penguins*. On 26 October, the *Argus* in Melbourne published a multiply signed letter of protest from writers and others 'vitally interested in Australian creative talent'. The signatures of the hoaxers were absent. Harold Stewart remembers they did draft their own letter to the *Advertiser*, pointing out that 'if anyone ought to be prosecuted it was the authors, but then since we were quoting Shakespeare, the Oxford Dictionary, and the Bible, perhaps they should be indicted'. It was never sent.

A few weeks later McAuley explained to Brian Elliott:

Harris's little court drama was a pity. By a rather strained extension of the word literature, the police attack on his and Ern's effusions constitutes an attack on literary freedom, which no one can view

*The law was not changed to take account of literary and artistic merit until 1953. But when Ern Malley's poems were brought back into print in 1961, the South Australian Crown Solicitor advised the Attorney-General that he should give no undertaking that distributors of the book in South Australia would not be prosecuted. In 1974 the law was changed again in South Australia. The Classification of Publications Act specifically incorporated the rights of adults to read and view what they like. See Peter Coleman, *Obscenity, Blasphemy, Sedition*, Angus & Robertson, Sydney, 1974, 34.

with equanimity. Clive Turnbull, in an article on the Dobell and Harris cases, saw fit to raise the question whether Stewart and myself foresaw the courtroom sequel – a suggestion unworthy even of a journalist. A letter of protest against the police action was sent to the papers by a number of people who described themselves, rather quaintly, as 'vitally' interested in Australian creative talent etc . . . Among the vitalists was Henrietta Drake-Brockman: she at first 'supposed we would not want to sign it'; then, having been told the contrary, thought we should not sign it, because it was our 'work' which was under attack! Our only course would have been to write a separate letter. But in those circumstances, the purpose of the letter would have been less to promote Harris's cause than to clear ourselves of the grubby imputations of the Turnbulls and Brockmans – a rather unworthy motive. You might explain this to Harris, though I don't imagine he nurses any such suspicions.

There was no appeal.

By the end of November 1944 invading Allied armies were opening up a huge front on German soil. The Russians were advancing through Hungary. American planes bombed Tokyo at will. On 29 November Eisenhower and Montgomery met near the Dutch frontier to design the final defeat of Germany. On the same day, in Adelaide, the South Australian Commissioner of Police announced he had awarded a special mention to Detective Vogelesang for 'zealousness and competency in securing evidence for the prosecution of an indecent publication'.

AFTERMATH

Max Harris moved to Melbourne early in 1945. He would always be at risk of further prosecution if he continued to edit *Angry Penguins* in his own city. The magazine could no longer be offered for sale in South Australia. Bitter at the treatment meted out by the panjandrums of Adelaide, he threw himself into his work with Reed & Harris: the partners launched a weekly newspaper called *Tomorrow*, and a polemical literary monthly, *Angry Penguins Broadsheet*. The firm continued to publish books, and there was talk of opening a bookshop. Harris was ebullient as ever, though he was often strapped for cash and lodged for a time with the Brotherhood of St Laurence. He and Nolan cadged free rides on trams driven by Nolan's father. Harris would slip past the gate-keeper at the Melbourne City Baths at the top of Swanston Street for a free steam bath, and knew which restaurants would feed him for nothing just before they closed for the night.

Harris landed on his feet after his drubbing, but he began to find it harder to believe in the manifest destiny of *Angry Penguins*, and his own self-evident genius. Doubts about his work and writing gnawed at him. *Amo, Amas, Amat*, a new book of his poetry that Nolan had agreed to illustrate, was delayed and then abandoned. He and Reed assembled three more issues of *Angry Penguins* after Ern Malley, the last in July 1946. The magazine was as handsome as ever, but had lost its focus. The end of the war lifted the lid on the pressure-cooker, and the cultural imperatives that had driven the Angry Penguins were slackening. Harris decided to start again from scratch.

In October 1946, while the Reeds were on holiday in north Queensland, Nolan wrote from Melbourne with the news that Harris had resigned from the partnership and decamped to Adelaide. Reed was 'bewildered and shattered': he phoned Nolan from Townsville who told him 'you must understand Max had to do this'. Reed & Harris, now losing thousands instead of hundreds of pounds each year, was wound up, and ceased all its operations. The following year Nolan went to Sydney and in 1948 he married John Reed's sister Cynthia. The couple left Australia for London soon after. Nolan's relationship with both Sunday and John Reed was destroyed, and they were never reconciled.

In Adelaide Harris dropped his role of bohemian modernist. In partnership with Mary Martin he became a bookseller, one of the best in the country. In 1952, in his early thirties, he announced he had stopped writing poetry because 'he didn't have anything to say any more'. *Angry Penguins*, he confessed, 'built up an astounding monolith of obscure cult-ridden subjectivism, incredible in fervor for such a small country as Australia'. Later, he underlined this, admitting to 'excesses, absurdities and intolerable posturings' and declaring that 'the poetic output of the modernists was of nugatory value'. The hostility of McAuley, Stewart and Hope was 'justified in critical essence even if irresponsible in animus'.

In 1953, Harris reluctantly agreed to help John Reed and Barrett Reid, a poet who had contributed to the Ern Malley edition of *Angry Penguins*, edit their new magazine, *Ern Malley's Journal*. The title was defiant but by the third issue the editors began to worry whether the audience had taken the point. They ran an article with the dismal heading 'Who was Ern Malley?' and explained the whole sad story to readers who had forgotten or never knew. No further issues of *Ern Malley's Journal* appeared after 1955, but the Reeds never abandoned their patronage of new painters and contemporary art. In the late fifties they established a Museum of Modern Art in Melbourne which flourished for a time but then closed its doors eight years later. John and Sunday Reed died within ten days of each other in December 1981. Heide II, their new home on their Heidelberg property, became a public museum and park for their extensive collection of modern Australian art.

In 1955, Harris broke his silence with a slim new book *The Coorong*. Over the next two decades he helped to found and edit a couple of literary magazines, *Australian Letters* and *Australian Book Review*. His editorial work is the keystone of his literary achievement, though he became most famous as a columnist for Rupert Murdoch's *Australian*, a pot-stirrer who held court before a popular audience until illness forced his retirement at the beginning of 1992. Sometimes he would write in the same kind of shorthand as the journalists who beat him up in 1944, but the jejune modernist also liked to shoot from the hip back then. 'His chief failing is a loss of nerve,' his old friend Geoffrey Dutton said, commenting on Harris's 'tendency to take the easy way out, to take sides with the Philistines he so abhorred as a young man, and who so gleefully denounced him at the time of the Ern Malley affair'. ('Poppy-lopping' is how Harris lists his recreation in *Who's Who in Australia*.) Before he died John Reed confided that the hoax was 'a very devastating experience' for Harris. 'I think it did something to him which, you know, he never recovered from.' Harris continues to write poetry but rarely publishes it. 'You're vulnerable in your poetry,' he told an interviewer. 'I don't want it to be available to those who don't wish me particularly well.' But he kept his sense of humour – he once announced a novel in progress entitled 'Biography of a No-Hoper', and a few years later declared a forthcoming book of poetry would be called 'Poetic Gems', after the famously bad nineteenth-century Scots poet William McGonagall. *Poetic Gems* appeared in 1979, but the novel was never published in full.

The hoax was the imaginative pinnacle of Harris's publishing life, the moment when all his literary dreams came true and then turned into a nightmare. He survived: Ern Malley became his scarlet letter, which he now wears with a kind of pride and affection. Whatever he thinks of his own early work, he has never disowned the hoax poems, and continues to sponsor new editions, in the belief that Ethel Malley gave him permission to publish Ern's poetry until 1994, fifty years after the hoax.*

It must be dificult, whatever the evidence, to disbelieve in the existence of somebody who has sent you real letters with real stamps on them and real postmarks. In the first issue of *Ern Malley's Journal* Harris confessed:

I still believe in Ern Malley.

I don't mean that as a piece of smart talk. I mean it quite simply. I know that Ern Malley was not a real person, but a personality invented in order to hoax me. I was offered not only the poems of this mythical Ern Malley, but also his life, his ideas, his love, his disease, and his death . . . in Rookwood cemetery. Most of you probably didn't think about the story of Ern Malley's life. It got lost in the explosive revelation of the hoax. In the holocaust of argument and policemen, meaning versus nonsense, it was not likely you closed your eyes and tried to conjure up such a person as the mythical Ern Malley . . . a garage mechanic suffering from the onset of Grave's Disease, with a solitary postcard of Durer's 'Innsbruck' on his bedroom wall. Of someone knowing he is to die young, in a world of war and death, and seeing the streets and the children with the eyes of the already dead.

A pretty fancy. It can have no meaning for you. But I believed in Ern Malley. In all simplicity and faith I believed such a person existed, and I believed it for many months before the newspapers threw their banner headlines at me. For me Ern Malley embodies the true sorrow and pathos of our time. One had felt that somewhere in the streets of every city was an Ern Malley . . . in Hamburg, Vienna, Rome, Cleveland, Bombay . . . a living person, alone, outside literary cliques, outside print, dying, outside humanity but of it. And setting it down. The Germans talk about Weltschmerz. Always that sense of Weltschmerz expressed itself for me in some such person as Ern Malley.

As I imagined him Ern Malley had something of the soft staring brilliance of Franz Kafka; something of Rilke's anguished solitude;

*After *The Darkening Ecliptic* appeared in *Angry Penguins* in 1944 and was republished in book form by Reed & Harris in the same year, further editions appeared in 1961 (Lansdowne Press, Melbourne), 1970 (Martin Publications, Adelaide), 1974 (Mary Martin Publications, Adelaide), and 1988 (Allen and Unwin, Sydney). In 1992, Angus & Robertson announced another edition of the poems.

something of Wilfred's Owen's angry fatalism. And I believe he really walked down Princess Street somewhere in Melbourne. I believed that the children there picked their noses in the sun with their left hands.

I can still close my eyes and conjure up such a person in our streets. A young person. A person without the protection against the world that comes from living in it. A man outside.

On a balmy evening in March 1988, I attended the launch of a new edition of *The Darkening Ecliptic* in a chic Adelaide bookshop, presided over by Max Harris. A mustachioed man in owl-eyed glasses, dressed in an old grey suit and grubby white shirt with a red bow-tie — Ern Malley himself, we were told — recited the poems in a loud whine. Ethel Malley, in frock and hat, looked on. Ern launched into 'Petit Testament', with its talk of transfigured sadness, of the inevitable graph, of a nightmare become real. The audience chuckled. I stole a glance at Harris, a plump, elegant figure in his late sixties, cigarette in hand, resting on his silver-capped cane in a corner of the crowded room. He tilted his body forward, head at a slight angle as if to hear better — though Ern was shrieking so loudly he might have woken the dead:

> I said to my love (who is living)
> Dear we shall never be that verb
> Perched on the sole Arabian Tree
> Not having learnt in our green age to forget
> The sins that flow between the hands and feet
> (Here the Tree weeps gum tears
> Which are also real: I tell you
> These things are real).

With a cherub's half-smile, Max Harris opened and closed his mouth in time with Ern, 'Here the Tree weeps gum tears/Which are also real.' Ern Malley paused for effect. Max Harris paused too and then, 'I tell you,' he mouthed, to himself, to nobody, to his love who was living, 'These things are real.'

'As to whether I'm sick of the nonsense, words fail me,' James McAuley confessed at the end of November 1944. He and

Harold Stewart were eager to put the hoax behind them. Early in 1945 McAuley went to Canberra to help prepare future administrators of New Guinea for their tasks, and he continued with this work in Sydney after V-Day. Stewart served out his war in the directorate. Both men began to seek their separate truths in religious experience, in search of a metaphysic with millennia behind it. In particular they were reading René Guénon, the French scholar in comparative religion, and the Anglo-Sinhalese, A. K. Coomaraswamy, who worked for thirty years at the Boston Museum of Fine Arts and who wrote extensively on Eastern art and religion until his death in 1947.

For Stewart, especially, who was learning Chinese and reading deeply in Taoism, these men showed the way. After he was demobbed he stayed for a while with his old friend Alf Conlon in North Sydney, who was finishing his medical degree and would later go into practice. But towards the end of the forties Stewart went back to Melbourne where he lived for the next quarter century, working in a bookshop and writing his poetry in isolation. His audience was tiny, and to most he was known dimly as the co-creator of Ern Malley. His literary identity in Australia progressively diminished, and his influence on other writers was nil. Stewart had loathed the way Ern Malley thrust celebrity on him and the result was that he became invisible to the public. 'I made a firm resolve that I would simply withdraw from the whole literary world in Australia and have nothing further to do with it,' he told me, 'and I never have. You stop being a private person, you can no longer have any solitude and silence to get on with the real business of writing poetry, you're a figure of fun, pestered by journalists morning, noon, and night. I've gone out of my way all my life to avoid fame.'

In 1956, Stewart published a sequence of poems based on Orpheus and Eurydice, the last time he touched Western themes. *A Net of Fireflies* and *A Chime of Windbells*, two highly successful collections of haiku in translation, appeared in the sixties. Each sold in excess of 50,000 copies. For years he dreamed of emigrating to the East, and immersing himself in its traditional culture. Stewart made a pilgrimage to Japan in 1961 – the first time he had been out of Australia – and settled in Kyoto five years later. For a long time he lived in a single room in a private hotel but now has a three-roomed apartment in the north-east of the city, not far from the imperial retreat at Shugakuin.

Stewart is a treasury of information about Kyoto, its art, literature, religious and philosophic traditions, architecture, topography, climate. I have never met anyone who knew so much about plants, birds, food, about different ways to make paper, to prepare ceramic glazes, or interpret details of dress. He adores facts – citing Blake's 'every minute particular is holy' – and has an elephantine memory. All this is evident in *By the Old Walls of Kyoto*, a long poem Stewart published in 1981 in homage to the ancient capital of Japan and to his deepening faith in Buddhism. Stewart loves to tell the story of seeing some tourists negotiating their way around Kyoto clutching an open copy of the book. The explanatory essays in *Old Walls* are astonishingly dense, written with the determination of the initiate to omit nothing from his account of a culture he has lovingly absorbed from scratch. Stewart has learned to write poetry more plainly as he has grown older, though his work has never lost its painterly qualities, and its ability to linger over intricate detail.

Stewart's life in Kyoto is austere and saintly: what fires his imagination are dramatic tales about the great religions of Asia, about Hindu holy men who teach by silence or Buddhist monks who traverse hot coals unscathed. He is now engaged on what he considers the culmination of his life's work, a long poem on the East called *Autumn Landscape-Roll*. His work stands alone. No writer of this century has influenced him. A tiny fraction of his readers are *au fait* with his subject. Stewart has no nostalgia for Australia and will never return. He sometimes seems to think of his Australian years as a previous incarnation. 'I have never written a single line about Australia,' he told me. 'Isn't that strange? It probably seems strange to an Australian. It's a country that repels me. I find it very alien and hostile. As a small child of five or six, I was taken to see the bush and I burst into tears of inconsolable grief and had to be taken home.' Stewart has long grown weary of the hoax. 'One day someone is going to have a brilliantly original idea,' he remarked. 'They're going to write a book about the life and works of James McAuley or Harold Stewart, or both, without mentioning Ern Malley.'

After the war James McAuley worked in Sydney at the Australian School of Pacific Administration, training patrol officers for duty in New Guinea. He visited the island many times and it was the crucible in which he forged his conversion to Catholicism in 1952. In New Guinea McAuley saw a 'primitive', integrated, culture struggling with the influence of the West, but also came into contact with European missionaries whose faith in the Christian mystery awed him. He set out to heal the dislocations which haunted his life and poetry, to insist his own society recover spiritual traditions he believed it had not properly observed since the middle ages. Some of his old friends were incredulous at his conversion – 'he went out like a light', Amy Witting recalled. Later, in response to his 'Letter to John Dryden' – 'Thus have I written hoping to be read / A little now, a little when I'm dead' – she wrote 'A Letter to James McAuley' which concluded:

> Your eyes I fear are permanently shut.
> At least you reach your goal, of being read,
> This present moment, after you are dead.

Alec Hope told McAuley the 'existence of god' was 'a hunger not a fact'. Yet he congratulated his friend for his courage in converting, though 'the spectre of yourself a few years ago muttered "insipid, foolish, repellent" in your ear'. A few months later, however, he chastised McAuley for his narrowing outlook: 'Your cultural pyramid seems to me to have the nice authority of a simple geometrical figure but a living and complex organism such as the literary tradition of Western Europe can no more be forced into a simple geometrical shape than most complex organisms can.' For his part McAuley told Hope his own poetry was 'morally dangerous material'. Even Stewart, who understood better than anyone McAuley's search for a *via mystica*, grew impatient with him: 'Blast McAuley for a meddling, chauvinistic, Jesuitical, proselytizing, Popish pomposity! Why doesn't he save his own soul first?' he exploded to Hope.

McAuley the militant Christian was also a cold warrior. In 1955 he played his part in one of the key events of post-war Australian politics, the formation of the right-wing Catholic splinter group, the Democratic Labor Party, which split from the Australian Labor Party, led in opposition to Menzies' Liberal Party by Bert Evatt. McAuley now despised Evatt with a passion – 'The traitors' tribune, bigots' Galahad / The greatest blot this country ever had' – and became involved in party politics. He wrote letters to newspapers, fought with the Catholic hierarchy who were determined to avoid any schism in Labor ranks, and chaired a committee which helped form the New South Wales branch of the DLP. *A Vision of Ceremony*, a book of poems he published in 1956, celebrated his faith, savagely defended his politics and raged against the kind of liberal, sceptical thinking he once identified with. McAuley postulated his aesthetic credo:

> Scorn then to darken and contract
> The landscape of the heart
> By individual, arbitrary
> And self-expressive art.
>
> Let your speech be ordered wholly
> By an intellectual love;
> Elucidate the carnal maze
> With clear light from above.

The imperious tone was characteristic. McAuley's insistence on thumping the pulpit in his poetry may have sometimes deceived him about the tenor of his language. 'Elucidate the carnal maze' sounds like an overblown Malleyism to me. Perhaps the lesson of the hoax for McAuley was that poetry could have a dramatic public impact, could change people's lives and jolt them into action. His poetry turned doctrinal, and his literary judgements were fierce: a friend who admired *The Waste Land* was taken aback when McAuley dismissed its author as that 'post-Shelleyan goon squad cheerleader'. When occasion demanded McAuley would rustle up the spectre of Ern Malley to make his point. Reviewing his fellow Catholic Vincent Buckley's first book of poems *The World's Flesh* in 1955, he compared Buckley with Malley and lashed out at the neo-romantic forties with their 'appalling Anglo-American series of galvanic twitchings simulating vitality, spasms of ineffectual violence, incoherent complexities, unclued scrawls, nauseating coagulates and colloids of opaque imagery, mere Rorschach blotches'.

McAuley still saw himself as an outsider: except now he was defending institutions he scorned in his youth. In 1956 he became founding editor of the conservative quarterly *Quadrant*, and three years later published *The End of Modernity*, a jeremiad against what he saw as the decadence of post-Renaissance culture. He became Professor of English at the University of Tasmania, and in 1964 published *Captain Quiros* which many thought might be his *magnum opus*, the grand mythic poem to unite an heroic narrative with the evocation of religious and intellectual passion. But the poems McAuley subsequently wrote, some of them the best things he ever did, were not like this at all: they were brief, personal lyrics, plain and modest, outlining their own contracted landscape of the heart. 'I make no comment; I don't know; / I don't know what there is to know', he said in one of his last poems. There were moments of paralysing doubt. ' "Dark night" is too grand a phrase,' he told Alec Hope in the sixties, 'but there is the loss of all natural appetite for religious exercises, much soreness and fatigue, and prayer only in darkness', and complained of 'being held fast, out of sight by the God I don't feel at all interested in or cognizant of'. But McAuley survived his doubts: he never abandoned his religious faith or his political convictions.

Harold Stewart and Max Harris never met. McAuley encountered the ex-Angry Penguin for the first time at an international conference of magazine editors in Sydney sponsored by

Quadrant in late August 1962, almost two decades after the hoax. There was anticipation of flying sparks but instead they talked through the night with the aid of a large quantity of whiskey. The two men became friends. 'I think Max naturally took a certain amount of hurt from it and I have never been in retrospect comfortable about that,' McAuley said of the hoax a few months before his death, 'but I think one could say, and I think Max would probably also say, over a long life, various things happen, that was one incident, and you survive most things.'

James McAuley grappled with the ogre of modernism more strenuously than any other poet of his generation in Australia. He stared into the same black hole as Baudelaire and Eliot – and then averted his gaze. I think his own stability depended on this: he never did anything by halves, and once remarked that the production of art by surrender to the irrational forces of the unconscious 'has its own personal dangers' and 'can upset or destroy a personality'. Ern Malley was a parody of that process of disintegration, but McAuley believed in the urgency of the warning he posted. He seemed to think he had escaped the implications of his libertarian youth, with its terrible dreams and cold remorse, by the skin of his teeth:

> Beware of the past;
> Within it lie
> Dark haunted pools
> That lure the eye
> To drown in grief and madness . . .
>
> . . .
>
> Fear to recall
> Those terrible dreams
> That sickened the heart
> Or tore with screams
> The shocked affrighted air . . .

He never trusted the mountains and cliffs of fall in his own mind, and he knew that contradictory identities wrangled within him. 'I am not resigned / To be what I do', he wrote in the fifties. 'Living, I seem to live / Outside my nature'. He had a strong sense of evil in himself and in others. The Church allowed him to tame his demons – the intensity of his conversion suggests how desperately he needed to believe – but it is at least arguable that when McAuley put his work at the service of God the force of his language was diminished. The proselytizer overwhelmed the man who had seen into the heart of darkness and recoiled in horror. Those bare, bleak and oddly moving poems of his final years, with their refusal to judge, suggest that McAuley knew this too. One need only look at a late photograph of his handsome and ravaged face to realize what a mercurial and complex man he was. James McAuley died of cancer on 15 October 1976. For many Australians he was the most remarkable person they had known.

Ern Malley was not the first caricature of 'revolutionary' modernism but he is the most interesting. In 1885, two French writers, Gabriel Vicaire and Henri Beauclair, produced *Les Deliquescences*, eighteen 'decadent' poems by a non-existent symbolist poet named Adoré Floupette, which strikingly resembled the work of Mallarmé, Rimbaud and Verlaine in turn. Vicaire, disguised as the chemist Marius Tapora, Floupette's boyhood friend, subsequently wrote the poet's biography. According to Marius Tapora, Floupette grew up in provincial France, an overweight boy who was obsessed by spiders. He came to Paris and found his true destiny as a symbolist poet, perpetually drunk with the power, the colour and the music of words. He haunted the cafés and cultivated his decadent tendencies. On the wall of his room was Floupette's ultimate symbol, a painting of a huge spider, which sent shivers down Tapora's spine. A bouquet of eucalyptus was at the end of each leg and in the middle of its body was a large, dreamy eye.

Harold Stewart had never heard of Adoré Floupette when he helped create Ern Malley, and there is no evidence James McAuley had either. Nor did they know about a hoax that took place on the other side of the Atlantic, in 1916, when two

American poets of little significance devised a new literary movement called 'Spectra'. They wanted to send up imagism, Ezra Pound's invention, which had become the fad of 'Amygism' under the presidency of Amy Lowell. Arthur Davison Ficke took the pseudonym of Anne Knish and Witter Bynner called himself Emanuel Morgan. Knish contributed a manifesto defining the 'Spectric' method ('not so wholly different from . . . Futurist Painting') and a slender book of poems was sent out as the emissary of the movement. The poems were smart, inane, Chinesey – Ezra Pound's *Cathay* had appeared the year before – and rather charming. Morgan mimed philosophical depth while Knish could flip into bathos at will.

They fooled everybody: Pound, William Carlos Williams who corresponded with Emanuel Morgan, Alfred Kreymbourg, editor of *Others*, an avant-garde magazine that devoted a special issue to the movement. But in the end, after its unmasking, Spectra didn't matter: the imagists had moved on anyway, and the hoax turned into a benign joke. Witter Bynner continued to write intermittently in the person of Emanuel Morgan and was even prepared to admit that some of his best work appeared under that name. Ern Malley may be very funny but there is nothing charming either about his poetry, by turns limpid and tortuous, or about the motivation which created him. McAuley and Stewart meant business, and there was no chance, once the game was up, that either would step into Ern's shoes again.

Ern Malley also has things in common with the great eighteenth-century hoaxes: Chatterton, the 'marvellous boy', the best hoax poet in English; James Macpherson, the deviser of Ossian, whom Goethe adored and Napoleon preferred to Homer; and William Henry Ireland who shamelessly added to the output of Shakespeare. All have an affection for the incongruous, the tinny and hyperbolic. Obsessed with style, hoax poetry is synthetic and self-referential, like Chatterton's fake Chaucerian argot or Ern Malley's 'No-Man's-language' – a literal description of the hoax and a hint to its satirical intent. Hoaxers love to pepper their work with clues. Anne Knish defined the Spectric vision by suggesting how 'the ghosts which surround reality are the vital part of that existence', while Ern Malley warned that 'It is necessary to understand / That a poet may not exist'. Max Harris misread giveaways like this one, with its intimations of mortality, as the signature of his poet. All successful hoaxes play out a comedy of misplaced belief. On 20 February 1795, when Boswell first saw the fake Shakespearean documents concocted by William Henry Ireland, he went down on his knees and proclaimed, 'I shall now die contented, since I have lived to witness the present day.'

Hoaxes are often written fast, as Ern Malley was, by people who must feel something like the thief's rush of adrenalin. William Ireland contrived his mass of phoney papers in a period of five or six weeks. 'It remains almost inconceivable that one human being, boy or man, could have turned out that quantity in less than a month and a half,' gaped his biographer. The Spectra poems (60 pages of them) were written over ten quarts of Scotch in a hotel in Moline, Illinois, in ten days. Kenneth Koch, an early American enthusiast of Ern Malley, once wrote some poems with John Ashbery where each poet produced alternate lines. 'It's like having the muse in the room,' Koch says of collaborating at speed. 'You have to write fast or you bore the other person.' In 1944 Alec Hope told the editor of *Meanjin*, should he doubt the story about how quickly the poems were written, 'that McAuley and Stewart are both remarkably apt at improvised poetry and have practised it for years on a number of subjects. They are in addition remarkable blokes.' When Hope heard 'from a possibly reliable source that Maxie is off on another wild-goose chase' with the theory 'that Stewart actually wrote poems in illness as Ern Malley over a considerable period of time and subsequently used them for the hoax' he retorted: 'Don't say a word. If he follows this up he will stick his neck out for the axe a second time. I have correspondence enough on the progress of the hoax to blow the pants off his theory.'*

*Hope's correspondence about the hoax was destroyed by fire, along with his library and his papers, early in 1953.

The fidgety ghost might not have been visible but he was always there, clanking his chains off-stage. Ern Malley's negative influence in Australia peaked in the late fifties when there was no one local writers wanted to resemble less. In 1960 the poet and broadcaster John Thompson produced a radio feature on the hoax for the Australian Broadcasting Commission. It was the beginning of Malley's resurrection, and he began to re-emerge in his oddly stubborn way as a figure in his own right. In 1961, seventeen years after his first, spectacular manifestation, a new edition of the poems was published. By this time almost all talk of the 'experimental' and the 'avant-garde' had fallen silent in Australia. The advent of the cold war, the ascendancy of the English 'movement' poets, the difficulty for Australians in obtaining new American writing in the fifties, and the emergence of the university in Australia as the single most powerful sponsor of literary activity all combined to snuff out 1940s-style bohemianism and avant-gardism. Only the painters *Angry Penguins* had sponsored survived unscathed. The literary enemies of the Angry Penguins, 'traditionalists' like Hope and McAuley, who invented their own kinds of 'modern' poetry out of disdain for modern values, became the pre-eminent poets and critics in Australian letters.

Was the hoax so influential in itself as to suppress an entire trend in contemporary Australian poetry, or was it that the guardians of the flame, who fought tenaciously for the qualities they wished to preserve in poetry, were among the strongest poets in the country anyway? The suppression theory is widely believed. In 1988 the critic Don Anderson declared: 'The great blow against any possibility of the modernist enterprise in Australia was of course struck in 1944 by the Ern Malley hoax . . . the great catastrophe to our letters.' This strikes me as wishful thinking. It is impossible to prove that the hoax prevented the writing of first-rate poetry in Australia of any kind, though it is true that we shall never know what kind of 'modernism' Harris might have matured into had his development not been checked by his public humiliation. We know he did write some good poems after the hoax, none the less. The belief that Ern Malley was a kind of proof against modernism may have helped encourage some ephemeral 'school of McAuley' or 'school of Hope' writing in the fifties and sixties, but it stretches credibility to suggest minor work in one vein would have been major in another. Some writers have talked of feeling that the literary and publishing climate of the fifties was not sympathetic to poetry that risked looking strange or different from the 'norms' Hope and McAuley had established: this may be true, but to talk of the hoax as *the* determining factor in this state of affairs is simplistic. Besides, modernism has always thrived by presenting itself as the dissident voice arguing at the gate of stuffy, 'official', repressive culture. Ern Malley was surely the definitive red rag to any snorting modernist.

Enthusiasm for an 'avant-garde' in Australian poetry revived in the sixties and is yet to work itself out, or at least to be superseded. Sponsored by the Academy, 'modernism' is now part of the official literary culture, institutionalized as 'post-modernism', and the argument for experiment is a conventional one. But an avant-garde in Australian poetry remains a contradiction in terms. There is no poetry which enters the tradition by making everything that immediately preceded it seem untenable, as the *Lyrical Ballads* did the heroic couplet or *The Waste Land* did the Georgian pastoral. Just as it does not make sense to talk about Australia's greatest novelists, Christina Stead or Patrick White, in terms of a 'vanguard', the major figures of post-war Australian poetry – among them Hope, McAuley, David Campbell, Judith Wright, Gwen Harwood, Francis Webb, Peter Porter, Les Murray, Robert Adamson – cannot be satisfactorily discussed in terms of any revolutionary history. (And no Australian poet can hold a candle to White or Stead, though Malley sometimes brings to mind the flavour of White's early novels, written during the war, with their mercurial and highly coloured forays into stream-of-consciousness experimentalism.) A number of poets, including Alan Wearne, Laurie Duggan, John A. Scott, John Forbes, and John Tranter, matured in the sixties and seventies during a period of rapid assimilation. Their international models were largely French and American, especially Black Mountain and the New York school, though Pound, Stevens and Williams were also influential. This was the first time contemporary American poetry was widely imitated in Australia.

The reaction of Australian poets to Malley varies. Judith Wright (1915–), whose work has great traditional strengths, speculated that the poems were 'a good deal better than true hoax poems need be', and reasoned this was because work produced by poets amid 'hilarious excitement' was 'apt to contain flashes of really exciting prosody, and to have a degree of internal organization and (conscious or unconscious) allusion much higher than can be achieved by non-poetic minds applying themselves to verse'. 'A poem cannot be made out of isolated brilliant images,' she suggested, 'but the whole cadence and management of these verses was obviously expert, even without the images.'

Peter Porter (1929–) did not read Ern Malley until 1974: the poems struck him then 'as being only mediumly obscure and modern, and sometimes exhibited real poetic frisson. Each poem made sense and compared (say) with what we take for granted in Ashbery and a hundred others today the Malley archive could not be considered extreme.'

Les Murray (1938–), on the other hand, sees the poems as having no particular merit but simply as 'a hoax got up to discredit a movement. They were successful for a while in that, but it has to be faced: they did hurt a number of people, and condemn an enthusiastic editor to a lifetime of assertive and slightly pathetic self-justification, and they did bring about a temporary narrowing and deadening of the arts in Australia, and prolong the life of some pretty lousy anti-artistic attitudes here.'

John Tranter (1943–), who thinks his work has been influenced by Malley 'to some small extent', first read him in the mid-sixties, and was struck by the 'bizarre power' and the 'authority' of the verse. He recalls discussing with his contemporary Robert Adamson the idea that Malley was a precursor, a poetic father figure for their generation. 'He stood in relation to the poetry of the fifties rather the way we felt we stood in relation to that poetry too. It was a joke at the time for us to say that Ern Malley was one of Australia's best poets, but we both knew that it was more than a joke, we half-believed it.' In 1991 Tranter co-edited a Penguin anthology of modern Australian poetry which included *The Darkening Ecliptic* entire.

Ern Malley was read outside Australia too. By 1943 the American poet and visiting serviceman Karl Shapiro had tired of Harris: 'I simply couldn't put up with any more blather about Kafka and George and Rimbaud,' he said. The hoax delighted Shapiro 'as nothing else could'. It was 'a classic and a pretty important bit of demolition', he thought. The following year, back in the United States, he reported 'a sincere interest in Australian letters' though 'it wasn't encouraged any by Ern Malley'. But 1945, the year Shapiro won the Pulitzer Prize, was also the year John Ashbery discovered Ern Malley. 'I liked the poems very much,' Ashbery recalls. 'They reminded me a little of my own early tortured experiments in surrealism, but they were much better.' In 1961, the year of Ern Malley's Australian comeback, the American avant-garde put him into print. He appeared in *Locus Solus*, a magazine edited in France by the prose writer Harry Mathews and by Ashbery, Kenneth Koch, and James Schuyler, key figures in the so-called New York school of poetry. Koch phoned James McAuley for permission to publish 'Boult to Marina' and 'Sybilline' in a special collaboration issue of *Locus Solus*, which included everyone from Basho to Chatterton to Paul Éluard, who invented the 'exquisite corpse' poems. These were one liners written by groups of five poets who would each secretly inscribe a word on a slip of paper. Such sentences ensued as 'The exquisite cadaver shall drink the new wine.' In his discussion of the hoax in *Locus Solus*, Koch praised the 'profundity and charm' of Ern Malley's work and found it 'hard not to agree' with Harris's initial judgement of the poems. 'I remember I had a rather lively sense of Ern Malley as a real person when I first heard about him,' Koch recalls.

A decade later, in 1971, when he was in his early twenties, and deep into the work of Ted Berrigan, Ashbery, Koch and Frank O'Hara, the poet John Forbes (1950–) stumbled on this edition of *Locus Solus* in a second-hand bookstore in Sydney. He promptly went to the library and retrieved the poems of Ern Malley which he had never read. Forbes reacted against the 'myth' that Malley prevented the modernist revolution from taking hold in Australia: 'I had a fairly dismissive attitude to the entire corpus of Australian poetry up to that time,' Forbes remembers.'* 'My major feeling was that Harris and those guys must have been wimps. "This destroyed modernism!" Why did it destroy modernism? I have a better idea now why it did because I have a better idea of the social context in which poetry gets published, appreciated and talked about. But the idea that somehow you couldn't write modernist poetry because of this hoax seemed ludicrous to me.' Forbes maintains, however, that Malley exercised no influence on his own development.

Ashbery's and Koch's appreciation of Malley is a little like Baudelaire's fondness for Poe whom he imported into France and then shipped back to America as a *symboliste*. The Ern Malley Forbes read in *Locus Solus* was an altogether different poet from the scarecrow who seemed to cast a shadow over the possibilities of Australian poetry. The qualities McAuley and Stewart took care to insert in their fake – Malley's love of pastiche and ironic quotation, his cavalier refusal to think in a straight line, his skill at mimicking the sound of a Bad Poem – can all be found in the work of poets like Tranter or Forbes, and suggest that Ern was rather ahead of his own time. The hoax is, however improbably, the conduit across the Pacific between the New York avant-garde and the Australian poets who began to write under its spell.

For the Americans, Malley's credentials were more impeccable because he did not exist. Koch remembers that he and Ashbery thought of Malley as a secret exotic figure, precious because

*I once remarked to Forbes that someone ought to produce the Stuffed Owl of Australian poetry. 'Mate,' he said, 'you couldn't do it. It would be like Borges' map of the world, a one-to-one correspondence.'

he was outlandish, though neither poet thinks Malley had any influence on his work. Koch taught Ern Malley to his students at Columbia University for years and in the mid-seventies, at Brooklyn College, John Ashbery would, in the exam for the creative writing course he taught, print without attribution one of Geoffrey Hill's *Mercian Hymns* – densely constructed, massively serious, late modernism, if ever it existed – beside a poem by Ern Malley, and tell his students:

One of the two poems below is by a highly respected contemporary poet; the other is a hoax originally published to spoof the obscurity of much modern poetry. Which do you think is which? Give your reasons. Can obscurity ever benefit poetry? Do you think it possible that the intellectual spoof might turn out to be more valid as poetry than the 'serious' poem, and if so, why?

Ashbery remembers his students 'rather enjoyed the exam'. About half picked Ern Malley as the spoof – which means that half picked Geoffrey Hill.

To read Ern Malley is like crossing the street in a foreign city. You can't remember which way to look, and keep trying to second-guess the poems, to come to grips with the ambition to deceive and the effect of the deception. Malley can write very well and very badly, sometimes in the same line. That is a highly unusual phenomenon. Unevenness in art more often indicates a failure of the imagination and has a deadening rather than an enlivening effect. The poet Harris fell in love with has vanished for ever, but we can enjoy aspects of the poetry Harris missed altogether. Vivian Smith may be correct when he says that Ern Malley does not add up to 'a coherent work of art' but the hoax amounts to something far less common than mere incoherence and fascinating in itself: a pretend work of art. Once the game is up with such constructions anything may happen. Ern Malley knew this, and prophesied in the final line he ever wrote, 'Beyond is anything.' Malley has become a legendary figure in Australia, one of a handful of names – like Phar Lap, the tragic racehorse, or Ned Kelly, the noble bushranger – embedded in the national psyche. The more successful the hoax, the harder it is to obliterate, even when the truth is known. A good hoax is like a snapshot of the *Zeitgeist*.

Ern Malley demonstrates with peculiar force the impact of a fictional event on the people who believed in it; how they thought of themselves, how they lived their lives and made their art under the influence of this fiction. It cannot be reduced to a sequence of poems: the hoax was really a piece of performance art before the form was invented. Ern Malley invaded the real world in a way few real writers do, and in ways the hoaxers never imagined. They viewed his persistence with dismay, and must sometimes have wished they had spent that Saturday afternoon in 1943 dutifully reading reports on mosquito control. Does Ern Malley prove the intentionalist fallacy, a key tenet of the New Criticism, postulated in the 1940s, which states that the intention of the artist is irrelevant to the effect of the work of art? Would not the poetry have faded into oblivion by now were it as empty of value as Stewart and McAuley believed? But wait: we know about the intention of the hoaxers, which the poetry legibly declares. Their ambition was to deceive Max Harris, and they were entirely successful. Or perhaps Ern Malley fulfils Roland Barthes' more recent dream of the death of the author, superseded by the 'text' conceived of as 'a multi-dimensional space in which a variety of writings, none of them original, blend and clash'. Maybe, but the trouble with Ern Malley is that just when we abandon ourselves to the seductions of his language, the authors barge through the door, shouting 'Hands Up!'

Only an artist can make a riddle out of a solution, declared the satirist Karl Kraus. If McAuley and Stewart were justified in the critical point they wished to uphold, it is hard to avoid the conclusion that their agent Ern Malley muddied the waters. He is an enigma half a century of debate has not solved. Had they wished, the hoaxers could have written far more ineptly than Malley does. They did not construct a poet who could not write, or who was a bore, or who had nothing at all to say, but one who writes with panache in a way they thought spurious. Malley was *designed to attract attention* and that is just what he has done ever since Harris did backflips.

The Angry Penguins' theory – that the hoaxers, liberated from inhibitions operating in their 'serious' poetry, were in touch with previously untapped sources of creativity in the unconscious – has appealed to many but does not account for the nature of the verse. Ern Malley is hardly a good test of the irrational unconscious in action since much of the time he makes conscious and rational reference to his own status as a surrealist hoax. And, as Brian Elliott observed, the fact that the poems 'didn't make sense' was evidence that the hoaxers 'knew what they were about'. Ern Malley can't really prove anything about the value of free association as a viable 'method' for writing poetry, since his dream-like visions are hardly 'free' of the satire that interrupts them.

Whether he wrote poetry 'better' than the independent works of the poets who wrote him, as some have asserted, is arguable, but as doubtful as the claim that Malley has no merit at all. This is no longer the crucial issue it was in the days when his creators were two young men with only a handful of poems to their names: in the to and fro of debate, Malley's detractors have underestimated his work, and his supporters often overvalued him. Peter Porter remarked that the poems probably 'have more flair if not more competence than the serious works of their perpetrators'. Malley's tragicomic brio is as unmistakable as the mature accomplishment of McAuley and Stewart, who were in search of something more than flair. 'Only Ern Malley could write like a genius all the time,' Harold Stewart reminded McAuley in August 1944. Perhaps a more useful way to speculate about the value of Malley is to ask whether anything in his poetry can stand comparison with the strongest examples of the kind of work he satirizes, George Barker's *Calamiterror*, say, or Dylan Thomas's 'Fern Hill'?

Still, the hoax is the most fascinating thing *Angry Penguins* ever published. In cooking up their poet to a satirical recipe,

McAuley and Stewart threw into the brew a seasoning of anarchic intelligence and comic self-laceration. Writing pretentiously, they described a mind so aware of pretension that it debunks itself with aplomb. In the end, Malley is really unlike the sort of grandstanding, romantic surrealism he mocks. It pays to remember that two very different temperaments and personalities were constructing the work without bothering to smooth the edges. Like a medium possessed by a host of spirits, Ern Malley freely exhibits his multiple consciousness. There is not one Ern Malley but several, and they are all mutually exclusive characters. There is Ern Malley, the black swan of trespass, the native modernist talented enough to turn the poetic tradition of his country on its head. There is Ern Malley the jejune and modish experimentalist who does belly-flops in his attempt to look significant. There is the Ern Malley who bravely stares his own death in the face, and the Ern Malley who slyly tells the reader he never was. All these writers were essential to the hoaxers' fiction. Each contradicts the others and helps give the poetry its dizzy, speeded-up quality, as Malley rifles through his composite self.

Ern Malley the self-conscious fake is a more interesting writer than the moribund genius Harris thought real. If he was wrong about most things in Malley, Harris was right, as Brian Elliott pointed out years ago, to recognize him as 'a remarkable *tour de force*'. James McAuley agreed the hoax has a vaudevillian energy. Malley flips between being the Australian Jules Laforgue, the futile disconsolate mind that haunts the future while forgoing all the glory, and the Australian Groucho Marx, the mercurial wit who observes how the living stand upright by habitual insouciance and then wants to mourn at his own funeral.

Were Ern Malley real he would not be half as alluring as we now find him. As poet and cipher he represents, with whatever perversity or futility, the definitive moment in Australian literary modernism. Malley is the exception that proves the rule: he is the only genuinely avant-garde writer in a country which has never sponsored a literary revolution. After him a species of poetry became untenable for a while, though that would have happened anyway, I think. The hoaxers used the Swiftian tactic of constructing a more powerful image of modernist identity than had hitherto existed in Australia – admittedly, not a huge achievement – and then discrediting it. The hoax is the most decisive piece of literary criticism ever produced in Australia. But it was more than two people pissing on modernism, as they could have done in an essay – it was a creative act, no matter how tendentious, which became part of the idiom it satirized. From their opening line, most parodies advertise themselves as being modelled on an identifiable writer: 'As we get older we do not get any younger,' Henry Reed wrote in 'Chard Whitlow', his brilliant take on *Four Quartets*. 'Seasons return, and today I am fifty-five, / And this time last year I was fifty-four / And this time next year I shall be sixty-two.' To work as nonsense, the lines require us to recognize the intonation of T. S. Eliot. Ern Malley is better than 'Chard Whitlow'. Though he borrows freely, he doesn't resemble anyone except himself. He is the only writer I know whom one can approach expecting the worst and the best, and depart satisfied.

We are nearly certain Ern Malley never lived but his manuscript existed once. After Ethel sent Harris the poems in November 1943 he took care to post them registered mail to Reed. A methodical man, Reed had his secretary type copies of the manuscript – which inexplicably, he told Harris in March 1944, 'vanished into thin air'. There have been no reported sightings since and the baseless fabric of Ern Malley's vision cannot now be found. It is not among the Reed Papers with the other Malleyana. Perhaps Bob Cugley, the printer of *Angry Penguins*, destroyed it; or perhaps he returned it to Harris who left all his papers with Reed when he went back to Adelaide. Perhaps it was dumped in the Reeds' cellar at Heide, a storehouse for bundles of old papers, and prone to flood. Hundreds of sheets, those that were not already pulp, crumbled upon retrieval years later. Sunken, sodden, did the manuscript die a watery death, like the wraiths and wreaths of tissue paper it describes? Harold Stewart, who would not care to see it in any case, does not have a copy nor is there one among James McAuley's papers. There is no authority for the final line restored by the hoaxers and now accepted in all editions: 'I have split the infinitive' which in *Angry Penguins* read 'I have split the infinite'; but James McAuley went to the trouble of correcting his own copy and Harris agrees it was the one instance where he 'improved' Malley.

Did it ever exist? Yes, but the sense of a collective hallucination is powerful. The vanishing manuscript is one of Ern's better tricks. He is always going to have the last laugh.

THE DARKENING ECLIPTIC
by ERN MALLEY

'Do not speak of secret matters in a field full of little hills.'

Old Proverb

Durer: Innsbruck, 1495

I had often, cowled in the slumberous heavy air,
Closed my inanimate lids to find it real,
As I knew it would be, the colourful spires
And painted roofs, the high snows glimpsed at the back,
All reversed in the quiet reflecting waters –
Not knowing then that Durer perceived it too.
Now I find that once more I have shrunk
To an interloper, robber of dead men's dream,
I had read in books that art is not easy
But no one warned that the mind repeats
In its ignorance the vision of others. I am still
The black swan of trespass on alien waters.

Sonnets for the Novachord

(i)

Rise from the wrist, o kestrel
Mind, to a clear expanse.
Perform your high dance
On the clouds of ancestral
Duty. Hawk at the wraith
Of remembered emotions.
Vindicate our high notions
Of a new and pitiless faith.
It is not without risk!
In a lofty attempt
The fool makes a brisk
Tumble. Rightly contempt
Rewards the cloud-foot unwary
Who falls to the prairie.

(ii)

Poetry: the loaves and fishes,
Or no less miracle;
For in this deft pentacle
We imprison our wishes.

Though stilled to alabaster
This Ichthys shall swim
From the mind's disaster
On the volatile hymn.

If this be the norm
Of our serious frolic
There's no remorse:

Our magical force
Cleaves the ignorant storm
On the hyberbolic.

Sweet William

I have avoided your wide English eyes:
But now I am whirled in their vortex.
My blood becomes a Damaged Man
Most like your Albion;
And I must go with stone feet
Down the staircase of flesh
To where in a shuddering embrace
My toppling opposites commit
The obscene, the unforgivable rape.

One moment of daylight let me have
Like a white arm thrust
Out of the dark and self-denying wave
And in the one moment I
Shall irremediably attest
How (though with sobs, and torn cries bleeding)
My white swan of quietness lies
Sanctified on my black swan's breast.

Boult to Marina

Only a part of me shall triumph in this
(I am not Pericles)
Though I have your silken eyes to kiss
And maiden-knees
Part of me remains, wench, Boult-upright
The rest of me drops off into the night.

What would you have me do? Go to the wars?
There's damned deceit
In these wounds, thrusts, shell-holes, of the cause
And I'm no cheat.
So blowing this lily as trumpet with my lips
I assert my original glory in the dark eclipse.

Sainted and schismatic would you be?
Four frowning bedposts
Will be the cliffs of your wind-thrummelled sea
Lady of these coasts,
Blown lily, surplice and stole of Mytilene,
You shall rest snug to-night and know what I mean.

Sybilline

That rabbit's foot I carried in my left pocket
Has worn a haemorrhage in the lining
The bunch of keys I carry with it
Jingles like fate in my omphagic ear
And when I stepped clear of the solid basalt
The introverted obelisk of night
I seized upon this Traumdeutung as a sword
To hew a passage to my love.

And now out of life, permanent revenant
I assert: the caterpillar feet
Of these predictions lead nowhere,
It is necessary to understand
That a poet may not exist, that his writings
Are the incomplete circle and straight drop
Of a question mark
And yet I know I shall be raised up
On the vertical banners of praise.

The rabbit's foot of fur and claw
Taps on the drain-pipe. In the alley
The children throw a ball against
Their future walls. The evening
Settles down like a brooding bird
Over streets that divide our life like a trauma
Would it be strange now to meet
The figure that strode hell swinging
His head by the hair
On Princess Street?

Night Piece

The swung torch scatters seeds
In the umbelliferous dark
And a frog makes guttural comment
On the naked and trespassing
Nymph of the lake.

The symbols were evident,
Though on park-gates
The iron birds looked disapproval
With rusty invidious beaks.

Among the water-lilies
A splash – white foam in the dark!
And you lay sobbing then
Upon my trembling intuitive arm.

Documentary Film

Innumerable the images
The register of birth and dying
Under the carved rococo porch
The Tigris – Venice – Melbourne – the Ch'en Plain –
And the sound track like a trail of saliva.
Durer:
'Samson killing the Lion' 1498
Thumbs twisting the great snarl of the beast's mouth
Tail thrashing the air of disturbed swallows
That fly to the castle on the abraded hill
London:
Samson that great city, his anatomy on fire
Grasping with gnarled hands at the mad wasps
Yet while his bearded rage survives contriving
An entelechy of clouds and trumpets.
There have been interpolations, false syndromes
Like a rivet through the hand
Such deliberate suppressions of crisis as
Footscray:
The slant sun now descending
Upon the montage of the desecrate womb
Opened like a drain.
The young men aspire
Like departing souls from leaking roofs
And fractured imploring windows to
(All must be synchronized, the jagged
Quartz of vision with the asphalt of human speech)
Java:
The elephant motifs contorted on admonitory walls,
The subtle nagas that raise the cobra hood
And hiss in the white masterful face.
What are these mirk channels of the flesh
That now sweep me from
The blood-dripping hirsute maw of night's other temple

Down through the helpless row of bonzes
Till peace suddenly comes:
Adonai:
The solemn symphony of angels lighting
My steps with music, o consolations!
Palms!
O far shore, target and shield that I now
Desire beyond these terrestrial commitments.

Palinode

There are ribald interventions
Like spurious seals upon
A Chinese landscape-roll
Or tangents to the rainbow.
We have known these declensions,
Have winked when Hyperion
Was transmuted to a troll.
We dubbed it a sideshow.

Now we find, too late
That these distractions were clues
To a transposed version
Of our too rigid state.
It is an ancient forgotten ruse
And a natural diversion.
Wiser now, but dissident,

I snap off your wrist
Like a stalk that entangles
And make my adieu.
Remember, in any event,
I was a haphazard amorist
Caught on the unlikely angles
Of an awkward arrangement. Weren't you?

Night-Piece

(Alternate version)

The intemperate torch grazed
With fire the umbel of the dark.
The pond-lilies could not stifle
The green descant of frogs.

We had not heeded the warning
That the iron birds creaked.
As we swung the park-gates
Their beaks glinted with dew.

A splash – the silver nymph
Was a foam flake in the night.
But though the careful winds
Visited our trembling flesh
They carried no echo.

Baroque Exterior

When the hysterical vision strikes
The facade of an era it manifests
Its insidious relations.
The windowed eyes gleam with terror
The twin balconies are breasts
And at the efflux of a period's error
Is a carved malicious portico.
Everyman arrests
His motives in these anthropoid erections.

Momentarily we awake –
Even as lately through wide eyes I saw
The promise of a new architecture
Of more sensitive pride, and I cursed
For the first time my own obliteration.
What Inigo had built I perceived
In a dream of recognition,
And for nights afterwards struggled
Helpless against the choking
Sands of time in my throat.

Perspective Lovesong

It was a night when the planets
Were wreathed in dying garlands.
It seemed we had substituted
The abattoirs for the guillotine.
I shall not forget how you invented
Then, the conventions of faithfulness.

It seemed that we were submerged
Under a reef of coral to tantalize
The wise-grinning shark. The waters flashed
With Blue Angels and Moorish Idols.
And if I mistook your dark hair for weed
Was it not floating upon my tides?

I have remembered the chiaroscuro
Of your naked breasts and loins.
For you were wholly an admonition
That said: 'From bright to dark
Is a brief longing. To hasten is now
To delay.' But I could not obey.

Princess, you lived in Princess St.,
Where the urchins pick their nose in the sun
With the left hand. You thought
That paying the price would give you admission
To the sad autumn of my Valhalla.
But I, too, invented faithfulness.

Culture as Exhibit

'Swamps, marshes, borrow-pits and other
Areas of stagnant water serve
As breeding-grounds . . .' Now
Have I found you, my Anopheles!
(There is a meaning for the circumspect)
Come, we will dance sedate quadrilles,
A pallid polka or a yelping shimmy
Over these sunken sodden breeding-grounds!
We will be wraiths and wreaths of tissue-paper
To clog the Town Council in their plans.
Culture forsooth! Albert, get my gun.

I have been noted in the reading-rooms
As a borer of calf-bound volumes
Full of scandals at the Court. (Milord
Had his hand upon that snowy globe
Milady Lucy's sinister breast . . .) Attendants
Have peered me over while I chewed
Back-numbers of Florentine gazettes
(Knowst not, my Lucia, that he
Who has caparisoned a nun dies
With his twankydillo at the ready? . . .)
But in all of this I got no culture till
I read a little pamphlet on my thighs
Entitled: 'Friction as a Social Process.'
What?
Look, my Anopheles,
See how the floor of Heav'n is thick
Inlaid with patines of etcetera . . .
Sting them, sting them, my Anopheles.

Egyptian Register

The hand burns resinous in the evening sky
Which is a lake of roses, perfumes, idylls
Breathed from the wastes of the Tartarean heart.
The skull gathers darkness, like an inept mountain
That broods on its aeons of self-injury.
The spine, barbed and venomous, pierces
The one unmodulated cumulus of cloud
And brings the gush of evanescent waters.
The lungs are Ra's divine aquaria
Where the striped fish move at will
Towards a purpose darker than a dawn.
The body's a hillside, darling, moist
With bitter dews of regret.
The genitals (o lures of starveling faiths!)
Make an immense index to my cold remorse.

Magic in the vegetable universe
Marks us at birth upon the forehead
With the ancient ankh. Nature
Has her own green centuries which move
Through our thin convex time. Aeons
Of that purpose slowly riot
In the decimals of our deceiving age.
It may be for nothing that we are:
But what we are continues
In larger patterns than the frontal stone
That taunts the living life.
O those dawn-waders, cold-sea-gazers,
The long-shanked ibises that on the Nile
Told one hushed peasant of rebirth
Move in a calm immortal frieze
On the mausoleum of my incestuous
And self-fructifying death.

Young Prince of Tyre

'Thy ear is liable, thy food is such
As hath been belch'd on by infected lungs'
Pericles

Inattentive, suborned, betrayed, and shiftless,
You have hawked in your throat and spat
Outrage upon the velocipede of thriftless
Mechanical men posting themselves that
Built you a gibbet in the vile morass
Which now you must dangle on, alas.

The eyeless worm threads the bone, the living
Stand upright by habitual insouciance
Else they would fall. But how unforgiving
Are they to nonce-men that falter in the dance!
Their words are clews that clutched you on the post
And you were hung up, dry, a fidgety ghost.

The magpie's carol has dried upon his tongue
To a flaky spittle of contempt. The loyalists
Clank their armour. We are no longer young,
And our rusty coat fares badly in the lists.
Poor Thaisa has a red wound in the groin
That ill advises our concupiscence to foin.
Yet there is one that stands i' the gaps to teach us
The stages of our story. He the dark hero
Moistens his finger in iguana's blood to beseech us
(Siegfried-like) to renew the language. Nero
And the botched tribe of imperial poets burn
Like the rafters. The new men are cool as spreading fern.

Now get you out, as you can, makeshift singers:
'Sail seas in cockles, have an wish for't.'
New sign-posts stretch out the road that lingers
Yet on the spool. New images distort

Our creeping disjunct minds to incredible patterns,
Else thwarting the wayward seas to fetch home the slatterns,

Take it for a sign, insolent and superb
That at nightfall the woman who scarcely would
Now opens her cunning thighs to reveal the herb
Of content. The valiant man who withstood
Rage, envy and malignant love, is no more
The wrecked Prince he was on the latter shore.

Colloquy with John Keats

'And the Lord destroyeth the imagination
of all of them that had not the truth with them'
Odes of Solomon 24.8

I have been bitter with you, my brother,
Remembering that saying of Lenin when the shadow
Was already on his face: 'The emotions are not skilled workers.'
Yet we are as the double almond concealed in one shell.
I have mistrusted your apodictic strength
Saying always: Yet why did you not finish Hyperion?
But now I have learned not to curtail
What was in you the valency of speech
The bond of molecular utterance.

I have arranged the interstellar zodiac
With flowers on the Goat's horn, and curious
Markings on the back of the Crab. I have lain
With the Lion, not with the Virgin, and become
He that discovers meanings.

Now in your honour Keats, I spin
The loaded Zodiac with my left hand
As the man at the fair revolves
His coloured deceitful board. Together
We lean over that whirl of
Beasts flowers images and men
Until it stops . . . Look! My number is up!
Like you I sought at first for Beauty
And then, in disgust, returned
As did you to the locus of sensation
And not till then did my voice build crenellated towers
Of an enteric substance in the air.
Then first I learned to speak clear; then through my turrets
Pealed that Great Bourdon which men have ignored.

We have lived as ectoplasm
The hand that would clutch
Our substance finds that his rude touch
Runs through him a frightful spasm
And hurls him back against the opposite wall.

Petit Testament

In the twenty-fifth year of my age
I find myself to be a dromedary
That has run short of water between
One oasis and the next mirage
And having despaired of ever
Making my obsessions intelligible
I am content at last to be
The sole clerk of my metamorphoses.
Begin here:

In the year 1943
I resigned to the living all collateral images
Reserving to myself a man's
Inalienable right to be sad
At his own funeral.
(Here the peacock blinks the eyes
of his multipennate tail.)
In the same year
I said to my love (who is living)
Dear we shall never be that verb
Perched on the sole Arabian Tree
Not having learnt in our green age to forget
The sins that flow between the hands and feet
(Here the Tree weeps gum tears
Which are also real: I tell you
These things are real)
So I forced a parting
Scrubbing my few dingy words to brightness.

Where I have lived
The bed-bug sleeps in the seam, the cockroach
Inhabits the crack and the careful spider
Spins his aphorisms in the corner.
I have heard them shout in the streets
The chiliasms of the Socialist Reich

And in the magazines I have read
The Popular Front-to-Back.
But where I have lived
Spain weeps in the gutters of Footscray
Guernica is the ticking of the clock
The nightmare has become real, not as belief
But in the scrub-typhus of Mubo.

It is something to be at last speaking
Though in this No-Man's-language appropriate
Only to No-Man's-Land.
Set this down too:
I have pursued rhyme, image, and metre,
Known all the clefts in which the foot may stick,
Stumbled often, stammered,
But in time the fading voice grows wise
And seizing the co-ordinates of all existence
Traces the inevitable graph
And in conclusion:
There is a moment when the pelvis
Explodes like a grenade. I
Who have lived in the shadow that each act
Casts on the next act now emerge
As loyal as the thistle that in session
Puffs its full seed upon the indicative air.
I have split the infinitive. Beyond is anything.

Notes

The National Library of Australia, Canberra,
is referred to as NLA.

1 The Death of Ern Malley

5 'raw . . . so crude in their feelings' D. H. Lawrence, 28 May 1922, *The Collected Letters of D. H. Lawrence*, ed. Harry T. Moore, Heinemann, London, 1962, 705.

– 'Australia would be a lovely country' Lawrence, 22 June 1922, *Collected Letters*, 711–12.

– 'to study elementary anatomy' Henry Lawson, ' "Pursuing Literature" in Australia', *Bulletin*, January 1899, reprinted in *Autobiographical and Other Writings 1887–1922, Collected Prose*, Vol. 2, ed. Colin Roderick, Angus & Robertson, Sydney, 1972, 115.

6 By mid-1940 *Christian Science Monitor*, 10 July 1940, 5.

– 'terribly afraid' Lawrence, 13 June 1922, *Collected Letters*, 707.

8 'young girls sat on the curbs' *Sydney Morning Herald*, 5 November 1943, quoted in *Over-Sexed, Over-Paid, and Over Here: Americans in Australia 1941–1945*, John Hammond Moore, University of Queensland Press, St Lucia, 1981, 226.

– 'The present decay of morals' *Sydney Morning Herald*, 8 March 1943.

– 'THE FLESH' *Advocate*, 4 October 1944, 9.

– 'excursions into the subconscious mind'; 'moll-houses, barrell-houses' *Advocate*, 5 July 1944, 5, 11.

2 Enfant Terrible

10 'soft deep eyes' John Reed, unpublished autobiography, Reed Papers, La Trobe Library, Melbourne, Pre-Accession 1168.

– 'Slender and handsome as Flecker's Hassan' Hal Porter, *The Paper Chase*, Angus & Roberton, Sydney, 1966, 176.

11 The English master, J. S. Padman Interview with Max Harris, 7 February 1989.

13 'As owners of a great van Eyck' Quoted in Leonard Cox, *The National Gallery of Victoria 1861–1968: A Search for a Collection*, National Gallery of Victoria, Melbourne, 1970, 164.

14 'the most interesting of the *Jindyworobak*' *Bulletin*, Red Page, 14 December 1938.

– 'I am afraid that my position'; 'secretary of the Jindys' Max Harris, letter to Ted Turner, 11 April 1939, NLA H. H. Pearce Collection, Series 2, MS 2765/2/10.

– 'quiet fanatic' Porter, *Paper Chase*, 176.

15 'English idiom' Rex Ingamells, *Conditional Culture*, F. W. Preece, Adelaide, 1938, 7.

– 'so aggressively foreign' Brian Elliott, letter to Clem Christesen, 11 April 1944, Meanjin Archive, Baillieu Library, University of Melbourne.

– 'Australia is still the Unknown Land' Rex Ingamells, 'The Australian Outlook', *Meanjin Papers*, Vol. 1, No. 8, March 1942, 11.

16 'Moorawathimeering', Rex Ingamells, *Selected Poems*, Georgian House, Melbourne, 1945, 63.

– writer of jargon Harris's attack ('Dance Little Wombat') appeared in *Meanjin Papers*, Vol. 2, No. 2, Winter 1943, 34.

– 'Each moment of isolationism'; 'the present *attitude* to poetry' Harris to Turner, 11 April 1939, NLA.

17 'disenfranchised by his lack of residence' Herbert Read, *A Coat of Many Colours*, George Routledge and Sons, London, 1945, 219.

19 'a handsome and charming young coot' Rex Ingamells, letter to Clem Christesen, 21 September 1942, Meanjin Archive.

19–20 'I am iconoclastical'; 'cause hostility, criticism, dislike' Max Harris, letter to Ted Turner, undated.

20 'near Dadaistic' Harris to Turner, undated, NLA. The talk was given on Monday, 24 June 1940, and the description of its contents was by Arts Association Secretary Geoffrey Dutton. See Margaret M. Finnis, *The Lower Level*, Adelaide University Union, 1975, 186.

– suffered the indignity See Harris to Turner, undated, NLA, 'I am in the shit . . .'

– 'this town hates my guts' Interview with Catherine Veitch (née Caris), 17 March 1992.

21 'Most of the verses' Harold Stewart, 'Harris Harrassed', *Honi Soit*, 21 May 1942, 2.

– 'producing a magazine' Harris to Turner, undated, NLA.

22–3 'my life is lived with artists'; 'He may be egocentric' John Reed, letter to JDB, 10 May 1944, Reed Papers, 10/18,3.

24 'should arouse . . . a massive . . . response' This and the following quotations from George Fraser, 'Apocalypse in Poetry', *The White Horseman: Prose and Verse of the New Apocalypse*, Routledge, London, 1941, 14, 3, 15.

25 Lawlor was its advocate See Richard Haese, *Rebels and Precursors*, Penguin, Ringwood, 1981, 1988, 30ff and 61ff.

– 'Tartarean drench of verbosity' Max Harris, 'Eliminations', *A Comment*, No. 7, September 1941.

26 'may I show you the faraway blister' Adrian Lawlor, *A Comment*, No. 8, November 1941.

– 'swinish disciples of equality and fraternity' Alister Kershaw, *A Comment*, Nos 9 and 10, January 1942.

– once gave a public performance The anecdote is taken from Haese, *Rebels and Precursors*, 111.

– 'unending self-abnegatory groan' These and the following quotations from 'No Levelled Malice', Kershaw's introduction to *The Lonely Verge*, Warlock Press, Melbourne, 1943, 1ff, 26.

27 As chief *Angry Penguin* Interview with Geoffrey Dutton, 30 July 1988.
– 'We are in a position' John Reed, letter to Max Harris, 25 January 1944, Reed Papers, 10/18,5.

3 *Jim and Harold*

28 'the first McAuley was an Irish soldier' Interview with James McAuley by Catherine Santamaria, 5 May 1976, NLA, Tape Recording Collection 576/1.
– 'dammed up his Irish blood' James McAuley, 'Because', *Collected Poems 1936–1970* Angus & Robertson, Sydney, 1971, 200.
– 'daily as the *Sydney Morning Herald*' James McAuley, 'Because'.
29 'profound horror' James McAuley, 'Some Aspects of Modern Poetry', *Fortian*, June 1934, 24–6.
30 'a thirty-page answer' Harold Stewart, letter to the author, 15 November 1992.
– 'rivals . . . We were both editors'; 'I have never been so bored . . .' Harold Stewart, letter to the author, 15 November 1988.
– 'I had no money at all' Interview with Harold Stewart, 23 January 1989.
31 'Among the extreme Expressionists' Harold Stewart, *Honi Soit*, 18 September 1941, 2.
– 'That was a period' Interview with Harold Stewart, 25 January 1989.
– 'He did all his own reading' Interview with Norma McAuley, 26 November 1988.
– 'I thought McAuley' Interview with Tess van Sommers, 1 August 1988.
– 'He was so impressive' Interview with Amy Witting, 4 July 1989.
– 'had some of the mannerisms' Donald Horne, *The Education of Young Donald*, Penguin, Ringwood, 1975, 229.
32 McAuley sometimes used to walk See Peter Coleman, *The Heart of James McAuley*, Wildcat Press, Sydney, 1980, 1, and Horne, *Education*, 226ff.
– 'meagre rooms in the western suburbs' van Sommers, 1 August 1988.
– He sang in an alto voice Harry Jackman, 'Jim and the Kiaps', *Quadrant*, March 1977, 73.
– 'and played "Rhapsody in Blue" on the carillon' Horne, *Education*, 226.
– he riled loyalists Interview with Douglas McCallum, 5 July 1989.
32–3 'Readjoice and begad!'; 'But then you were faithful to Joseph' James McAuley, undated letters (1939?) to Ulick and Joan King, in the possession of Joan Dunbar.
33 'the McAuley group' van Sommers, 1 August 1988.
– 'It was very chauvinist' Witting, 4 July 1989.
34 rather secretive Norma McAuley, 26 November 1988.
– 'almost without mannerism' Horne, *Education*, 229.
– 'He's a very strong character'; 'The two halves of his life' Witting, 4 July 1989.
– 'took as his subject' James McAuley, *Union Recorder*, University of Sydney, 28 October 1937, 245–6.
– 'Pound's outstanding achievement' James McAuley, 'The Book of Ezra', *Hermes*, magazine of the University of Sydney, XLIV, 1 Lent Term, 1938, 10–12.
– 'convinced disciple' James McAuley, 'The Journey of the Magus', *Hermes*, XLIII, 1 Lent Term, 1937, 12–17.

35 'the only prose work' This and the following quotations from McAuley letters to Dorothy Auchterlonie, 1938–9, NLA, MS 5678.

36 a friend remembers him describing a dream The friend was Joan King.

– 'There was a banished part of himself' Witting, 4 July 1989.

37 'a big man in a stove-pipe hat' NLA, Palmer Papers 1174, Series 28, Folder 15.

– 'that inward stir' This and the following quotations from McAuley letters to Auchterlonie, NLA, MS 5678.

– 'Aspects of the Moon' McAuley's letter may have been written on 7 November 1938.

38 'We came from a crooked town, my dear' James McAuley, 'Rhyme's End', Under Aldebaran, Melbourne University Press, 1946, 31.

– 'earning a small living' McAuley to Auchterlonie, NLA, MS 5678.

39 'acrid despair' These and the following quotations from McAuley's unpublished MA thesis, Fisher Library, University of Sydney.

– 'He wanted to be a conscientious objector' Interview with Dorothy Green, 31 July 1988.

40 An acquaintance remembers him Interview with Bill Pritchett, 18 July 1989.

– 'a thin, slight, pale, intense young man'; 'several heavily disguised'; 'as a sort of mock wake' Russel Ward, A Radical Life, Macmillan, South Melbourne, 1988, 137, 138.

41 'film running in your own mind'; 'I had to ask myself' McAuley with Santamaria, 5 May 1976.

– 'Ballade of Lost Phrases', James McAuley, Collected Poems, 18.

42 'timid with people' Interview with Manning Clark, 7 July 1988.

– 'craggy cheeks' Manning Clark, The Quest for Grace, Viking, Ringwood, 1990, 129.

– 'When he spoke he spoke' Clark interview, 7 July 1988.

43 'What you hated in those days' Witting, 4 July 1989.

– 'Anderson taught so many of us to think' James McAuley, ABC TV Spectrum interview with Tony Morphett, taped 25 September 1966, Mitchell Library, Sydney, MSS 1511.

44 'replicas of the innovations'; 'moping maudlin moonlit nights'; 'he has written sentimentally bad poems' Oliver Somerville, letters to Harry Hooton, 11 August, 10 March, 24 August 1942, Mitchell Library, Sydney, MSS 569.

– 'all the outward marks of genius' Witting, 4 July 1989.

– He smoked 'violently' Interview with Ronald Dunlop, 4 July 1989.

45 'I've always been on the fringes'; 'I am gregarious' Somerville to Hooton, 11 August 1942, Mitchell Library, MSS 569.

– 'the most suburban bank clerk'; 'I am really, as McAuley'; 'it beats all mine' Somerville to Hooton, June 1944, 24 August 1942, Mitchell Library, MSS 569.

46 'The educated mob exudes' Oliver Somerville 'Ballade', Hermes XLVI, 1 Trinity Term, 1940, n.p.

48 'authentic utterance' Dulcie Renshaw, Honi Soit, 17 August 1942, 2.

50 'I sometimes think the war forces us' Sidney Nolan, letter to Sunday Reed, Reed Papers, La Trobe Library, Melbourne, 6/18,11.

51 'There the blue-green gums'; 'The people are hard-eyed' James McAuley, 'Envoi', Collected Poems 1936–1970, Angus & Robertson, Sydney, 1971, 6.

- 'A Nation of trees'; 'A vast parasite' A. D. Hope, 'Australia', *Collected Poems*, 13.
- 'He is capable of producing' McAuley to Green, NLA, MS 5678.
- 'I liked Emily Dickinson's' Stewart to author, 30 November 1988.
52 He introduced Horne to Pound and cummings Horne, *Education*, 229.
- 'It took me years' This and the following quotations from Stewart to author, 15 November 1988.
53 'Now in that brazen zenith' from Harold Stewart, 'The Ascension of Fêng', *Phoenix Wings*, Angus & Robertson, Sydney, 1948, 21. Stewart has subsequently revised this passage, as he has most of his early poetry.
- 'Anubis-headed, the heresiarch' McAuley, 'The Incarnation of Sirius', *Under Aldebaran*, 15.
54 published in an 'experimental way' Frederick T. Macartney, 10 August 1942, NLA, MS 1174, Series 28, Folder 15.

4 *A Strange and Sinister Figure*

55 'Dear Sir, When I was going through' The letter, which no longer survives in manuscript, was published in facsimile in *Angry Penguins*, December 1944, 10–11.
57 'At this stage I knew nothing' Max Harris, *Angry Penguins*, Autumn 1944, 2.
- 'Thank you for sending me' Max Harris, letter to Ethel Malley, 2 November 1943, McAuley Papers, in the possession of Norma McAuley.
58 'Here's a pretty terrific discovery' Harris to Reed, 8 November 1943, Reed Papers, La Trobe Library, Melbourne, 17/18,2.
59 'Sunday, Nolan and another friend' Reed to Harris, Reed Papers, 17/18,2.
60 'He plucked and held the scented rose' Alister Kershaw, *The Lonely Verge*, Warlock Press, Melbourne, 1943, 15.
- 'Dear Mr Harris, Thank you for your letter' Malley to Harris, Reed Papers, 17/18,2. Part of this letter was published in *Angry Penguins*, Autumn 1944.
63 'an explanation of his complete silence' Harris, *Angry Penguins*, Autumn 1944, 2.
65 'These poems are complete' Reed Papers, 17/18,2. The 'Preface and Statement' was published in *Angry Penguins*, Autumn 1944, 7.
66 'Yes, with reservations' Brian Elliot, letter to Clem Christesen, 14 September 1944, Meanjin Archive, Baillieu Library, University of Melbourne.
- 'the sort of highly derivative' J. I. M. Stewart, quoted in John Thompson, 'The Ern Malley Story', an ABC Radio feature published in Clement Semmler, *For the Uncanny Man*, F. W. Cheshire, Melbourne, 1963, 164.
66–7 'I was absolutely carried away' Interview with Geoffrey Dutton, 30 July 1988.
67 'read them carefully' Interview with Catherine Veitch, 17 March 1992.
- 'Ern Malley prepared for his death' Harris, *Angry Penguins*, Autumn 1944, 3. The other quotations in this section are from the same source.
69 'The wind masters the waves' Reed Papers, 17/18,2.
70 'a heart-rending unfinished last poem' Harold Stewart, 'The Truth About Ern Malley', Colin Simpson Papers, NLA, MS 5252.

- 'It was a big moment' Reed to Harris, 26 November 1943, Reed Papers, 11/18,5.
- 'quite definitely never' Reed to Harris, 29 November 1943, Reed Papers, 11/18,5.
- 'princess of Princess Street' Harris to Reed, undated, Reed Papers 12/18,11.
- 'reluctant' Reed to Harris, 3 December 1943, Reed Papers, 11/18,4.

71 'no doubt about the quality' Reed to Harris, 1 December 1943, Reed Papers, 11/18,2.
- 'they were the product' Interview with Sidney Nolan, 5 April 1991.
- 'Been reading the Malley' Nolan to Reed, Reed Papers, 7/18,15.
- 'help you to see things' Nolan to Sunday Reed, 17 August 1943, Reed Papers, 6/18,11.

72 'Painted this afternoon'; 'painting as hard' Nolan to Sunday Reed, undated, and 12 October 1942, Reed Papers, 6/18,11.

73 'had a very intimate relationship' Nolan, 5 April 1991.
- 'of all things loneliness' Nolan to Sunday Reed, 12 January 1944, Reed Papers, 6/18,11.
- 'Your brother was one of the most remarkable' Harris to Malley, undated, McAuley Papers.

74 'I have not received an answer' Harris to Malley, undated, McAuley Papers.

74-5 'I am sorry I couldn't reply' Malley to Harris, 14 January 1944, Reed Papers, 17/18,2.

75 'There are no photos of Malley' Harris to Reed, undated, February(?) 1944, Reed Papers, 11/18,2.
- 'old', 'creased' Stewart, 'The Truth About Ern Malley', NLA, MS 5252.

76 'Ern – The plot is sprung' Reed Papers, 17/18,2.
- 'The handwriting is cultured' Harris to Reed, February(?) 1944, Reed Papers, 11/18,2.
- 'Grave's disease' *Voices*, Australian Issue, Summer 1944, 46.
- 'Malley will possibly be more important' Harris to Reed, 1 December 1943, Reed Papers, 10/18,5.
- 'Malley is of such terrible significance' Harris to Reed, just before 28 February 1944, Reed Papers, 11/18,2.

77 'the epic suffering' Harris, *Angry Penguins*, Autumn 1944, 4,2.
- 'addressed the Art Association' Elliott to Christesen, 23? June 1944, Meanjin Archive.
- just over £250 to set up and print   I am grateful to Jeff Prentice who showed me copies of accounts kept by Bob Cugley, printer of *Angry Penguins* and all Reed & Harris publications from 1943. Cugley became a legend in the trade for his sympathetic attitude to publishers and writers denied a voice by the mainstream press. 'Every ratbag in Melbourne sooner or later finds his way here,' he once said. His firm, The National Press, closed its doors in 1983 and Cugley died in 1987, at the age of 85. In his last recorded statement about the hoax, he confided, 'I'm the only bloke who ever met Ern Malley.' What he meant cannot be glossed.
- John Reed expected . . . to lose about £100 Reed to Harris, 25 May 1944, Reed Papers, 11/18,4.
- 'I have posted you a copy' Reed to Harris, 31 May 1944, Reed Papers, 11/18,2.

77–8 'the most outstanding journal' Harris to Reed, 5 June 1944, Reed Papers, 11/18,2.

78 'It seems to me that the next six months' Harris to Reed, 2 June 1944, Reed Papers, 10/18,5.

5 A Wonderful Jape

82 'that sometimes the shortest way' Sid Deamer in *Alfred Conlon*, compiled by John Thompson, Benevolent Society of New South Wales, Sydney, 1963, 7.

– 'the moving force' Peter Thompson in *Alfred Conlon*, 49.

– 'magnificent fun' John Kerr, *Matters for Judgment*, Sun Books, South Melbourne, 1988, 116.

– 'with a solemn, rather owlish expression' Hugh Gilchrist in *Alfred Conlon*, 3.

– 'He was given to using' Interview with Alan Crawford, 3 July 1989.

– 'Sometimes he would admit' Gilchrist in *Alfred Conlon*, 3.

– 'To hold out specific promises' Alf Conlon, *Honi Soit*, 20 July 1939.

83 In February 1942 This and much of the following information is derived from Richard Hall, *The Real John Kerr*, Angus & Robertson, Sydney, 1978, 36–63.

– 'snatching an hour's sleep at dawn' Unsigned article, 'The Master Puppeteer' by Peter Ryan, *Nation*, 26 September 1958, 13.

– 'Renaissance Court' James McAuley in *Alfred Conlon*, 25.

– 'would switch lights on' Interview with James McAuley by Catherine Santamaria, 5 May 1976, NLA, Tape Recording Collection 576/1,32.

84 'a kind of spell-binder, Svengali-like' Interview with Sir John Kerr, 5 July 1989.

– 'another naughty thing' Interview with Harold Stewart, 23 January 1989.

85 'to keep the Commander-in-Chief' Gavin Long, *The Final Campaigns*, Australian War Memorial, Canberra, 1963, 397.

– 'wasn't an appendage to the British Government' McAuley with Santamaria, 5 May 1976, 33.

– 'with a toothbrush and nothing else' Interview with Manning Clark, 7 July 1988.

86 'The Directorate has inquired into everything'; 'manpower position in universities' Australian Archives, Melbourne Permanent 742/1, 1/1/1808.

87 'travelling Malaria exhibitions' Australian Archives, Melbourne Permanent, 742/1, 211/6/30.

– 'Springs and seepages' From a New Zealand Army report on mosquito control, December 1943, Australian Archives, Melbourne Permanent, 742/1, 211/6/810.

– a compulsive talker Alec Hope in *Alfred Conlon*, 54.

– 'immensely grateful' McAuley in *Alfred Conlon*, 24.

88 'suggested in a way that he *had* written poetry' Thompson in *Alfred Conlon*, 48.

– 'a strong opponent of any sort of humbug' Gilchrist in *Alfred Conlon*, 52.

89 'and probably gave thereby the degree' John Thompson, 'The Ern Malley Story', an ABC Radio feature published in Clement Semmler, *For the Uncanny Man*, F. W. Cheshire, Melbourne, 1963, 177.

– 'we probably had two pens' Stewart, 23 January 1989.

91–2 'one of two or three'; 'We ranged from Picasso's'; 'What the poem claims' James McAuley, 'Albrecht Dürer: Self and the World', *Quadrant*, November 1976, 8–16.

93 'We'd think of a line or two each' Stewart, 23 January 1989.

94 'one another's style' James McAuley, in Thompson, 'The Ern Malley Story', 180.

– 'a macaronic medley of literary detritus' Stewart, 23 January 1989.

96 'Someone should try and locate the man' Elisabeth Lambert, letter to John Reed, 11 July 1944, Reed Papers, La Trobe Library, Melbourne, 11/18,7.

97 'imperfect rhyme'; 'let unstressed syllables'; 'hued you'd unsubdued nude denude' *A Pocket Dictionary of English Rhymes*, compiled by Walter Ripman, J. M. Dent and Sons, London, 1932, 120, v, 88.

99 'It was a hard day's work' James McAuley, quoted in Graeme Kinross Smith, *Australia's Writers*, Nelson, Melbourne, 1980, 319.

– 'It would have taken Shakespeare' Sidney Nolan, quoted in the *National Times*, 4 March 1974, 26.

100 'two army officers working in the same unit' Harold Stewart, in Thompson, 'The Ern Malley Story', 182.

– 'We carefully mistyped and erased' Harold Stewart, 'The Truth About Ern Malley', Colin Simpson Papers, NLA, MS 5252.

– 'so they got sillier and sillier' Harold Stewart, in Thompson, 'The Ern Malley Story', 175.

– 'in fits of laughter' Interview with Norma McAuley, 26 November 1988.

– 'horrified' James McAuley, in Thompson, 'The Ern Malley Story', 174.

101 'laughed and said he doubted' James McAuley, *Quadrant*, January 1976, 26.

– 'an important public figure' Kerr, *Matters for Judgment*, 116.

– Born in Sydney in 1894 See Kylie Tennant, *Evatt – Politics and Justice*, Angus & Robertson, Sydney, 1981.

– 'with a kind of sardonic grin' Crawford, 3 July 1989.

102 'he had a no hands approach' Kerr, 5 July 1989.

103 'had to get to work and invent a life' Stewart, 23 January 1989.

– 'Edna was conceived as a character'; 'I invented Edna because I hated her' Barry Humphries, quoted by John Lahr, 'Playing Possum', *New Yorker*, 1 July 1991, 49, 56.

– 'apotheosis of the lower middle-class female' Stewart, 'The Truth About Ern Malley', NLA, MS 5252.

– 'as good as anything similar' Vivian Smith, *The Oxford History of Australian Literature*, Oxford University Press, Melbourne, 1981, 371.

104 'At the time I thought it was unlikely' Norma McAuley, 26 November 1988.

– 'The letters required much more literary skill' Stewart, in Thompson, 'The Ern Malley Story', 182.

105 'Another one of the books' Stewart, 23 January 1989.

107 'in the proportion of 8 to 1' *Black's Medical Dictionary*, 34th edition, 1984, 409.

– 'We just got it out of a medical dictionary' Stewart, 23 January 1989.

– 'I'd rather have an art of genuine humour' Quoted by Robert Hughes, *Donald Friend*, Edwards and Shaw, Sydney, 1965, 46.

108 'Art is a product of autarky' Herbert Read, *A Coat of Many Colours*, George Routledge and Sons, London, 1945, 114.

– 'It shows the signs' Interview with A. D. Hope, 31 July 1988.

- 'great favourite' Harold Stewart, letter to the author, 15 February 1989.
109 'the richly paradoxical character' Stewart, 'The Truth About Ern Malley', NLA, MS 5252.
- 'It was an airfield below'; 'as a later discovery of Ethel's' Stewart to author, 6 May 1989.
110 'You know, the lady by the stream'; 'I'd never seen a Dali before' Stewart, 23 January 1989.
111 'practical joke'; 'American snobbism' Donald Friend, *Diaries*, 16 November 1943, NLA, MS 5959, Item 26.
111–12 'peat-and-potato-eating'; 'reproduction of an American primitive portrait' Donald Friend, *Painter's Journal*, Ure Smith, Sydney, 1946, 64–5.
112 who 'adored' it NLA, 5959. An extensive search of the *Christian Science Monitor* between 1937 and 1942 failed to find Friend's article. Yet it was certainly published. Friend's sister Gwen remembers once owning a cutting. The 'primitive' painting itself was lost in storage in the late forties, and has not been sighted since. It is reproduced in Friend, *Painter's Journal*, 65.
- 'That gave me the idea' Stewart, 23 January 1989.
- 'the coupling of two realities' Max Ernst, *Beyond Painting and Other Writings by the Artist and His Friends*, Wittenborn, Schultz, Inc., New York, 1948, 13.
114 'a lot of nonsense' Hope, 31 July 1988.
- 'deliberately phoney constructions' Hope, letter to Clem Christesen, 25 June 1944, Meanjin Archive, Baillieu Library, University of Melbourne.
- 'to send them to *Angry Penguins*' Hope, 31 July 1988.
- 'Yes, I'd love to do *The Vegetative Eye*' Hope to Christesen, Meanjin Archive. The letter is dated 6 March 1943 but this must be in error, since the book was not published until very late in that year.
- 'The Boy Scout School of Poetry' A. D. Hope, 'Cultural Corroboree', *Southerly*, Vol. 2, No. 3, November 1941.
115 'I never thought to find myself' Hope to Christesen, undated, Meanjin Archive.
- 'of whom I know so little'; 'excellent – the only really exact critic'; 'You do publish quite a lot of criticism' Hope to Christesen, 1 January 1944, Meanjin Archive.
- 'this piece of tomfoolery' A. D. Hope, *Native Companions*, Angus & Robertson, Sydney, 1974, 48–9.
115–16 'nearly all the characters'; 'The great names' A. D. Hope, 'Confession of a Zombi' *Meanjin*, Vol. 3, No. 1, Autumn 1944, 44–8.
116 'pretentious and illiterate verbal sludge', A. D. Hope, 'The Bunyip Stages a Comeback', *Sydney Morning Herald*, 16 June 1956, 15.
- 'The whispering innuendos' Max Harris, *The Vegetative Eye*, Reed & Harris, Melbourne, 1943, 84.
117 'a serious piece of criticism'; 'The best touch from my point of view' Hope to Christesen, 25 June 1944, Meanjin Archive.
118 'donkey work'; 'I can't remember where'; 'When you are a journalist' Interview with Tess van Sommers, 1 August 1988.
- 'who could be trusted' Tess van Sommers, letter to the author, 2 August 1988.
- 'sheaf of their failures' van Sommers, 1 August 1988.
- 'wonderful jape' Thompson, 'The Ern Malley Story', 164.

6 Malley Who?

119 'not a jumped-up type' This and the following quotations from interview with Brian Elliott, 30 May 1988.

123 'It is a sheer joy' Copy of a letter from Harold Stewart, Donald Friend, *Diaries*, 27 June 1944, NLA, MS 5959, Item 26.

124 'My eye fell on this frightful Sidney Nolan' This and the following quotations from interview with Tess van Sommers, 1 August 1988.

  – 'in a state of frightful excitement' Tess van Sommers, in John Thompson, 'The Ern Malley Story', an ABC Radio feature published in Clement Semmler, *For the Uncanny Man*, F. W. Cheshire, Melbourne, 1963, 165.

125 'Jimmy never really forgave me' van Sommers, 1 August 1988.

  – 'It was the egregious Herbert' James McAuley, copy of letter to Brian Elliott, 27 November 1944, McAuley Papers, in the possession of Norma McAuley.

126 'the biggest literary hoax' John Reed, letter to Max Harris, 19 June 1944, Reed Papers, La Trobe Library, Melbourne, 11/18,2.

  – 'a Nembutal-stupefied sleep at 2' Harris to Reed, 16(?) June 1944, Reed Papers, 11/18,2.

129 'Lady, three white leopards' Stephen Spender, 'Remembering Eliot', in *The Thirties and After*, Macmillan, London 1978, 242.

130–1 'Everything points to Adrian'; 'Latest Malley news'; 'This apparently points'; 'I heard an indirect story this morning' Reed to Harris, 19, 21, 23 June, 3 July 1944, Reed Papers, 11/18,2, 10/18,3.

131 'a short-sighted Pomeranian dog' The *Age*, 17 June 1944, 2.

133–4 'I suppose by now'; 'I am rather pleased' A. D. Hope, letters to Clem Christesen, 22, 25 June 1944, Meanjin Archive, Baillieu Library, University of Melbourne.

134 'Max has taken my part' Brian Elliott, letter to Clem Christesen, 23(?) June 1944, Meanjin Archive.

136 'I hope it is no aspersion' J. I. M. Stewart, letter to *On Dit*, 23 June 1944.

7 A Serious Literary Experiment

142 'I think the enclosed' James McAuley, letter to Tess van Sommers, 19 June 1944, Colin Simpson Papers, NLA, MS 5252. Quotations from the draft versions of the statement published in *Fact* are also from documents in the Simpson Papers. I am grateful to Tess van Sommers who showed me her copies of McAuley's letter and the drafts.

143 '*Meanjin*'s reaction to the "affaire Malley"' *Meanjin Papers*, Vol. 3, No. 2, Winter 1944.

144 'keep your spirits up' A. D. Hope, letter to Clem Christesen, 25 June 1944, Meanjin Archive, Baillieu Library, University of Melbourne.

  – 'unsatisfactory, since it was cobbled up' Interview with Harold Stewart, 23 January 1989.

145 as Hugh Kenner has shown in *The Counterfeiters*, Indiana University Press, Bloomington, 1968.

  – 'confused by the presence' Brian Elliott, 'A Summing Up', *Meanjin Papers*, Vol. 3, No. 2, Winter 1944, 117.

146 'I am not a modern painter' William Dobell, quoted in *Angry Penguins*, Autumn 1944, 106.

147 'I felt the newspaper statement' Brian Elliott, 'A Summing Up', *Meanjin Papers*, Vol. 3, No. 2, Winter 1944, 119.

150 'rather terrific' Interview with Sidney Nolan, 5 April 1991.

152 'the substantiation of the poems' John Reed, letter to Max Harris, 27 June 1944, Reed Papers, La Trobe Library, Melbourne, 10/18,3.

153 'to make a newspaper holiday' James McAuley, draft statement for *Fact*, Simpson Papers.

— 'disgusted by the way the press' Stewart, 23 January 1989.

— '*The Argus* reported' 3 July 1944, 3.

154 'dissipate the too prevalent charlatanism' Bernard O'Dowd, *Herald*, 4 July 1944, 5.

— 'poetry should express simple thoughts' Letter to the Editor from Lieut. H. Burkitt, *Herald*, Thursday, 6 July 1944, 8.

155 'the complete cultural bankruptcy' Noel Counihan, 'Pretentious Penguins Exposed by Hoax', *Guardian*, 14 July 1944, 7.

— 'Only the complete lack of talent' Vic O'Connor, *Communist Review*, August 1944, 302–3.

— 'decadent Australian Anderson products' Vic O'Connor, letter to Bernard Smith, 18 August 1944, in the possession of Bernard Smith.

156 'extremely interested' John Reed, letter to Harry Roskolenko, 10 November 1944, Reed Papers, 11/18,9.

— 'I TOO WOULD HAVE BEEN' *Angry Penguins*, December 1944, 5. Read's cable arrived on 24 August 1944. Neither the cable nor the subsequent letter has survived in the original.

158 'the leading authority' Adrian Lawlor, letter to John Reed, 29 August 1944, Reed Papers, 10/18,3.

— 'heretic' John Anderson, 'Poetry and Society' (1945), in *Art and Reality*, ed. Janet Anderson, Graham Cullum and Kyman Lycos, Hale and Iremonger, Sydney, 1982, 77–81.

159 'sickened with horror' Richard Ellmann, *Oscar Wilde*, Hamish Hamilton, London, 1987, 447.

160 'ingenious hypothesis' James McAuley, letter to Brian Elliott, 27 November 1944, from a copy in the possession of Norma McAuley.

— The sport of enjoying bad poetry For further discussion of *The Stuffed Owl* see Hugh Kenner's *The Counterfeiters*, especially the opening three chapters.

— 'So past the strong heroic soul away' From Tennyson's 'Enoch Arden', *The Stuffed Owl*, J. M. Dent and Sons, London, 1960, 8.

— 'eerie supernal beauty' Lewis and Lee, *Stuffed Owl*, ix.

162 'Spade! With which' From Wordsworth's 'To the Spade of a Friend', *Stuffed Owl*, 1.

163 'spoils anyone for modern poetry' 'The Talk of the Town', *New Yorker*, 4 November 1944.

— The *Nation* remarked 18 November 1944, 618.

— 'These men have not lived in vain' 'Janus', *Spectator*, 30 June 1944, 584.

8 *Persona Non Grata*

167 'the malicious vapourings' Max Harris, letter to John Reed, 27 June 1944, Reed Papers, La Trobe Library, Melbourne, 11/18,2.

－ 'disposed to dismiss' Reed to Harris, 27 June 1944, Reed Papers, 10/18,3.

－ 'I've said all I desire' Harris to Reed, 1 July 1944, Reed Papers, 11/18,2.

167 'the utmost concession' Harris to Reed, 25 July 1944, Reed Papers, 11/18,2.

－ 'no end' Harris to Reed, 10 July 1944, Reed Papers, 11/18,2.

－ 'Another of the clan' Harris to Reed, 1 July 1944, Reed Papers, 11/18,2.

－ 'Hope on V. Eye very nice' Brian Elliott, letter to Clem Christesen, 3 July 1944, Meanjin Archive, Baillieu Library, University of Melbourne.

168 'the fluidity and emotive control' Max Harris, 'East Lynne at Uncle Tom's Cabin; or Plays at the Hut', *On Dit*, 30 June 1944, 2.

－ 'not robust but highly strung'; 'dark blue eyes and raven hair' *Australian Dictionary of Biography*, Vol. 9: 1891–1939, Melbourne University Press, 1983, 150–53, 149.

169 'not happily cast' Sidney Downer, *Advertiser*, 4 September 1934.

－ 'I took a bottle of ink' Patricia Hackett, quoted in *News*, 5 September 1934.

170 'peculiar pictures' Charles Abbott in *Parliamentary Debates of South Australia*, Vol. 1, 1942–3, 21 July 1942, 102.

－ 'Quite possibly the whole thing'; 'I haven't yet seen the article' Reed to Harris, 12, 19 July 1944, Reed Papers, 10/18,3.

－ 'a remarkable experience' Harris to Reed, 28 July 1944, Reed Papers, 11/18,2.

171 'It does not seem enough' Reed to Harris, 25 July 1944, Reed Papers, 10/18,3.

－ 'certain inescapable things' Harris to Reed, 28 July 1944, Reed Papers, 11/18,2.

172 'were caught in Adelaide' A. J. Hannan KC, 'Our Second Hundred Years', a printed pamphlet of a speech read before members of the Insurance Institute of South Australia, Monday, 22 June 1936.

173 'It is the culmination'; 'the doctor who is sympathetic'; 'battled his way through to a psychiatrist' Reed to Harris, 23 June, 5, 11 July 1944, Reed Papers, 10/18,3.

－ 'John Reed was influenced' Sidney Nolan, letter to Malcolm Good, 14 July 1944, Reed Papers, 10/18,3.

175 'Without Ern Malley' Sidney Nolan, 'Beyond is Anything', ABC TV documentary, 1974.

－ 'your heightened perception' Interview with Sidney Nolan, 5 April 1991.

176 In December 1942 he did a painting For discussion of Nolan's works of this period see Elwyn Lynn, *Sidney Nolan–Australia*, Bay Books, Sydney, 1979; Richard Haese and Jan Minchin, *Sidney Nolan: the City and the Plain*, National Gallery of Victoria, Melbourne, 1983; and Jane Clark *Sidney Nolan: Landscapes and Legends*, International Cultural Corporation of Australia, Sydney, 1987.

－ 'did make sense' Nolan, 5 April 1991.

177 'really good poetry' A. R. Chisholm, 'The Case of Ern Malley', *Angry Penguins*, December 1944, 8.

－ 'blind to the brilliance' Brian Elliott, 'The Merit or Lack of It', *Angry Penguins*, 10.

－ 'acts of recognition' Albert Tucker, 'Clear the Air', *Angry Penguins*, 13.

178 'was justified' H. M. Green, 'The Anopheles', *Angry Penguins*, 16.

— 'not poetry at all' Dorothy Green, 'The Cloud-Foot Unwary', *Angry Penguins*, 16.

— 'I suggest 1,000 copies' Harris to Read, 10 July 1944, Reed Papers, 11/18,2.

— Tipper was also the first The details about Tipper's singing and cycling are from Richard Haese, *Rebels and Precursors*, Penguin, Ringwood, 1981, 1988, 177.

178–9 'really delightful'; 'the Tipper (primitive painter) idea' Reed to Harris, 11, 3 July 1944, Reed Papers, 10/18,3.

179 'full of fight, & not retracing' Harris to Reed, 10 July 1944, Reed Papers, 11/18,2.

— 'but yesterday Mullens' Reed to Harris, 16 January 1945, Reed Papers, 10/18,3.

— 'What did you mean by asking' A. D. Hope, letter to Clem Christesen, undated, Meanjin Archive.

180 'We are police officers' All quotations are taken from the transcript of *Harris v. Harris* in the Adelaide Police Court, File No. 7548 of 1944, the only surviving copy of which is deposited in the Reed Papers.

9 *Indecent, Immoral, Obscene*

182 'available for tender minds' Max Harris, letter to John Reed, 16 August 1944, Reed Papers, La Trobe Library, Melbourne, 11/18,2.

182–3 'NO REFERENCE'; 'PARSON HERE HAS RATTED' Harris to Reed, 25, 29 August 1944, Reed Papers, 11/18,2.

183 'most strongly' J. I. M. Stewart, *Myself and Michael Innes*, Norton, New York, 1988, 108.

— 'For goodness sake, don't let us'; 'It is not any picnic' Reed to Harris, 25, 28 August 1944, Reed Papers, 10/18,3.

— 'if a policy of persecution'; 'personal reactions' Harris to Reed, 30, 24 August 1944, Reed Papers, 11/18,2.

184 'whether the tendency of the matter' Quoted in 'Reasons for Judgement' of L. E. Clarke Esq., SM, 20 October 1944, 3, Reed Papers.

— this was the first official attempt This and subsequent information derived from Peter Coleman, *Obscenity, Blasphemy, Sedition*, Angus & Robertson, Sydney, 1974.

185 'crowded as a picture theatre' Harris telegram to Reed, 5 September 1944, 2.19 p.m., Reed Papers, 11/18,2.

— 'hordes of Catholics' Harris to Reed, 7 September 1944, Reed Papers, 11/18,2.

— 'quite a number of modern books' All quotations are taken from the transcript of *Harris v. Harris* in Adelaide Police Court, File No. 7548 of 1944, Reed Papers.

186 'popped' Harris to Reed, 11 September 1944, Reed Papers, 11/18,2.

189 Williams had already tried to silence Detail from *Truth*, Adelaide, 9 September 1944.

— 'I want to make it clear' reported in *Argus*, 6 September 1944, 4.

192 'MILLHOUSE THRASHED DUMB DETECTIVE' Harris to Reed, 5 September 1944, 2.19 p.m., Reed Papers, 11/18,2.

- 'terribly pure'; 'rather queer' Harris to Reed, 7 September 1944, Reed Papers, 11/18,2.
- hissed at and cat-called Von Harris, quoted in Peter Ward, 'The Intellectual Swaggie', *Australian*, 17 February 1979, 9.
193 'an intellectual burst' Harris to Reed, 11 September 1944, Reed Papers, 11/18,2.
- 'chaos and confusion' Harris telegram to Reed, 18 September 1944, Reed Papers, 11/18,2.
197 'as an ally' Herbert Read in 'Surrealism and the Romantic Principle', Introduction to *Surrealism*, printed in *Selected Writings of Herbert Read*, Horizon Press, New York, 1964, 260.
199 'a beautiful example of the English language' Sidney Nolan, quoted in John Thompson, 'The Ern Malley Story' an ABC Radio feature published in Clement Semmler, *For the Uncanny Man*, F. W. Cheshire, Melbourne, 1963, 179.
206 'oppressive respect' Stewart, *Myself*, 109.
207 'DEFENCE WEAK' Harris to Reed, 4 October 1944, Reed Papers, 11/18,2.
- 'confused'; 'dithering' Reed to Harris, 4, 5 October 1944, Reed Papers, 10/18,3.
- 'indecent' All quotations are taken from Clarke, 'Reasons for Judgement'.
210 'MAGISTRATE GAVE VICIOUS' Harris to Reed, 20 October 1944, Reed Papers, 11/18,2.
- 'The guardians of our morals' Reed to Harris, 21 October 1944, Reed Papers, 10/18,3.
211 'Harris obscenity hunt' A. D. Hope, letter to Clem Christensen, 28 August 1944, Meanjin Archive.
- 'if anyone ought' Harold Stewart, letter to the author, 15 November 1992.
- 'Harris's little court drama' James McAuley, letter to Brian Elliott, 27 November 1944, from a copy in the possession of Norma McAuley.
212 'zealousness and competency' *News*, 29 November 1944.

10 *The Black Swan of Trespass*

216 'bewildered and shattered' John Reed, unpublished autobiography, Reed Papers, La Trobe Library, Melbourne.
- 'he didn't have anything to say any more' Max Harris, 'The Faded Years', *Direction*, I, May 1952, 6.
- 'excesses, absurdities and intolerable posturings' Max Harris, 'Angry Penguins and After', *Quadrant*, Vol. 7, No. 1, 1963.
- 'the poetic output' Max Harris, 'Conflicts in Australian Intellectual Life 1940–1964', in *Literary Australia*, ed. Clement Semmler and Derek Whitelock, F. W. Cheshire, Melbourne 1966, 26.
217 'His chief failing is a loss of nerve' Geoffrey Dutton, *Snow on the Saltbush*, Viking, Ringwood, 1984, 140.
- 'a very devastating experience' John Reed, unpublished interview with Richard Haese, 1973, Reed Papers, 13/18,6.
- 'You're vulnerable in your poetry' Max Harris to Craig McGregor, 'Conversation with Max Harris', *National Times*, 29 August to 3 September 1977, 19.

- 'Biography of a No-Hoper' The *Age*, 8 October 1960; 'Poetic Gems' *Australian*, 13 August 1979, 7.
219 'As to whether I'm sick' James McAuley, letter to Brian Elliott, 27 November 1944, from a copy in the possession of Norma McAuley.
220 'I made a firm resolve' Interview with Harold Stewart, 23 January 1989.
221 'I have never written a single line' Stewart, 23 January 1989.
222 'he went out like a light' Interview with Amy Witting, 4 July 1989.
- 'Thus have I written' James McAuley, 'Letter to John Dryden', *Collected Poems 1936–1970*, Angus & Robertson, Sydney, 1971, 95.
- 'Your eyes I fear' Amy Witting, 'A Letter to James McAuley', quoted in Peter Coleman, *The Heart of James McAuley*, Wildcat Press, Sydney, 1980, 55. Witting submitted the poem to McAuley at *Quadrant*. He rejected it.
222 'existence of god'; 'the spectre of yourself'; 'Your cultural pyramid' A. D. Hope, letters to James McAuley, undated, 8 April, 26 December 1952, McAuley Papers, in the possession of Norma McAuley.
- 'morally dangerous material' McAuley to Hope, 24 June 1955, Hope Papers, NLA, MS 5836.
223 'Blast McAuley for a meddling' Harold Stewart, letter to A. D. Hope, undated, Hope Papers, NLA, MS 5836.
- 'The traitors' tribune, bigots' Galahad' James McAuley, 'The Leader', quoted in Coleman, *Heart*, 57.
- 'Scorn then to darken' McAuley, 'An Art of Poetry', *Collected Poems*, 70.
224 'post-Shelleyan goon squad' Peter Hastings, 'A Kind of Tolerance', *Quadrant*, March 1977, 49.
- 'appalling Anglo-American series' *Sydney Morning Herald*, 12 March 1955, 11.
- 'I make no comment' McAuley, 'Childhood Morning – Homebush', *Collected Poems*, 225.
- ' "Dark night" is too grand a phrase', McAuley to Hope, undated, Hope Papers NLA, MS 5836.
225 'I think Max naturally' Interview with James McAuley by Catherine Santamaria, 5 May 1976, NLA, Tape Recording Collection 576/1.
- 'has its own personal dangers' James McAuley, quoted in John Thompson, 'The Ern Malley Story', an ABC Radio feature published in Clement Semmler, *For the Uncanny Man*, F. W. Cheshire, Melbourne, 1963, 178.
- 'Beware the past' McAuley, 'Warning', *Collected Poems*, 100.
226 'I am not resigned' McAuley, 'Time Out of Mind', *Collected Poems*, 179.
- the most remarkable person Donald Horne makes this point in his tribute to McAuley, *Quadrant*, March 1977, 31.
- two French writers The story can be found in *Les Deliquescences: Poèmes décadents*, d'Adoré Floupette, avec sa vie par Marius Tapora, introduction et notes par N. Richard, A. G. Nizet, Paris, 1984.
- there is no evidence David Brooks speculates about Floupette's influence on Malley in 'Notes and Documents', *Australian Literary Studies*, Vol. 15, No. 1, May 1991, 78–80.
227 'not so wholly different from' The story of Spectra is told by William Jay Smith in *The Spectra Hoax*, Wesleyan University Press, Middletown, 1961.
228 'I shall now die contented'; 'It remains almost inconceivable' Bernard

Grebanier, *The Great Shakespeare Forgery*, Norton, New York, 1965, 127, 120.

— The Spectra poems Smith, *Spectra Hoax*, 17.

— 'It's like having the muse' Interview with Kenneth Koch, 24 April 1990.

— 'that McAuley and Stewart are both'; 'from a possibly reliable source' A. D. Hope, letters to Clem Christesen, 25 June 1944, undated, Meanjin Archive, Baillieu Library, University of Melbourne.

229 'The great blow against any possibility' Don Anderson, *Island*, Nos 34/35, Autumn 1988, 92.

231 'a good deal better' Judith Wright, *Preoccupations in Australian Poetry*, Oxford University Press, Melbourne, 1965, 195.

— 'as being only mediumly obscure' Peter Porter, letter to the author, 10 January 1990.

— 'a hoax got up' Les Murray, 'James McAuley – A Personal Appreciation', *The Peasant Mandarin*, University of Queensland Press, St Lucia, 1978, 188.

— 'to some small extent' Interview with John Tranter, 8 July 1989.

232 'I simply couldn't put up'; 'as nothing else could'; 'a sincere interest' Karl Shapiro, letters to Clem Christesen, 4 October 1943, 13 January, 11 August 1945, Meanjin Archive.

— 'I liked the poems' Interview with John Ashbery, 21 November 1990.

— 'profundity and charm' Kenneth Koch, *Locus Solus*, II, Lans-en-Vercors (Isère), France, 1961, 203.

— 'I remember I had a rather lively' Interview with Kenneth Koch, 24 April 1990.

233 'I had a fairly dismissive' Interview with John Forbes, 22 May 1989.

234 'One of the two poems' Brooklyn College, Department of English, MFA Comprehensive Examination (Poetry), 1976.

— 'rather enjoyed the exam' Ashbery, 21 November 1990.

— 'a coherent work of art' Vivian Smith in *The Oxford History of Australian Literature*, Oxford University Press, Melbourne, 1981, 371.

235 'a multi-dimensional space' Roland Barthes, trans. Stephen Heath, 'The Death of the Author', *Image Music Text*, Fontana, Glasgow, 1977, 146.

236 'didn't make sense' Brian Elliott, quoted in Thompson, 'Ern Malley Story', 169–70.

— 'have more flair' Porter to author, 10 January 1990.

— 'Only Ern Malley could write like a genius' Harold Stewart to James McAuley, 3 August 1944, McAuley Papers.

237 'a remarkable *tour de force*' Brian Elliott, *The Landscape of Australian Poetry*, F. W. Cheshire, Melbourne, 1967, 259.

238 'vanished into thin air' Reed to Harris, 2 March 1944, Reed Papers, 11/18,2.

Index